W9-BEU-627

AN INSTINCT FOR WAR

AN INSTINCT FOR WAR

Scenes from the Battlefields of History

ROGER SPILLER

THE BELKNAP PRESS OF HARVARD UNIVERSITY PRESS

CAMBRIDGE, MASSACHUSETTS, LONDON, ENGLAND

Copyright © 2005 by the President and Fellows of Harvard College
All rights reserved
Printed in the United States of America

First Harvard University Press paperback edition, 2007

Library of Congress Cataloging-in-Publication Data

Spiller, Roger J.
An instinct for war : scenes from the battlefields of history /
Roger Spiller.
p. cm.
ISBN-13 978-0-674-01941-6 (cloth: alk. paper)
ISBN-10 0-674-01941-5 (cloth: alk. paper)
ISBN-13 978-0-674-02419-9 (pbk.)
ISBN-10 0-674-02419-2 (pbk.)
1. Battles—Fiction. 2. War—Fiction. I. Title.

PS3619.P548157 2005
813'.6—dc22

2005045214

For Rene and G.

CONTENTS

PROLOGUE

Some of this actually happened and some of it didn't, but all of it is as true as I can make it. Well before history there were stories, and after history has disappeared we will still tell stories if we are able. It is through these stories, some simple and some not so simple, that we have always created and advanced knowledge of ourselves and the world which encompasses us.

Stories about war must be some of the oldest kinds of stories— stories to entertain, to glorify, to condemn or to lament, stories even to educate.

The stories in this book speak of war in a certain way. They are meant to show how we have thought about its nature, its many shapes, and its conduct since we became sentient about war. Each tells of a moment when war changed importantly, sometimes even profoundly. The stories are told in the voices of those who in their own time thought expertly about war. Whether they loved or hated war or were simply caught up in it, the idea of war took over their thoughts, and in the thinking they found something new to say.

1

A SWORD IS DRAWN

At the edge of history itself, numberless years ago, war lives in a primeval state, beyond the reach of human understanding. Is war a force of nature? Or is it a mystery, born of the supernatural powers swirling about the ancient world? In old China, priests intone prayers, astronomers read the stars, and learned travelers spin their fantasies, pretending to foresee what shape the monster will next assume. So the wars of ancient China are fought for centuries, in a neverland closer to faith than reason. Must war continue so forever? A court historiographer believes he knows the answer and ventures to enlighten the great Han emperor—at some cost.

Once, a great and famous general fought and lost a desperate battle. The emperor demanded the general's execution. After investigating the defeat, the grand high chronicler hastily won an audience with his sovereign.

"Excellency, I am happy," said the chronicler, but his voice quivered all the same. The emperor was frowning.

"And why is this, Ssu ma ch'ien?" the emperor asked, and sternly.

"I bring news from my researches," replied the courtier, "that will save our general from the executioner."

The emperor shifted his tiny form on the throne. He had been saddened and made anxious by the defeat, which indeed was so serious its true significance was even now not fully known. Someone had to pay for this disaster. The enemy was out of reach and too strong. The general was not. If the general did not bear responsibility, who?

The chronicler himself was anxious, but not for reasons of state. History proved that contending with the emperor could be dangerous. So unconventional were the emperor's habits of mind, so unpredictable, that disputation could be suicidal. He did not even respect the gods; he was often heard uttering the most blasphemous remarks. He belittled the court's astronomers and soothsayers. When he was irritated, he had noses cut off. The executioner's sword awaited all; only the emperor's hand stayed its invitation.

So it was with some delicacy that the grand high chronicler pressed on: "My examination of the great battle shows that events conspired to defeat our army. The gods did not smile favorably upon our exertions and foiled our ambitions from the outset. The moon was red, and so our army was correctly placed outside, in the Yin position, as we began. But the color escaped the moon to clad the body itself in a red halo, which of course gave the advantage to the enemy. Indeed, all under the Nine Mansions seemed to be in an uproar. A recounting of our mishaps proves our commander's innocence. Allow me to elaborate."

The chronicler told of a tumultuous storm that swept down the valley where the battle was to occur. Unexpected and strong winds demolished the flags and signals and blinded the general's commanders. A torrent drowned what had been firm, dry ground and disturbed the formations of the troops.

Four traitors had chosen this moment to defect, and in full view of the front ranks. The brazenness with which they paraded their treachery caused these troops to lose heart.

Meanwhile, the enemy's formations seemed to be shaken by the torrent as well. These men ran about in great panic, but they fled in the wrong direction—indeed, toward our own men, who in their confusion believed that the enemy had launched a wild, ferocious assault.

This was too much to bear. Trapped between the torrent and the onrushing enemy, battered by the winds, beyond the succor of their comrades and commanders, the front ranks left their places of safety for the great masses to their rear. And as a snowball becomes an avalanche, so did panic compound itself in the face of the enemy.

The enemy's commanders easily discerned these developments, so at this moment they saw fit to order their troops forward. The enemy troops who had been milling about were now given purpose and direction. From all the eight directions, they joined in the assault with renewed energy. Most of our soldiers were killed, their heads mounted on pikes.

From his place, the chronicler saw the emperor's eyebrows ascend, ever so slightly. "Have I gone too far? Have I been too forthright in my report?" the chronicler wondered. Before he dared answer himself, the chronicler hurried to conclude: "These events were plainly beyond the powers of our general to affect, and so he might as well be held to blame for the torrent, the windstorm, the traitors, and the fortuitous confusions of the enemy—which, in truth, were as great as our own.

"I hope this brings comfort to the emperor's troubled mind," the chronicler offered.

"I am comforted," replied the emperor, "but I am also stimulated to consider this matter anew." With a wave of his hand, the emperor dismissed his chronicler, who left the throne room as quickly as decently could be done.

Nothing more was heard of the affair from the emperor for some time. The general languished in his cell. News of the chronicler's entreaties had flown throughout the court. The emperor had been known to vent his rages in the most horrible and reckless manner, rages that were sated only when hundreds had been summoned to the executioner's block or boiled alive. In truth, the chronicler's interference had placed them all in danger, and the other courtiers cursed him quietly but fluently for disturbing the imperial peace. In such an atmosphere, the most innocent signs were taken for portents, and bootless speculation silenced all the other business of state.

On the day the general was to be executed, the emperor summoned all his court to the Great Hall. Once the court was assembled, the unfortunate general was brought before the throne. The general's head was bowed. He remained silent as if contrite, but the truth was that his self-righteous arrogance still upheld a fragile dignity.

The general was no supplicant, even now. He had not petitioned for clemency, nor had he offered any extenuating defense of his own actions. Nor, indeed, had he persuaded the grand high chronicler to plead his case. The other courtiers knew already that the chronicler was the author of his own folly.

Anciently, other defeated generals had grasped for any way to save themselves. They blamed the gods and spirits above all, then their subordinates, and then even the enemy for not conforming to their desires for victory. When all these defenses had failed, they had shrieked and cajoled the emotions of all who heard them. And in their final moments as they were dragged before the executioner, they had even offered up their wives and children as sacrifices for their misdeeds.

The general had resorted to none of these devices. He was widely known as a righteous man, simple in his tastes and intellect, as devoted to the gods as to his emperor. If the gods had smiled upon him thus far, he was sufficiently humble to know that they were by no means obliged to favor him forever. He had assumed on the occasion of his defeat that for reasons known to them only, the gods had finally abandoned him. Men, he thought, are moved by the earth, just as the earth is moved by heaven, just as heaven is moved by the Way. And so he was resigned to his execution, perfectly content that in this, as in all other things, he was conforming to the wishes of powers higher than himself. Such habits of personality and temperament were taken as evidence of his great and righteous character.

Indeed, the general's appearance in court, dressed in his finest robes, though still clearly in custody, caused a moment of hope to ripple among the courtiers. Perhaps the emperor had after all been swayed by the chronicler's arguments. Should clemency now be granted, the gods would be appeased. An act of imperial mercy would cheer the common people from whom the army was drawn. The emperor's praises would be hailed and harmony would once again mark his reign. And, not least, a valuable servant of the imperial house would be saved. Bit by bit, the courtiers convinced themselves that they, too, could be saved from the fear they had lived with since the dispatch rider had arrived with the awful news of the defeat.

The emperor entered the Great Hall and called for his chronicler to come forward and stand by the general. The imperial guardsmen, whose presence cast a menace over the assembly, withdrew from the hall. The optimists among the courtiers took this to be a good sign. But then the emperor spoke.

"Chronicler, you have served me well. Perceiving an injustice that would impair the harmony of my dominions, with due solicitude for my own mandate as hegemonic emperor under all the Nine Mansions of Heaven, you have sought to advise me on the correct path. This is the first duty of a wise and good counselor."

"And yet it is the fate of good counselors, as it is of good generals, that they often do not understand how I, and only I, have been destined to discern how the world of dreams may be manifested in the world of the commonplace. My destiny is special because it is informed by my special knowledge. No one may share my destiny; this knowledge is my burden, and mine alone."

"Therefore, what may seem to the common person a sensible view of events may in the light of my knowledge appear as a vulgar perversion of the true path, so that I might see the right way of events and use this gift for the benefit of my dominions."

No breeze disturbed the gowns of the court. Even the birds seem to have perched quietly to hear the emperor. All believed they were in the presence of genius and profundity. Had anyone ever been witness to such wisdom?

The emperor gazed over his court, and smiled. Later, trying to recall this instant, some courtiers thought the smile was more a grimace, but this interpretation depended only on knowing the outcome of the event.

The emperor continued: "All of you know that this general stands before me under sentence of death. Some of you may know that the grand high chronicler is here because he sought to convince me that I might see justice differently, that circumstances might absolve the general of the offense for which I have condemned him. But if our world were governed by justice alone, your emperor and all his dominions would have achieved a state of perpetual joy long ago. Alas, it is not to be so."

"I shall review the brief that the chronicler has put before me, not for your judgment but for your enlightenment, for it is of utmost importance that you understand the course I have determined to take and why that course is the true way."

The emperor then succinctly and effectively recounted the chronicler's version of the disaster, neither omitting nor embellishing any point. The chronicler noticed, not without some embarrassment, that the emperor presented the facts far more smoothly than he had.

The emperor continued: "As we now know, the result was not merely a battle lost but the loss of valuable weapons and equipment of all kinds fitted for an army of this size, as well as the territory these arms were meant to protect. And now we are vulnerable because of our great expenses, and because our adversaries now occupy the disputed lands, which were important to us because these lands point the way through an easily crossed terrain toward our own dominions. But even this is not so serious as the loss of several thousands of our soldiers."

"Thus, we are doubly, trebly in danger because of our defeat. It will be said, and indeed I am informed that it has been said among you, that the gods did not intend the general to win this day, so that they contrived to doom the battle. On its face, this reason seems correct. So sudden, so unexpected, and so dangerous a meeting of misfortunes could only have been arranged by the gods. Who are we to hold a mere general to blame for what followed?"

"From times of old to the present time, this reason has been called into service on such occasions as this. Over the long course of our earthly careers, we have been accustomed to the notion that the gods control our fate. And in order to live within the light of their favor and in order to obey the true way, we have devised rituals for their placation, and not incidentally our own protection from unfavorable incident."

Then the emperor looked fixedly at his general: "The gods did not kill these soldiers. Our enemies killed them. You made it possible for our enemies to kill them. Our enemies were doing your work."

The emperor rose from his throne. The audience, taken by surprise, instinctively drew back. He walked quietly toward one of his senior counselors, who remained frozen to the spot. In the blink of an eye, the emperor had drawn the counselor's sword. Ah, some thought, the emperor is going to execute the general here and now, before our eyes. Instead, the emperor merely returned to his throne and stood before it, turning the sword this way and that, as if inspecting it.

"Anciently," the emperor finally said, "our swords were made by only a few great masters. Devoting their lives to this calling, these masters observed strict rituals of manufacture that had been handed down to them by the older ones. These rituals produced exquisite weapons. But the making of these swords depended upon the conditions in which they were conceived. Let one element of the ritual change, and the swords would appear as travesties of what their masters had intended. Often, when mishaps occurred, the masters killed themselves in despair. For, not knowing the reason for these rituals, the masters were unable to know why they had failed, and why misshapen swords had been made."

"Because the masters wished to keep their sacred rituals secret, it was only with difficulty that we discovered the real nature of swordmaking. We found that anyone could craft a sword if he knew why he must do a certain thing at a certain time, and how different materials could make different blades. This discovery was of utmost importance to us."

"The priests and old masters were very angry with us, accusing us of heresy and blasphemy, and threatening us with the gods' disfavor. Sadly, their protests led to their demise."

"And when the dead hand of ritual was chopped off, we learned that swordmaking was indeed only a craft, that there was nothing sacred about it at all. We learned, too, and happily, that far more craftsmen could make many more swords than we had hitherto believed. The priests had told us only so many were possible within a certain amount of time."

"So began the growth of our arsenals, filled with weapons whose quality was as good as those made in the old way. We were able to send greater armies against our enemies, and we have expanded our dominions and extended the benefits of our rule farther than we might otherwise have imagined. And we have been able to do this because we have supplanted superstition, ritual, and tradition with reality."

"And now we fire our metals for a certain length of time, not because the gods warrant it so, but because we know that certain kinds of metal demand certain kinds of firing. By drawing our sword from the darkness of superstition, we have exposed its edge to the pure light of reason. We have more and better swords, and the gods have not protested," said the emperor.

The Great Hall was quiet. Only the most acute sense could discern a restlessness among the courtiers. Of course, no voice had risen while the emperor spoke. Indeed, as the emperor seemed to be in another of his uncertain moods, one might prefer simply to disappear altogether. Who could say what might set him off toward an even more dangerous mood. The fluency of his address seemed to underscore how finely balanced was this occasion, suspended as it were between the cool tones of wisdom and snarling ferocity.

Among the thick-headed, brows were furrowed, their inward perplexity reflected on their faces. They looked about pitifully to the other courtiers for some sign of understanding, but there was little to be discovered. Those who did understand were happy to keep their suspicions well to themselves and felt that, whatever happened, at least their curiosity had been aroused. Better to allow events to run their course.

As if he had read their thoughts, the emperor resumed: "I know you are impatient with me. What has swordmaking to do with the general before us now? Secretly, you are insisting that I conclude so that I might then dismiss you and allow you to return to your concubines or your duties. Only some of you will have understood what I have said thus far, and you may for the present be smugly content. As for the rest of you, more is required."

Not a few of the courtiers winced. Even the beetle-brows among them feared they had somehow offended their sovereign, but how?

Satisfied that he had unbalanced even the self-satisfied few, the emperor gathered his gowns about him and sat down, still turning the glistening blade slowly, back and forth. "During our preparations for this campaign I observed our military experts as they worked. Our experts observed the heavens closely. Who knows how many nights they aimed their thoughts toward the Nine Mansions of the sky? And of course the Moon obliged our experts—at least momentarily."

"Our experts observed carefully the mountains in our army's path, for, as everyone knows, one must avoid fighting on any mountain's eastern side, for that is a death position. And then, too, our experts took careful note of the rivers before us, because, as everyone knows, water flowing northward is death water. Much preferable is eastward-flowing water. That, as everyone knows, is living water. When the armies drew near to one another, our commanders—at the general's direction—took great pains to place their formations where the Yang is most powerful and to avoid Yin positions at all costs. Those were the most dangerous, as everyone knows. Everyone knows that these are the ways of making war. But no one knows why," the emperor said.

"I say these silly ideas do not show the true path of war. I say no righteous army warrants these pitiful methods of propitiating gods who are uninterested in us or in our earthly doings. Twenty generations have passed since the Master Sun gave us his thoughts on the arts of war. You still do not see that the correct way of war is to study war so that we may see war only for what it is and nothing more, to see that an army is righteous with true knowledge, and that a righteous army commanded by righteous generals and full of righteous soldiers will achieve victory, whereas an army that does not know the way, that is commanded by generals who do not know the way, fought with soldiers who do not know the way, is doomed to defeat. I say that true righteousness is knowing what is real, and not what is suspected or feared."

"And so, with auguries cast, the incantations sung, the priests and prophets consulted, our experts—with our general overseeing the whole affair—declared our army ready for the coming war. The general gave the order to march."

"Our general saw war as a simple matter, as simple as life itself. To him it was enough if time-honored practices had been observed. That these practices derived from no particular reason was of no moment to him. Indeed, to have probed too deeply into some of these rituals would have been regarded as a reckless act of impiety."

"Throughout time, these habits—for that is what they really are— took less and less account of those matters which seemed beyond the power of mortals to influence. Those were best left to the gods themselves. As time passed, our conception of what was necessary and what was possible in war became ever more confined, and always those things that were difficult to understand were ignored in favor of those that were simple."

"In the present case, our general gave no thought to the weather because he could not control it. He gave no thought to treasonous activity because he could not influence the venality of scoundrels. He gave no thought to the enemy because someone else commanded that army. He gave no thought to the inadvertencies of combat because accidents and crises have always been a part of war and lie beyond hope of manipulation."

"Surely, all these matters were in the hands of the gods. And if the gods were propitiated, these matters would not work an evil influence upon our hopes for victory."

"Yet how convenient and how like the swordmakers of old to blame the gods for a fouled instrument of war, and so to absolve themselves. That is the true heresy: to accuse the gods for our own shortcomings. For that alone, this general should be executed."

"On the other hand, if we were to employ reason instead of ritual, if we were to assume responsibility for our own actions and not cringe before the powers of superstition, we would not be so content with the story given us by our grand high chronicler, who has—out of loyalty to me, it is true—actually conspired in this heresy. You may say his explanations depended upon natural causes only, but he has only attributed to the blind forces of nature and human folly the same influences we assign to the gods. Both natural and supernatural forces possess the same invulnerability to human influence and so serve the same function for us—they make it possible for us to hold ourselves blameless for our own ignorance."

"And perhaps it will be argued hereafter among the court that only a god could possess the powers necessary to conduct a successful war. Yet, anciently, twenty generations ago, the Master Sun wrote that the true way of the strategist is to seek battle after the victory has been won, and that he who struggles and fights toward victory is doomed to defeat. With Master Sun's wisdom so long in our hands, it is unworthy of us to burden the gods with these matters. Their compass is the universe; ours is only the dominions of our kingdom. It is right that we should take a hand in the making of our own fortunes now that we have grown to such a state, having passed our infancy as human beings."

"No doubt some of you are blaming me for setting this disaster in motion. You would not do so within my hearing, I wager, but in any gathering of this kind one may assume the presence of such views, judgments easily and covertly made. And, after all, I did have a part to play in this drama, a part for which the threat to my dominions now serves as punishment. After the chronicler pled for my general's life, I was moved to contemplate all the events of this war and the reasons for them. For his encouragement, I am grateful."

"I reexamined, first, my reasons for choosing my general and found that they were not reasons at all. I realize now that I selected him to command merely because he had won many hard battles in the past, because I thought of him as a craftsman of war. Yet, the Master Sun would not have approved of him. Battles should merely complete the victory long since set in motion by strategem; a general who fights hard thinks too little."

"Too many of my other generals—including some of you here—had been the children of chance or superstition. Your successes had nothing to do with your skills. You, Lord Shang: you are supposed by the people to be a child of the supernatural world, full of magical powers. I have heard it said you can raise a powerful wind at your will, with which you can put up a storm of dust anytime you desire. Your soldiers say you can see one hundred *li* in every direction and tell the future besides. Some would say you should be kept in my service even if you do not have such powers, but I say that would be a lie; you are kept because I regard you as a barely adequate commander."

"However, I supposed that this general who stands before me was different somehow, more like those who now fabricate our swords than the old masters who husbanded their mysteries to the disadvantage of all. And in the high councils of strategy before the war, the general spoke with such confidence that I, too, was carried away by the hope of success. I see now that his only real success was in misrepresenting his own cleverness, and that he appealed to me because he was lacking in timidity. His aggressiveness masqueraded as knowledge."

"As events showed, this general had deceived everyone all his life. He was no better than some of you, and perhaps worse, because he had no appreciation of the powers that were available to him, had he only reached into the regions of war that he supposed had been reserved for the gods."

"There were no gods there. Only reason could be found there, as elsewhere. He did not reach out to it; he pretended power when he had none."

"Ultimately, it is for this deception that he now stands condemned. And for failing to see this deception, the grand high chronicler must share in the general's punishment. That is the true path. That they will both be punished is imperative. They have failed to see that reason may defend us against what they supposed was unknowable; that reason may make understandable what the gods will not; and that reason may shield one's eyes against the blinding glare of reality."

"Thus, what appeared to our general and our chronicler as a confluence of misfortune would have been a great stage of opportunity. A general who trusted not to fortune or fate or superstition would have sought to wring favor from every circumstance. This general would have placed his army where it was not vulnerable to the natural elements, and where the enemy would suffer their full blast. He would have composed his plans so as to anticipate treason, so that any traitor might carry only fiction to his new masters. This general would have trained his commanders and his signalmen so that if one failed to perform, another was immediately at hand. And he would have prepared his troops and their commanders to have confidence in themselves and in their ability to meet the worst their enemies might imagine."

"These are my expectations and they are sensible, only what I have the right and power to demand. And they are not beyond the reach of any ordinary human."

The emperor chose this moment to stare directly at his general and the chronicler. To the emperor, the general's eyes now looked only dull and stupid. In the chronicler's eyes, there was now the kind of dreamy fear the emperor had seen so often.

The chronicler had listened to the emperor with the keenest attention, listened to the tones, inflections, the nuances in his sovereign's words, estimating at each point whether he was doomed or not. With the passing of each phrase he had gradually realized that he would be punished in some way.

In the time a breath could be drawn, thoughts from every direction assaulted the chronicler. By day's end, he and all his family could be dead, his house pulled down or given to someone else. All his writings, now declared flawed with incorrect thinking, could be destroyed, lost to posterity forever. Of all the possibilities, this one seemed most to unsettle the chronicler: to be forgotten, to leave no trace of his life's work. To never have existed, to disappear seemed to him even worse than death.

But to have been betrayed by one's own intellect! What a travesty of fate. His mouth was invaded with the taste of dry grass. For his entire life, the chronicler had believed that the intellect was the best of all defenses against life's turns, that the intellect revealed the true path of one's existence, and that those who were blessed with intellect, as he was, were to an infinitesimal degree closer to the gods themselves. He now saw that none of this was true, that his life had been founded upon magician's smoke. No matter how the day might end, the chronicler knew for certain that he would never again trust his own mind.

These recriminations crossed his face as a light might flicker, yet somehow the emperor understood when the chronicler had reached the end of his reveries. The fear in the chronicler's eyes had been replaced by the same dullness one could see in the general's.

"I shall now announce my decision," the emperor declared abruptly. "Both the general and the grand high chronicler shall be spared their lives, families, and possessions. Though conventional and tradition-bound, still they can be of some use to me."

"But for indulging their laziness of mind, for refusing to engage their imaginations and their powers of reason in the service of their emperor, they shall be castrated, and their condition will be a lesson to you all for the future."

"And as for the rest of you now assembled here, I will have no more of superstitions and portents, auguries and prophesies, fortune-telling and ill-disguised resignation to the supposed will of the gods. You will leave the gods to their own dominions, and you will devote your energies to mine."

With that, the emperor lifted his fingers slightly. The imperial guardsmen came forward and removed the convicted from the Great

Hall. Moments later, the screams of the general and the chronicler punctuated the silence. Then, with a final, menacing gaze, the emperor parted his gowns and took his leave.

As the members of the imperial court left the hall, many walked in thoughtful, or stunned, silence. It seemed the emperor had said that the making of war would depend no longer upon the good will of the gods. Now, war was a story with many true paths and endings, all made by those who must take a part in the telling of the story.

And shuffling quietly along with the rest, one courtier was heard to whisper to another, "The gods rained good fortune upon us today. The emperor could have as easily blamed all of us, and then where would we be? This day could have been our last."

"Yes," his companion replied. "But who knows the ways of the gods as well as the emperor?"

2

THE TESTAMENT

The war between the Greeks is in its final agonies. For the Athenians, a descent into a long night of tyranny awaits. On the verge of defeat, a disgraced general is secretly summoned from exile. He is called upon to speak to Athens' newly elected commanders, young citizens who must lead their cause to its dark fate. He must arm them against their future, if he can, with the wisdom of his hard-won knowledge. How strong is such an armor?

I, Thucydides, son of Olorus, do in my sixtieth year record this account of my last public appearance, before the assembled commanders of the Athenians. I have done so because of my belief that certain matters left unsaid in my history of the great war may now reasonably be said, these matters bearing upon the nature of experience and its relations with fact and the ordered arrangement of stories that we sometimes call history. I consider it of some importance that these observations be recorded for the benefit of those who come after me.

And as I have spoken at some length of experience, its true character, its advantages and disadvantages, the reader will see that I have not been reluctant to detail my own experience, so that the reader may form a useful impression of me, one that will enable him to assign to my prejudices their due weight.

17

As a preface I should only say that I was born of a noble family and had reached my maturity when the great war began. I fought in some of the earliest engagements against the Spartans and their allies. I survived these engagements in good health, and after a period of time I was elected *strategos* by the Athenian grand assembly, the *Ekklesia,* having been promoted by acquaintances among the *boule,* or Council of 500. Eventually, I was given command of a small flotilla whose purpose was the protection of some of our most important outposts and colonies.

I had not been long in command before I was required to launch an expedition against our enemies. My expedition was rife with difficulties, some of which I made for myself, and some of which I did not. The expedition was a failure. The most unfortunate events followed in the train of my failure, events from which our empire has yet to recover.

Quite naturally, my superiors in Athens were displeased with my performance, and although there was no imputation of treason, still I was exiled from Athens for twenty years. I repaired to my country estate, which I had been allowed to keep, and there began to work in earnest upon the history that I completed not long ago. Upon the strength of this history, my old friend Nicias, who had read my work and commented upon it with some favor, petitioned for my temporary release from exile and arranged for my return to Athens.

Shortly after arriving, I was asked by Athenagoras to appear before a group of newly appointed commanders to discuss aspects of war that they could otherwise only learn by doing—a proposition which, in Athens' present unfortunate straits, would have been most unwise. Any misstep now might prove fatal for our empire, so prostrated by years of war is it. I was charged to act, in effect, as an antidote to our commanders' lack of experience.

On these grounds I accepted Athenagoras' invitation, although not without some reluctance. While far away in exile I had come to serve as a convenient source for blithe judgments among my former comrades in Athens. "See the example of Thucydides," they would say, and then attach to this phrase the most outrageous propositions. Orators in the *Ekklesia* found this method most useful when they had exhausted their originality, a rare enough quality in any of our public speakers. These annoyances, which always reached me wherever I might be, when combined with the mental and physical burdens of composing my history, led me to fear that whatever I might say would be lost upon those who still lived in this world.

Then, too, I suspected that much of what I might have to say was knowledge of a kind these new commanders might fear to have. Still, Athenagoras' goals were noble and positive: even if I did not hope for much, he still wished that what I could say to his charges might afford them some measure of protection—a way, so to speak, of constructing their defenses in advance. So while I was reluctant and anxious, in the end my affection for Athenagoras and my sympathy for these young commanders—who, in truth, were as yet innocent—counterbalanced my hesitations.

I was not at all surprised to find that when I stood before the commanders I sensed a deep hostility to my presence. During the usual formalities of introduction, the audience kept to a sullen mood. Just as I began my address, I heard a low voice say "blasphemous traitor." For some reason I cannot even now conceive, I smiled broadly, and so began my address.

"Athenian commanders: Once I was one of you. I stand before you now, much the humbler man than when I first took command to lead our fellow citizens in battle against the Spartans. This was long ago, when you were only children, if you were alive at all."

"Athenagoras has charged me to recount my experiences and to say what I have learned from them, if anything. My experiences are not what I would have wished, nor what Athens would have wished for me. Doubtless you know of my unhappy expedition to Amphipolis and my consequent exile. But that is all you know for certain. Before I leave here today, you will know more, and you will know it more nearly correctly."

"Some of you question my presence here. Why would Athenagoras have invited a failed *strategos* to speak? Somewhere, on the very edge of your mind where you cannot quite catch the thought, you have the feeling that a virtuous person could not fail so dramatically as I have done. No. It must be that this failure was only the most public evidence of a whole life of incompetence, the emergence of my true character, cast upon the great stage of history. If our counselors had been more careful with their appointments, you think, this disaster need never have happened. What could such a person have to say to us?"

"But you are only giving voice to your own pride, and this is a minor offense, easily forgiven. I will assume you owe your appointments as commanders to excellent records of service and conduct in battle—either that, or to a fortunate connection with those who hold such offices in their gift. In any case, you believe your appointments to have been only just, right, and appropriate. You look forward to discovering a field where you may display the talents you think you possess."

"Some of you may be so moved by the prospect of defending Athens that her welfare is uppermost in your minds. Fidelity to the ideals of our democracy is your wellspring. You believe passionately that this ideal is worth any sacrifice."

"Others among you may think that if you serve your own ambitions well enough, you will naturally serve those of Athens too. You are not quite so fervent, so hot-blooded as your higher-minded colleagues. You believe those who do not reveal their passions so readily are of the more reliable temperament for active service. I will say frankly that I prefer to serve under the passionate sort of commander than this kind. Cold hearts did not perish with Leonidas at Thermopylae."

"But I understand that among the leaders of our democracy, views of my sort are not widely held. Our leaders say in public that they want heroes, but I have good reason to believe that what they really want and depend upon are those who display little imagination in any direction, those who can be relied upon to do only what they are told. Certainly, such people are less trouble for any leader. The passionate ones are always very annoying and often quite inconvenient."

"Of course you feel that you are well equipped, intellectually and physically, for the challenges you will meet, and why not? Athens has as much confirmed these preconceptions by virtue of your appointments, so that if you did have any secret doubts, they would have been swept away by the mantle that has been laid upon you."

"Do not imagine that I am slyly insulting you or that I disrespect you. As I have said, once I was much like you. You cannot imagine that events will ever get the better of you. You are certain that you will remain master of any event that fate or the gods will throw in your path. That is one reason why some of you hold me in contempt: you believe I lost control of myself in the face of the enemy. To you, that is an ineluctable fact."

"You have formed this impression of me, however, by means that can only be considered unreliable. You may have heard of my expedition from common people in the streets. They know of Amphipolis as one of the great defeats Athens has suffered in this long war. Amphipolis is frequently brought to their attention, in company with other well-known tragedies, on feast days and other occasions. Merely to remember Amphipolis is enough to evoke the deepest regrets and recriminations. This form of knowledge is the least useful: neither author nor proof is ever available to anyone who might wish to inquire about the truth of the matter. It is knowledge easily possessed; knowing it poses no burden for its owner. It is so light that it merely floats in the air, ready to attach itself to any opportunity for self-deception that happens to be available."

"Indeed, this kind of knowledge is so insubstantial that it can hardly be understood as knowledge at all. The poets have been its best friends, for it supplies them with themes for their songs. And although our poets may write of these things, their purpose is not so much to tell the truth by being loyal to it. Instead, they take pride in the way they can make stories out of the air. To them, the common-places that usually compose the truth are an impediment. They do not trust the ordinary truth to hold their audience in the amphithe-ater. So they fill up their stories with drama. Once, not so long ago, these stories were thought to be no different from history itself. That is why I devoted so much energy to discovering the truth, no matter how mundane, in my own history. I wanted exactness above all."

"Let us say that you pay little heed to the gossips of the streets and that you look to the poets chiefly for amusement, not enlighten-ment. You may have learned of Amphipolis in more dignified quar-ters instead, in the quiet councils and salons of our city. 'Poor Thucydides,' your informants will say, 'see the bad end to which his failure has brought him, and poor Athens too.' This sort of knowl-edge, too, has its flaws, for it is born of malice. It is meant to elevate its speaker at the expense of its subject. As I have already suggested, orators at our great assemblies make reference to Amphipolis al-ways in words very unflattering to those of us who led the expedi-tion. I would be surprised if you had not been impressed by the dra-matic effect of the story when they told it. Why should not these accounts be regarded as true—or true enough?"

"For all I know, some of these accounts might well be true, so far as their speakers believe them to be. But if they speak the truth, it is only by accident, for here again the truth is not the purpose of their speech. Their purpose is to win advantage over their opponents by forcing them to defend what happened at Amphipolis, and we all know how desperately any public figure would want to avoid that."

"It is by these means that we prejudice truth, deforming it for vul-gar reasons having to do more with present vanities than with genuinely knowing what happened. Whatever you think or how you came to think it, I say that Amphipolis was no mere story, to be embellished or changed for the effect of the moment out of vainglory or pride or self-righteousness. Amphipolis was a true experience to me. For nearly twenty years I have done more than tend my olive groves. Although my history was well begun before Amphipolis, afterward my need—indeed my lust—to continue it would not abate."

"Considering what I have said so far, you may be misled to think that my failure is the greatest difference between us. That is not so. It is your pride. There is more to life than only one event. What seems so important to others may be of little moment to the one who lives it. You regard me with distaste, perhaps. You would hope that my fate does not befall you, and you would be disconsolate if it did. But I will say to you that all my experience made me, and that I am happy for having lived it. I am the sum of my experiences, and it is impossible that we should choose which experiences will make us. We must take them as they find us."

"Experience possesses many parts, as many facets as a gem. We think, without thinking too much, that experience will protect us from calamity. Indeed, that is the very reason Athenagoras invited me here. We overvalue experience, or rather, we regard it too positively. For life exposes us to both good and bad experiences. We esteem the good and try to forget the bad. Or else, having survived a bad experience, we content ourselves with the belief that even a terrible experience can be of some value. But that is rarely so. The one who can tolerate the pain of looking directly at a bad experience is rare. Most of us would prefer to banish it from our minds forever. If we were given a choice between having a bad experience that we might put to future use, or a good experience that we could not use at all, we would probably choose the good experience anyway, if only to avoid the pain."

"And if we were allowed to choose between having a bad experience of our own or contemplating someone else's bad experience, we would all avail ourselves of the more pleasant opportunity. Not only could we learn without pain, but we may also gloat over our own good fortune. No doubt my presence here today serves some of you in this particular way."

"I have come to regard experience as a kind of mishap, much like an earthquake or a storm in the mountains. While we may be involved in these matters, we cannot predict them. Even if we could, we would still be largely at their mercy. We may by quick running escape them, but to imagine ourselves in command of them would be folly."

"Were we to estimate how much any ordinary day follows our intentions from the day before, we might be surprised. Very little of what one does, even in the best ordered of lives, is intended. We may begin a day thinking that we will attend to this field or walk to a neighbor's house, only to be turned aside by a duty that we think needs attention sooner. But that involves only one creature's unpredictability. It may be that one begins a day thinking that such and so must be done, only to see visitors arriving unexpectedly. One's plans must be set aside for the sake of courtesy. Perhaps, after seeing to the comfort of our guests, we may try to return to our original plans, but now the day is well advanced, so we trim our ambitions for this particular field or postpone our visit to our neighbor. The future never conforms to our expectations, and in this respect the future is quite reliable. It will never oblige us completely. So we are, in a manner of speaking, peculiar sorts of victims, victims who are not altogether without complicity."

"It may be that some of you are curious now, whereas before you were content to nurse your hostility toward me. Animosity of this sort is quite seductive: it does not depend upon knowledge and costs little to possess, but it is highly satisfying. One is enveloped in a comfortable superiority. On the other hand, if we try to wean ourselves from this stupor we are bound to feel a little uncomfortable."

As I spoke I noticed my audience change its stern pose to a more relaxed form. Here and there some had found a spot to recline and had dozed off contentedly. A few others had moved closer to me as the assembly had gradually given up its formality. These were still standing; some were smiling, as if I had said something aloud that they had only cherished as a secret belief. Some had faces like storms: one could watch the tossing waves take shape and pass from brow to chin. Naturally, these were the ones I expected to take part now.

I was not disappointed. Close by stood a youngish man, of dignified but not pretentious bearing. A scar, not too old, coursed down his neck to nearly meet another that looked out from the edge of his plain tunic. His eyes were bright, but they impressed me more by the depth they seemed to possess. Since I had first seen him, I had known somehow that he would be the first to speak, although others were clearly moved to talk as well. More with a movement than any word, he made his wish clear to me, and I was interested to see that when he began to talk, some of the others toward the end of the plaza looked up from their ease with an interest they had not shown until then. Glad to rest, I motioned for him to speak, and so he did.

"I wish to say that so far as I am concerned you are welcome here. You are right to say that there are those who would wish you were elsewhere. We need not respect their wishes. We may instead fear for the safety of those they lead, and for the safety of Athens."

"As for myself and perhaps for others among us, I wish to know of Amphipolis. I believe I have understood what you have said so far, but you will see that as we are about to assume command we are mostly interested in yours. Athenagoras has told us of his intentions: he desires that we learn as much as we might from you, and that we later use as much of what we have learned as we possibly can use. This seems only right and sensible to me. I have commanded in battle, but my commands have been small until now. Before long I must leave with a very large command to once again contest the Spartans on the Megaran Plain. With me I will have my sword and *hoplon* and my faith in my fellow citizens, but in my mind I must have more if I am to serve Athens as I am expected to serve." So the young commander spoke.

A second young man came forward, rather impatiently, or so it seemed. "I am called Theramenes. And if I admit I have understood little of what you have said so far, you must forgive me. I do not fear to appear ignorant before my comrades, for I believe that they too are confused about your meaning. I cannot see how what you have said thus far can be of use to us, who are to be officers of responsible service."

"My friend Thrasybulus, who has just spoken, I do understand. I too am interested to learn of your expedition to Amphipolis. I only know of Amphipolis from speeches on feast days. I see now that what I heard then may not have been true, and in any case I did not hear anything I could use. I take your coming here, which you did not have to do, as proof of your willingness to share with us what you know."

Just then shouts arose from the rear of the plaza, where several officers had taken their ease with wine and now were, perhaps, too much at ease. "Amphipolis!" they shouted, "We will hear from the great sage of Amphipolis!" There was much laughter. Crocks were thrown against the wall. A table overturned with a crash. Elsewhere in the assembly, titters of nervous embarrassment could be heard. One of the more avid listeners detached himself and went to speak to the revelers. I could not make out exactly what he said, but his tones were delivered with vehemence—so much so, indeed, that he began to scuffle with two of the drunks. Swords were about to be drawn when another man intervened in the row. The two drunks slowly made their way toward a gate at the rear wall, glowering stupidly at my defender. I heard later that one of them had been of a family close to Cleon, my old political adversary.

And now a chorus went up among those closest to me. "Speak of Amphipolis!" they chimed. "Amphipolis!" And so I did.

"If you sail north from Artemesium as though making for Potidaea and bear slightly eastward instead for Torone, you will in a short time raise the headland at Mount Athos—all assuming the best weather, for as some of you know, the winds in these parts are unpredictable in summer and dangerous in winter. The offshore winds are made fickle by the wild coastline, and the onshore winds are sometimes born in the land of the Cimmerians, beyond the Pontis. So, much depends upon the time you make way. But if you can manage to double the headland at Athos and make northwest along the coastline for the place where the River Strymon reaches the sea, you will find Eion, the outpost that guards Amphipolis, which is but three miles upriver."

"Thrace and Macedonia meet at this place, and the meeting has ever been a dangerous one. It commands the only bridge across the Strymon for some distance; your fathers may have heard it called by an earlier name, the Nine Ways. Athens established a colony at this place only six years before the great war began. We could take gold and timber from this district, and before long Amphipolis was a colony of some importance to our empire. Its resources were of course sufficient unto themselves to attract our interest, but Amphipolis was a strategic resource as well. Apart from its important position between Thrace and Macedonia, from Amphipolis we could maintain our connections with Thasos and Samothrace and Imbros, and as you well know these islands take us straight past Troy into the Hellespont and Propontis and even beyond, into the rich Cimmerian lands. Indeed, such had been the progress of our trade in the years before the war, after Xerxes and his Persians were defeated at Marathon."

"In the seventh year of the war I was elected as one of the ten *strategoi*. I suspect now that I was elected partly because of my own family's connections with these districts, where we had interests in the mines and other things, but this I cannot prove now. It seems obvious upon reflection, but that does not mean that I am right to think this was the main reason. Like all citizens of Athens, I had been fighting for some time, and not without success."

"In the year of my election, Amphipolis had been taken by the Spartans under the command of Brasidas, as adept and brave a general as Sparta has ever raised. That summer, Brasidas left Megara and struck out toward Thessaly with a small army of helots and mercenaries. When we were informed of his movements, we could not discern his intentions. Why would anyone with such a mixed force, so brittle in its way, range so far from Sparta? Never had the Spartans resorted to sending such a large detachment so far away by land. And because this had never happened before, we did not believe such a thing would ever happen. We could at least comfort ourselves with the knowledge that each step took Brasidas farther from the comforts of home. Eventually, his army would desert him."

"However, as time went by it became clear to us that this peculiar army was far from fading away. With the assistance of traitors and opportunists, his army increased its numbers. Brasidas passed quickly through the Thessalian districts and into Macedonia, where he began to take cities that were under the influence of those whom we believed to be our allies."

"You see, then, how at every turn our expectations were disappointed. When we learned Brasidas was in Thessaly, we felt sure no Spartan army would survive a clash with Thessaly's cavalry. And when the Thessalians did not stop him, we were sure that at least the Macedonians would bring him to a halt once and for all. But we did not reckon upon the perfidy of their king, Perdiccas, who brought

Macedonia to the Spartan side. Thus reinforced, Brasidas eventually came upon Amphipolis."

"Brasidas conducted himself brilliantly. Even now, after all that has transpired in the wake of these events, I cannot see much fault with his campaign. The first snow of winter was in the air when he found himself within a day's march of Amphipolis. No army moves in this sort of weather. By day's end, Brasidas very wisely paused to allow his soldiers a meal and some small rest. And then he pressed on into the night, guided by traitors from within the city to the bridge that guards its western approach. This he forced with little effort. Thereupon, for some reason, he went to ground without entering the city. By then, however, cries of alarm had been sounded in Amphipolis. Eucles the Athenian held command of the city, and upon learning of the enemy's approach made haste to send a courier to Thasos, where an Athenian flotilla lay at anchor."

"I was in command of that flotilla, seven triremes in all. With these ships and the men attached to them, I had been instructed by Athens to guard her interests in Thrace from the mouth of the River Strymon to the Pontis. The courier's arrival was the first notice I had of the Spartan expedition."

"Upon hearing the news I immediately put to sea, aiming for a landfall at Eion. I reckoned that Amphipolis might have held out against Brasidas until I arrived. I thought I could employ Eion as a base of operations as well. I had no idea of the strength of Brasidas' army, only the breathless estimates given to me by Eucles' courier. Nor had I any idea of how many of the local towns had surrendered to Brasidas. I do not remember considering this matter at all. My mind was full of nothing but haste, and indeed we made the harbor at Eion after a half-day's hard sailing."

"Of Brasidas, I knew rather more. I knew Brasidas well enough to understand that he was not like other Spartans; indeed, he was so unlike his countrymen I could hardly imagine why he would have been entrusted with the command of so vast a campaign. Only later did I learn from other acquaintances in Sparta that he was the object of powerful envy and suspicion. Some there considered it quite a joke that his army began its life with seven hundred helots whom the Spartans were happy to see go away from their city, and thereby weakening the helots' hostility their rulers so feared. The superiors of Brasidas felt much the same way about him: better all round that he should be successful elsewhere."

"Brasidas' fast, hard marching, and his success on every field of battle were evidence enough of his military skills. What was most remarkable, for a Spartan, was his diplomatic talent. Instead of immediately laying waste to all who resisted his march, he had instead told the people of Macedonia and Thrace that he had come to liberate them from Athenian despotism. Once in command of a place, he did not go out of his way to create more resentment from those whom he had defeated. Instead, he allowed the vanquished to come and go as they pleased, to keep their property and their standing in the city, and he promised them freedom from retribution by their enemies. In these ways, he won battles without ever having to fight them. Had he done otherwise, he might well have arrived in Thrace in a state of exhaustion. As it was, however, he arrived stronger than ever."

"We were not long in Eion before we learned that Brasidas had finally entered Amphipolis. True to his custom, the rule he created was one of virtue and tolerance. Before he had been in the city only a few hours, he quickly issued decrees meant to uphold his presence and endear him even to his enemies."

"Seeing that we had established ourselves at Eion, Brasidas immediately launched an attack against our defenses, and again, and again. Both by boat and by land, he sent his troops against us. After several pitched battles, we managed to hold Eion, but that was the most we could do. We could offer no relief to Amphipolis. And so, the war in these districts proceeded with little further drama, except that Brasidas conducted forays into the countryside and turned still more towns against Athens. Athens still held Eion for the moment."

Now Theramenes spoke again, his voice full of protest: "And yet you were summoned to Athens, relieved of your command, and sentenced to exile. How could such a thing happen? It seems to me that you had done all that could be done. Brasidas was so strong he could not be dislodged from Amphipolis, but then you arranged for the protection of Eion against him. Who could have wanted more from you?"

"Indeed, more was wanted," I replied. "Somehow, news of the disaster had already reached Athens by the time of our arrival there. A great number of citizens met us at the port. I had not even seen to my moorings before a courier conveyed the summons to account for my failures at Amphipolis. The reverses we had suffered before I even arrived at Eion counted for little in my defense. I was thought to be all the more liable because these explanations were taken for flimsy excuses. When it was demanded that I give the reason Brasidas had managed to arrive at Amphipolis before me, I replied that I had known nothing of his progress or success. Cries went up, encouraged by Cleon, who as a *strategos* knew very much more about the Spartan's movements than I had ever known."

"When I gave as my opinion that the loss of Amphipolis could as easily be laid at the feet of the *strategoi*, Cleon led the others in an even more vehement attack upon me. He seemed all the more intent upon my conviction, and he had long been a great favorite of the people. Indeed, my interrogators seemed less interested in learning the truth of the story than in somehow turning my misfortune to their benefit. My long association with Pericles had made me Cleon's enemy; especially since Pericles had died several years before, I and the rest of my party had watched our influence wane as Cleon's had grown. For these and perhaps for other reasons that I do not know, my conviction seemed to have been decided upon well in advance. I was allowed to retain my property, but I was sent out from Athens and prohibited on pain of death from returning for twenty years."

"To me it appears the *strategoi* used your misfortune as a way of turning the people's heads from blaming them," Theramenes said. "Nothing that happened in Thrace could have been evidence against your conduct."

"That would be true," I replied, "if the truth of the campaign had been revealed as I have revealed it to you. Instead, very little was said of the campaign's military events. An ally of Cleon's suggested to the council that I had been timid in my reaction to Brasidas because I did not wish to alienate my friends and my family's commercial interests in the district. And, in truth, I did have such friends and interests throughout the district. But so deeply felt were my regrets at this time that I could hardly voice them. My attempts to defend myself before the assembly were feeble, a poor job all around."

"It was months before I could bring myself to think about this affair, and still longer before I began to think in anything like a clear way about it. You see, I had begun to believe what my enemies on the council had said about me: that as a general I was merely a pretender who owed his office to his wealth and nobility, and that I had not sufficient courage to meet Brasidas in battle. Even now, when I remind myself that if I had sallied forth against Brasidas, Eion would most certainly have been lost in the transaction, and all Athenian power in the district extinguished, I have twinges of guilt, even though I know these things to be true."

Thrasybulus now said, "But, nowadays, Cleon's expedition to Amphipolis is celebrated while yours is not. Accepting the story that you have told us, how can this be so? Among the people of Athens, Cleon is the hero."

"Yes," I answered, "in Athens I was forgotten except when some orator wished to use my experience for his purposes. Other events and men crowded into the public mind, while the history of

Amphipolis did not come to a halt. Indeed, subsequent events served to cast my expedition in a different light, and few were discerning enough to understand that if I had known the outcome of the events I was a part of, then perhaps I would have conducted myself differently."

"Two years after my expedition, in the tenth year of the war, Cleon commanded one of his own. He sailed against Brasidas with 30 ships, 1,200 hoplites, and 300 cavalry, and an equal number of soldiers from our allies. Thus equipped, he landed at Eion and set up camp. During a reconnaissance in force outside the walls of Amphipolis, Cleon was taken by surprise. Brasidas launched a fierce assault upon Cleon's columns as they were marching away, taking them in their flanks at several places. Six hundred Athenians were killed that day, and only seven Spartans, one of whom was Brasidas himself. Cleon was killed as well, cut down by an archer while running away from the fight. This I heard from one who was in combat with him there; but later, when his sacrifice was being praised in Athens, I heard no mention of this fact."

"Nowadays, if you were to visit Amphipolis, you would find no sign that it had been established by the Athenians. All memorials to its founder, Hagnon, have been torn down. In their place, Brasidas himself has been adopted by the city as its father. There are no memorials to Cleon at Amphipolis, nor to any Athenian. But Cleon's death in battle is celebrated here, and always there is the unspoken question: why did not Thucydides suffer the same fate? As if my death would have produced a different result, apart perhaps from the erection of yet another monument."

"What was the good of it all, then?" asked Theramenes. "What was it all for?"

"The deaths of Brasidas and Cleon caused a pause in the great war that we now call the Peace of Nicias. The loss of two important statesmen, when combined with the destruction that all sides had suffered, was enough to give rise to a peace party in the assembly.

All sides were allowed at least a brief respite. But of course that was temporary. We are again at war with renewed violence, and Athens stands in more danger than ever before. If courage and energy could produce a good result, one should already have been produced. But events cannot be tallied up in a straightforward way to achieve a certain result. The experiences that become history are ever a surprise, as we have learned if we are wise."

"And now I must conclude this assembly. I grow tired. I will return to my home in the country, there to tend my gardens and my history. And you must go forth, as your fathers have done before you, and attend to the defense of Athens."

Upon the crowd there fell a silence as complete as the one I had first met when I began to speak. But this silence was different, more considered. No traces of sullenness remained. As I made to leave the plaza, the young commanders gathered round me to see me off. One or another of them placed a hand on me, as if he might comfort me.

A few moments later, one of those who had been among the drunkards at the rear of the assembly pushed his way through the crowd and stabbed me in the back with a dagger. He was subdued and taken away. He said nothing, but the hatred in his eyes was sharper than his knife.

Since that day I have kept my promise to myself, shuffling round my gardens, resting my wound, which in truth is not so severe as it might have been. I have more visitors than I am accustomed to having, but my energies are failing, and if I cannot devote them to my histories, still I can attend to the simple courtesies demanded of me. The war is going very badly for Athens, but I hear that Theramenes and Thrasybulus are fighting well and promise to be among the best of the new commanders. I presume to take a sort of pride in their success. It is a small enough conceit for an old man at the end of a long and failed life.

3

THE LESSON

In which our hero, a Florentine bureaucrat and sometime poet, is imprisoned for conspiracy one fateful month in 1513, and while in jail considers how a virtuous republic may take possession of war's purposes.

"A torturer by rights should be a cultured man in these days and times, is it not so, signore?"

"Don't start with me again so soon, Rudolfo."

"Of course not, signore. I am no fiend. It is for the sake of conversation and learning that I have returned early. We have all the time we need for the rest of it."

"Another lesson for the both of us, then?"

"Well put, signore. Well put!"

"What are you doing?"

"Do not be disturbed, signore. I am merely arranging my tools. After our last lesson they were in some disarray."

"Much like myself, Rudolfo. Much like myself. But what has culture to do with your trade?"

"Signore?"

"Culture, Rudolfo. When you came in, you were saying something about the necessity for culture. I was a bit distracted at the time."

"Ah. Well, yes. My duty is not the mean sport most people think. The giving of pain in the service of the state is a very complicated affair. A thug or a common assassin may consort with the crudest of people, while my life is often touched by notables of the very best sort. Rather like yourself, if I may say, Signore Machiavelli."

"And that makes some sort of difference in your . . . modus operandi?"

"Oh my, signore! You wound me: someone of your rank merits an entirely different method. To begin with, I have no discretion over your life. Accidents may always happen, of course, but I mayn't simply dispose of you after I have taken what I was commanded to take. Too, it is only when you are actually on the chains that I am really at work. Much time will pass between us, and . . . "

"Would it were not so!"

" . . . and thus I must ensure that your brain is unharmed. My superiors have been quite firm on that point."

"I should not be here at all. I am no threat to anyone. Surely I proved that when I surrendered to the authorities. I am no *condotierro*. Before I was dismissed, I was merely a functionary in the government. Now, I only live out my adventures in my library, my gardens."

"So you *do* see the delicacy of my situation after all. You have come to me because you have dangerous notions. And yet, for my work, I must join my brain to yours, in order to tame it, after a manner of speaking. You must see how subtle, how dangerous it is for me, signore? How may I protect myself? Alas, sometimes I think my superiors believe I am one upon whom no imprint of reason could ever be made, a kind of cipher. But I am affected by my charges. Surely you must see by now that I am underestimated by my *commendatore*."

"I do not think I will contradict you, Rudolfo."

"You may find it an odd thing for me to say, signore, but without

my . . . *visitadores,* my life would be barren indeed, a desert of ignorance. From each one of them I have taken a great deal. Oh, I know
what they say up there: that some of these ideas, like yours, signore,
are treason without the dagger, or that they are heresy, or that they
are merely wrong and must be placed where they cannot harm the
people. And, it is true, my only real command is to drive these ideas
away, or, perhaps, to kill them . . . Please, signore, do not struggle so
against the chains; it only makes noise and fatigues you. You must
conserve your strength."

"I've no choice but to take your advice, Rudolfo."

"Wisely said, signore. Oh yes, I was saying how I have learned to
learn from the *visitadores.* And indeed I have learned the most
amazing things. The things that I've learned have actually made me
a different man."

"How are you different now? How were you before?"

"Ah, signore, I believe that I can say without fear of contradiction
that earlier in my life it would not have been pleasant to have met
me here. Yes, I wager that is the truth. Others would attest to it, if
they could."

"And, and now?"

"And now I am a good deal more thoughtful. In the beginning I
believed I was much like my tools. Meeting with resistance, I
merely overcame it."

"Do you mean to say, Rudolfo, that you used the same amount of
violence in every . . . in every instance?"

"Yes, signore. Mine was a simple life. But some of my
visitadores expired prematurely, before I had accomplished my task.
Others, I found, had nothing to offer in any case: in fact, my energies were entirely wasted. I was forced to give pain with no purpose."

"How were these tasks, as you call them, how were they made?
Who provided you with guidance?"

"My *commendatore*s, signore, but their advice was small enough. 'This one is to be treated roughly,' I might be told, or 'That one need not take much time.' Only rarely might I learn, from idle conversation with my colleagues, that a particular person had been arrested for a violent act. Of course, when I learned such things, my work was made easier. I met violence with violence. But with my more subtle orders, it is very difficult to see how they may be given practical shape. In an odd way, I must give those orders, vague or not, some sort of life."

"Did the reverse occur? When you found out that someone had been falsely accused, did your methods change?"

"Of course, signore. As you know, I am not one who takes any kind of pleasure in the physical aspect of my work. Often, it is quite disgusting to me. But I am serious about my responsibilities, and I try to be a thoughtful person. If opportunities for mercy reveal themselves, I certainly try to take advantage of them. Indeed, signore, you are yourself the beneficiary of my experience in these matters. Still, some of my colleagues insist that I make too much of my work, that I think about it altogether too much. For them, it is enough if they carry out their orders. They argue that their results are the same as mine. This may be true if we think only about the actual wreckage that comes about because of our work, but I have found that what I may learn is a great consolation—a kind of counterbalance against the obvious part."

"Rudolfo, what did your *commendatore* tell you about my . . . case?"

"I must take care, signore, not to violate my *commendatore*'s trust, so I will say only so much. Before you were given into my care, my *commendatore* said that you weren't to be allowed to die, that you were to be kept for a certain time—until our lord retrieved his good humor. I am allowed to cripple you if I must. And the *commendatore* said I should not allow you to go mad. So, you see, the *commendatore* is learning too. It is no longer enough for him to say 'Hurt this person in such and so a way' or 'Give his soul to the priests.'"

"Did the *commendatore* happen to say what I had done that so angered our lord?"

"Ah ha, signore, you are a rich one! Such a gentleman. I expected a far different question, the one that everyone asks: 'How long will I be kept here?' But you have not done so; you only wish to know the *why* of it. You see how much I can learn from my *visitadores,* the intellect, the chivalry? I knew nothing of these things when I was a rude soldier."

"Shall I take from your reply that you will not tell me what I ask? Would you reconsider? I wonder if my composition was defective. I wonder which of my ideas was objectionable. I would not want to surrender a good one by mistake, you see. These ideas are all I have remaining to me."

"Pray the *commendatore* does not hear you say such a thing. Have you not understood at all the reason for your predicament?"

"I only want to understand."

"But at such a cost. How can you be so unaware of the very cause that brought you here?"

"I cannot imagine with any precision what that might be. One may only speculate. I must assume that no mere point of theory would so excite our lord. No. Something I have said or written must have touched him in a personal way, as an insult might touch us and incite us to vengeance. But what if I have been misunderstood? All of this . . . suffering is to no good purpose. Nothing will be achieved, Rudolfo."

"I can see now that you suffer an illusion, Signor Machiavelli. No one idea brought you here. You are here because you have been named as a conspirator in a treasonous plot against our Lord Medici."

"Treason! You can't mean it! I have had no part in treason! I am a devoted citizen of Florence. For ten years I served the first citizen of our republic, Piero Solderini, the *gonfalonieri a vita* himself. A most terrible mistake has been made."

"I am grieved to say so, signore, but two of your fellow plotters have already been condemned to die. You have not been sentenced. The priests will not sing the *per voi s'ora* for you. Why, I know not, but I am grateful for it. I have grown fond of our talks."

"Rudolfo, what can one say? My mind is a tempest. What can be done to overturn this injustice?"

"Sire, I am a simple jailer. I am no advocate or judge. Before long, you will be called before the inquisitors. I have been named to handle the rope, I'm proud to say."

"The rope? Ah god, another torture?"

"Yes, sire, the *strappado*. You are to provide answers to the questions the inquisitors will pose to you. If these answers prove unsatisfactory or somehow incomplete, the inquisitors will signal me and I will pull the rope."

"But if the inquisitors suspect me of a treasonous act, and I deny it, I may be punished all the same!"

"That may be true, signore. It is hoped that the pain will encourage you to reveal the truth of the matter, to reveal your guilt."

"But I have no guilt. I am innocent."

"Ah, signore, you will forgive me, but almost all my charges say that. It is expected at first. Later, of course, the guilt is acknowledged."

"Even if it is not true?"

"But if the guilt is agreed to, how can it be false?"

"Never mind, Rudolfo. Tell me, how did this accusation against me come to be?"

"I have heard it said, signore, that your name was found on a list of those who were to conspire against our new lord."

"And who composed this list?"

"Sire, I have heard the names, but I should not say them."

"Rudolfo, have you heard of a party in Florence, the Optimates?"

"I cannot say that I have, sire."

"They are little more than wealthy thugs, without virtue or reason. They wish only to enrich themselves at the expense of the republic. I have had unhappy relations with this party. They would seize any pretext to rid themselves of me. Because of them I have been removed from my position in the chancery. Accusations of official theft have been leveled at me. Even before my arrest, I had been forbidden to leave the city."

"These are powerful men, signore?"

"They are. And they mean to have more power by associating themselves with the new regime. But I believe the new regime will not benefit by this alliance. On the contrary, I believe it will do much harm to the new regime."

"But, sire, if you have been arrested for treason it is because you have plotted against the new regime."

"Ah, Rudolfo, these are deep waters. I can barely swim in them myself. I may be drowning."

"A curious way to put it, sire."

"I believe the new regime might benefit from my knowledge, Rudolfo. My enemies know that they could be harmed by what I know. You may be right after all, Rudolfo. Perhaps it is all I know that has brought me here, rather than one particular thing."

"In any case, sire, you are here with me now. Perhaps you should not trouble yourself with these speculations. They may only defeat you in the end. Perhaps it is only bad luck that brought you here. Fortune for good or ill can never be predicted. You must content yourself."

"But you must understand, Rudolfo. I am no traitor. The new Medici can make Florence into a good state. My knowledge can help them. The power of good is the safest kind."

"No one could disagree, sire."

"You would think so, Rudolfo. But there are those who believe that power and goodness have little to do with one another. That gang, the Optimates, they believe so. To them, virtue is weakness. They do not see that goodness can be used by power, that power can benefit by goodness."

"Surely, this is a riddle, an amusement? Are you mocking me, signore?"

"Do not excite yourself, Rudolfo. I am in no position to mock anyone. But you see how power works in our own case? Let us say that you had been given no authority over me. Do you imagine that I would remain in the Bargello as long as I have?"

"What a curious question, sire. Of course not. But you are in chains."

"Indeed so. My chains keep me here, ready for you whenever you must work. And in between times, we talk a little. Think how we might talk otherwise."

"I cannot envision it, sire. You are well-born. I am not. We may pass one another in the Piazza della Signoria, but you would not even look my way."

"Exactly, Rudolfo. And what has changed all that?"

"Your chains, signore."

"Don't look so sad, Rudolfo. I assure you that I would be proud to make your acquaintance in any other place than this."

"Could it ever be, signore?"

"I think it could. Just as in our own case, Rudolfo, the state must make the acquaintance with ordinary people if it is to be good. Not that I would call you ordinary, Rudolfo. I never would have imagined a jailer like you."

"Ah, signore, you are behaving like a convict. One who is in my position hears such flattery all the time."

"You miss my point, Rudolfo. Ordinary people are not the ciphers my enemies believe them to be. Each person has value, and if all the people come together, then think of the great good that could be done in a state."

"I do not think all people are so good as you have imagined them to be, signore. I know this very well, because of my position."

"But if we could somehow arrange for life to be easier if one is good, do you think most people would choose to be so?"

"Yes, of course, but life has not made that possible."

"I say it can be done, Rudolfo."

"I do not see how, signore. Inside these walls, life looks dreary to me."

"The first and most absolute necessity is to have a state. We cannot get along without one. So, assuming there is a state, the state will possess a degree of power over life. How that power is composed will make all the difference, Rudolfo."

"Composed? I do not understand."

"If this power is composed of tyranny, then the people will be used and receive little in return. We should not be surprised if the people feel no kinship with their masters. And when the state needs protection, it must call upon someone to protect it. How have we done this in the past?"

"We hire soldiers, sire. I myself was a hireling for some years."

"And why did you become a soldier, Rudolfo?"

"Why, to get along, sire. I did not want to starve in the country. So many were starving around me, you see."

"I do see. I do. And the army that you fought with? How was it composed?"

"Of men much like myself, sire."

"To whom did you owe your service?"

"To the *capitane,* signore. He paid me."

"And not to the state?"

"No. We fought for different states. We were hirelings, you see."

"*Condotierri.* Yes."

"And did you ever fight for different *capitanes?*"

"Why, yes, signore, I did."

"And why was that?"

"What a question, signore! Because another *capitane* would pay me more."

"Would you say that you belonged to good armies, Rudolfo?"

"We fought well enough, signore, when we had to fight."

"No, Rudolfo. I want to know if your armies fought in a good cause."

"I do not know, signore. I fought for myself, and then for my *capitane.*"

"Let us say that you had not left your farm, say that you could live well enough and have a family, and that the state had enabled you to do so. Would you feel a certain gratitude toward the state?"

"I suppose so, but that could hardly be imagined."

"Imagine it so, for a moment. We know it is possible. The old Romans protected themselves in just this way. All Romans were bound to fight for their city. Let us say that the state to which you owed a certain gratitude was endangered. And because the state was in danger, your farm and family were as well?"

"I can imagine this well enough, signore. When I was a soldier, we laid waste to many farms and turned their families out into the cold. It was sad, but it could not be helped."

"Exactly so. Let us say that you and your fellow farmers could prevent such a thing from happening to you. Would you do it?"

"Yes, provided we had a chance to succeed against them. But in my experience, I never met farmers who acted this way."

"That was because they had not been prepared for this occurrence. They had no weapons. They had not been trained how to use them. They had no officers to lead them. But let us say all this was so, as it was with the old Romans. Let us say that you and your fellow farmers did have weapons and knew how to use them because your officers had taught you. What then?"

"Well, sire, there were always many more farmers than soldiers, it is true. We had our way with the farmers because they could do us no harm."

"And if all the farmers, so equipped, were put together into an army. What then?"

"I do not see how they could be used, sire. It is very difficult to arrange so large an army."

"If you are trying to move a boulder from your field, Rudolfo, and find that you cannot, what do you do then?"

"We break it up if we can, into smaller pieces."

"It is much the same with armies, Rudolfo. You break them up into smaller pieces."

"And you no longer have a boulder. I think I understand. But surely the power of an army lies in its number?"

"Not in the number only, Rudolfo, but in how that number is used. You said yourself that it is difficult to arrange any army. And if you want to have the army perform a duty, you must find ways to move it to and from the field. But while a farmer is happy to see a boulder lose its power, if you lead an army you must ensure that, even after it is broken up, it somehow keeps its strength."

"But, sire, what has this to do with goodness? An army is only a tool, to be used by whoever has power over it."

"Rudolfo, do you think an army fights better for a good cause or a bad one?"

"Sire, an army fights for any cause. I never cared overmuch about why we were fighting. One siege or battle looks much the same as another."

"And the soldiers themselves. Why do they fight?"

"I have already said: they fight for their *capitane*."

"Truly? I thought you said you fought to make a living."

"Well, yes, that is more nearly true."

"Did you like to fight? Did you look forward to fighting?"

"This is another of those questions, signore. I cannot for the life of me see why you would ask such a thing. Of course I did not like to fight."

"Then why did you? Was your employer, the *capitane,* always at your side, like a master with his apprentice?"

"No, of course it was not possible. For long times we were on our own. When we fought, we hardly ever saw our *capitane.* He was always on a horse and moved about rapidly."

"So, then, everyone fought alike? Did everyone stand his ground?"

"No, sometimes the battles were fierce. Many fled if they could."

"Did you ever run, Rudolfo?"

"What a thing to ask a man! I am fond of you, Signor Machiavelli, but you may well go too far if you do not take care of how you speak to me. Remember where you are. This place is not one of your fine gardens."

"Believe me, I mean no disrespect, Rudolfo. I know it is a hard thing to ask a man. Let me say this instead: I believe some men stand and others do not, but they are not always the same men. Some men stand on this day and not another. Others do not stand on this day, and yet on the following day fight like lions. No man is always brave, which is only to say that men do not always behave in the same way all the time. You must understand that I do not mean to insult you. I would not do so, even if I were not in chains, Rudolfo."

"Well, it is true enough, signore. There were times when I did not do as much as I could have. I do not think of myself as a hero, but neither am I a coward. I would kill any man who said I was."

"Have you killed in battle, Rudolfo?"

"Ah, sire, your question fills me with sadness. I have done what you say. In battle, one has little choice in such matters. I fought to defend myself, and that was well enough."

"Why does this make you sad, Rudolfo? I have heard that some exult in the clash of battle."

"I have never seen one who did, sire. The most terrible cries. Heartbreaking sights. Carnage. A slaughterhouse. A knight tried to ride me down with his horse once, but the crush was too great. He tried to hack me with his sword, but I crawled under his horse and found his stirrup on the other side and dismounted him. I caught him on the ground. His armor was so heavy he could hardly resist. I used my dagger to find a place under his arm and . . . "

"And did you not feel triumphant when it was over?"

"When the battle was over, I was tired and sad. I kept remembering how the knight had cried out . . . for his mother. It was a sorrowful day. Many died on all sides."

"You are a noble and fine man, Rudolfo."

"Sire, I am no such thing. I grew sick of fighting. I could not see the sense of it. That is why I came here, although sometimes I wonder if I did the right thing."

"Would you fight to defend your home and family, Rudolfo?"

"Who would not fight for that? But that is not the same as fighting with an army. I wonder why we need soldiers at all. Wherever they go is only sadness and destruction."

"The state needs their power, Rudolfo. Even the Pope has his army, you know."

"I still cannot see why, sire. Armies are a waste. Armies live in a perpetual wasteland. Have you ever seen a battle, a siege? Such ruin is not to be imagined."

"I have seen these things, Rudolfo. I was at Pisa. I saw Prato. I think there would be fewer of them if we had better armies and better states."

"I do not like to contradict you, sire. You are much more well-informed of these matters, but that seems contrary to the truth."

"If a state is sure of its power, as expressed by its army, it will not be so easily attacked—as our states have been. Look at us today, Rudolfo. We have French armies and Spanish armies and *condotierri* roaming about our lands at will. We are not our own masters.

We will never be our own masters until we are capable of protecting ourselves."

"But Florence has an army—or before Prato it did. The Spanish troops were too strong."

"True enough. The Spanish troops were too good for our militia. We need to weld our army to our state. How can we continue to contract for our future with hirelings, thugs who think only of their fortune, rather than ours? What if we had an army made of people who were willing to defend their homes, as you are?"

"Soldiering is expensive, signore. A mere foot soldier like myself does not require much, but a knight must be a wealthy man with horses and armor and aides and such. Only our noblemen can put up with such costs as these, as I am sure you know. And besides, even if I had money I could never ride in the cavalry. That service is reserved for the nobility."

"Yet you killed a nobleman, Rudolfo. Brought him to the ground and stabbed him in the armpit. How did his nobility help him then? Did you pause because you saw he was a knight?"

"Not for a moment, signore. I was quick upon him that day, and more besides. The advantages were with us."

"Rudolfo, I say a well-disciplined infantry is superior to cavalry. One might think otherwise, but your own experience reveals the truth. In our state, Rudolfo, do you think we could recruit more infantry or more cavalry?"

"More infantry, sire. There are more ordinary people to make up the infantry. There are not so many noblemen, so the cavalry will always be smaller."

"And more expensive?"

"Of course, more expensive."

"And who do you think wins battles these days, Rudolfo?"

"I do not know, sire. I know that on that particular day of which we have spoken, the infantry won."

"Yes, Rudolfo. The day of the infantry is coming. Just as the day of the new state is coming."

"But, sire, our new masters, the Medici . . . "

"They are new, Rudolfo. They must learn the ways of power. They must learn that it is not enough to have power, but to exercise it in defense of a good state . . . What is it, Rudolfo? You are looking distracted."

"You must know, Signor Machiavelli, that I must report our conversations to my *commendatore*. I fear that we have tread on dangerous ground."

"You will represent me well, Rudolfo. Of that I have no doubt."

"I will take my leave of you for a moment, sire."

"No lesson for the moment, then?"

"No, sire. Fare you well."

"Thank you, my friend."

"Good morning to you, signore."

"Good morning."

"And so we must begin."

"Wait, wait please. Where is Rudolfo? I am in his charge."

"Did you not hear the priests chanting the *per voi s'ora* last night, signore?"

"I did that. Whom were they praying for?"

"Why, for Rudolfo, signore."

"What? He was . . . ?"

"Yes, signore, he was beheaded."

"On what grounds?"

"I do not know, signore. Only that there was a ferocious row between him and the *commendatore*. Then he was arrested."

"How could this happen?"

"This morning, the executioner said he whispered that the lesson was over. I do not know what he could have meant."

"Never mind. Let us begin."

"As you wish, sire."

"Wait. What is your name?"

4

SCOUNDREL

A century after Machiavelli, war comes to a crossroads. In the afterlife, Albrecht von Wallenstein, scoundrel king of mercenaries, and Justus Lipsius, uncertain king of ideas, argue which path war should take— war for self and profit, or war for nation.

"So. You've come to a bad end, after all."

"Who, pray, are you, sir?"

"Let us say that I am someone you do not know who knows you well."

"There are many such people."

"*Were* such people."

"Were?"

"That is the way we speak here."

"Indeed? A sensible rule, under the . . . What is that sound?"

"Only the clouds and the sky changing shape. These encourage contemplation, we find. And you, sir, have much to contemplate."

"How you do sneer at me, as if I were a carcass."

"In your old place, I suppose that is what you were. You made many companions for yourself, too. Europe is a charnel house. Below Magdeburg, corpses choke the Elbe reeds. From Dresden to Prague, seven score gallows and wheels stand where vultures do now feed on the remains."

"Ha! I am no carrion, broken on the wheel. I spent my last moments sumptuously abed in my palace."

"Nay, you were not in Prague, but Eger, run through with a partisan, vomiting and cursing the stars and crying for quarter. And afterward, the big Irishman hurled your corpse from a window. You were defiled by the offal in the streets below."

"How . . . how do you come to know all this?"

"As I have said, I know you well."

"Was I betrayed, as Kepler said the stars foretold?"

"It was your friends, as you expected."

"Hell and death for all of them. I had no friends."

"True enough, at the last. Your old friends are quite beyond your reach now. You should in any wise be more charitable. Try to change."

"They were not beyond my reach once, by the stars and planets. My armies could have bested the legions of Rome. I owned sixty-six estates. My affairs cast a great shadow over all Europe. I could have kept my so-called friends in darkness forever, had I learned of their conspiracies."

"Far short of forever, count. You are about to learn how long forever lasts."

"Then for all of it, I shall damn the bastards who killed me."

"You will not. Eternity is not for wasting on such trifles."

"Damn your impertinence. You are too comfortable with me. You make as though you own this place and me besides. Who calls when you must answer? I will have his ear soon enough; we will make accommodations, and then . . . Why do you give yourself up to such laughter?"

"I do own this place and you besides, until I please otherwise."

"By God himself, I have heard enough of this . . . Why can I not move against you?"

"Alas, I spoke too soon, it seems."

"Had I my sword . . . "

"Yes. That was always your argument in the end."

"My sword, my talent for war and enterprise . . . "

"Your limitless ambition, your avarice: these virtues brought you here."

"I am the victim of murderers, that's . . . "

"Your own kind was the agent of your fall. Don't pretend to forget. There is no forgetting here."

"'Tis true. I can remember what I did not know. Has my history curved round, like an orbit?"

"Yes. You are at its beginning and ending, one and the same."

"Shall I live again? Then I shall draw and quarter that Irish bastard of a captain, Devereux, who did use his halberd on me."

"How quickly the old earthly poisons reappear."

"So. I shan't. Kepler's astrology lied."

"You wanted Kepler to tell you tales of fairies, and so he did. You needn't hang your head so. This place is not the doom some do imagine."

"Do not torture me. Ways aplenty serve better than this."

"As well you should know. You were expert in all of them."

"And this place, as you call it, is no place at all. It has no feel to it."

"If you must be literal, so be it."

"I would know your name if you would condescend to have one, spirit."

"As you were once called Albrecht von Wallenstein, so I once was called Justus Lipsius."

"I knew you not. How came you to know me?"

"This has been my place for a longer while. I have watched you in your . . . orbit."

"From mere insult to ridicule. I wager you were once as ignorant of this place as I am now. Mark me, I shall learn what you know, and then we'll see who has advantage."

"When you know, advantage will be of no use to you."

"So much for what you know. No matter where I am now, I once described a course through the universe that cannot be erased. My fame delivered me here with advantage aplenty."

"And such a disastrous course. You will be known for war and wreckage."

"I fought for my emperor and for God. Friedland is safe. My estates are prosperous and orderly."

"You fought for yourself. Friedland was your spoil, as now it is Trautmannsdorf's."

"Trautmannsdorf, that imperial quill-driver, has Friedland? My other estates?"

"Gone, apportioned now among your . . . friends: Piccolomini, Gallas, Butler, Gordon, Leslie, even Devereux."

"So much for gratitude. I gave Piccolomini 10,000 thaler after we fought at Lützen. I would have made an empire had these cowards not interrupted me. Your works, whatever they were, cannot have been greater than mine."

"That is not for me to say, nor you either."

"To whom will we answer, then?"

"I cannot say that we are anything but alone with ourselves, Wallenstein."

"Adrift among the stars?"

"Adrift, only."

"But what of time and fate? Where shall I go and when?"

"We are quite finished with all of that. I thought you understood. We are permitted to ruminate upon our accomplishments, as it were, for the benefit of those who follow. And it seems I have less to account for than you, Wallenstein."

"So I thought. You passed through life unnoticed, as ghostly then as now."

"I had not your thirst for fame, but none of that is of any moment."

"Yet I will be remembered by all of history. 'Tis most curious. I can see you at the edge of a candle's glow . . . You were a wretched scholar, by God!"

"Not wretched always."

"I know of books and their makers. From Bohemia to Italy, never did I know a one who was not miserable. Silly men. Petty men of no spirit or courage. They invented meaning where there was none to be had and took pride in their mean little lives. Yes, I can see you in that life. You wrote books and yearned for fame, much as did I."

"I did not yearn for fame."

"You did, Lipsius, and yet you had no courage."

"I wrote eighty-four books and four thousand letters."

"And changed sides for each one you wrote, I can see: Protestant hither, Catholic thither. Which way will our Lipsius jump? Does his quill go high today, or low, left or right?"

"I needed sanctuary for my work."

"With Europe aflame, Lipsius wants a cool spot? What arrogance!"

"I was master of my own domain, as you believed yourself to be."

"You were wretched, and you were alone. Your students fawned upon you, no doubt, but I taught thousands to follow me. I know your kind well enough, Lipsius. I suffered the acquaintance of scholars when I was a child at Aldorf, and after my mother and father died I was imprisoned in your company till I had the wit to attend my own mind. And when I had power I had men such as you ready to say to me what I would have them say, and cloak it all in the false dignity of knowledge."

"'Tis true that knowledge often does not deserve those who possess it. It seems that were knowledge a man, he would be a slave."

"I have never known a scholar so humble that he would submit to knowledge. You all pretend you are masters of it. But I see that you would yoke your knowledge to any patron at all. You lived a masquerade, Lipsius. How many creeds did you swear to? Calvinist, Lutheran, Catholic—it made no difference, did it?"

"I died a Catholic."

"You died afraid of life, clutching a crucifix, you pretender!"

"I was devoted to reason."

"Then your calculations were as faulty as Kepler's. Our times had no place for reason."

"Against all the riot, reason was our only defense. Religion spelled death and destruction. Reason and virtue. These could have been our salvation. Had I written more, had I . . . "

"Ink-swillers! Save me from their wisdom!"

"Who profits from your meditations?"

"Profit? No man knows more of it than I. I made war feed itself."

"And turned base metals into gold?"

"Do not scoff, Lipsius. Paper served well enough: the contracts I made with the emperor bested the best alchemists. Not even the emperor turned war into gold so well, and I gave him more than his money's worth. Had I served God thusly, I would be first among the saints of Heaven."

"Yet, Wallenstein, the emperor connived in your death. It was his warrant that Devereux acted upon."

"He . . . was made prisoner of his fears."

"He was the author of your miseries, no matter what service you gave, and why should a *condotierro* expect more? Betrayal is the rule in your tribe."

"I kept his faith till there was no more to be had. I defended him even before he became emperor. Do you not know of my actions in Hungary? At Gradisca against the Venetians? By God, my *cuirassiers* cut their way through twice to that city. Trautmannsdorf had reason enough to be grateful for my presence then. And Ferdinand: when Thurn and Gabor made their campfires on the hills above Vienna, he cowered in his palace while I defended his bridges. And at the White Mountain . . . "

"And after the twenty-seven were executed in the square at Prague, you made sure to receive your payment. Such devotion! You grew your power to such proportions that you endangered your beloved empire."

"And you, Lipsius, betrayed less? You swore as a Calvinist for a dozen years, you seditious old pedant, and then died with a crucifix clutched to your breast. Better to depend upon a wind vane for regularity than the loyalty of Justus Lipsius."

"Philosophy was my true creed, a philosophy that took no notice of temporal affairs. Zeno of the painted porch. Reason above all. Virtue its companion."

"And who knew of this secret faith?"

"No secret to those who knew of my books."

"And so, having read your books, your patrons forgave your treasons?"

"I wanted them only to understand. What care had Socrates for treason?"

"You make as though you are our Socrates? What effrontery! Once understanding, what would your patrons know?"

"They would know your reason of state no longer, but a state of reason."

"A scholar's silly word games in place of my *cuirassiers,* my heavy Reiters?"

"Your wars would be given a new shape."

"What a homely ambition, Lipsius. Was this all?"

"You should know enough of contracts, Wallenstein. I proposed a different kind, one between the state and those who defend it."

"I had such a contract with my emperor. He never had better, certainly not from Bucquoy, not Dampierre . . . "

"Mercenaries, who lived for loot and lust and the excitements of combat alone. You had no higher purpose. Machiavelli himself could not have imagined a worse band than this. Sforza himself would blush at your destructions."

"Name your higher purpose, then."

"Fighting for the love of country."

"Whose? The armies were made of many nations. My Croats, my Cossacks, my Poles, my Flanders-men, there could have been a thousand kinds. No other army could be made up."

"And what of those whose fields and villages you wasted, those whose children and wives you killed?"

"Not I. My instructions were strict: wanton plunder earned my soldiers the gallows and the wheel. Why, I've had a colonel's head at my feet for such."

"Wolves do now run free where you have marched."

"Soldiers will do as they do. It is in their nature."

"What if their nature were changed?"

"Ha! Easier to change the course of Mars itself."

"What if they were made to see to their own defenses, fighting for their own kind alone, so that their state might cherish and help to protect them?"

"This is beyond imagining. Where do you get such ideas?"

"The ancients imagined it. So ran the legions of Rome itself. Tacitus tells us so."

"Those were soldiers."

"Those were Romans."

"And who would tend the fields, if peasants were made to fight?"

"Who would tend the fields, after your soldiers slaughtered the peasants and spoiled the land?"

"When the lands are ruined, Lipsius, we will make peace."

"You will have peace when you have victory, Wallenstein."

"I could not see the end of it all. I fought for twenty years, and still the wars continued."

"Were the mercenaries gone, I could see the end of it. We could fight for peace, not for profit. War for peace, made by those who would enjoy it."

"Is this your virtue at war? If plunder and contributions do not pay the soldiers, they will not fight."

"My soldiers would be paid and trained besides, but by their own kind. And they will fight better than yours."

"What does a scholar know of such things? Was the great Lipsius beside me at Dessau Bridge without my knowing it? Did he charge with Isolani's Croats in their red capes? Or perhaps he did best Mansfeld with Gal's Hungarian horsemen?"

"The Romans taught me war, with their books. And I, in turn, taught my young scholars how they shaped their armies to defend what they loved, not plunder and kill what profited them."

"And your scholars then became soldiers, did they?"

"They did. Maurice of Orange was my student. And his cousin William Louis was my correspondent. You know of these scholars of war, and de la Guardie?"

"They made the Low Countries our university of war. And this de la Guardie, the one who tutored Gustavus Adolphus in his youth?"

"The same."

"Ah. I wondered at our pairing in this place, how it was made and what was the sense of it. This de la Guardie, he taught Gustavus the Dutch way of war. I heard first how it was done at Breitenfeld. Those damned musketeers, the way they handled their pieces, firing without cease, one rank, then another, and then another, till the first were reloaded. Tilly said it was a pretty piece of work. Even he took away a musket-ball in his arm. Pappenheim was wounded seven times, stripped and left for dead on the field. His men could not stand in the face of such firing. The artillery, the cavalry, all worked like actors on a stage."

"You saw my handiwork yourself on the fields of Lützen, did you not, Wallenstein?"

"Ah, God's truth I did, and used the Swedish way myself. But it was an evil day. If Pappenheim had not arrived when he did . . . "

"And did you read the Swedish musketeers and how they turned out to level their fire at you? How they performed their countermarch?"

"I did that. Without my cavalry . . . What did you call the turns of the musketeers?"

"A countermarch. I drew out how the Romans fought and fitted it to Maurice's army and said how they should use it with their muskets and arquebuses in battle. De la Guardie took it to Gustavus. You saw me through the fog and battle lines at Lützen, Wallenstein."

"I was looking for the king of snow and ice. I meant that he would melt in the German sun."

"There was no sun that day, though, was there, Wallenstein? He took your measure."

"I never saw an army handled so prettily, 'tis true. But he did not live to see it push me away from the windmills. One of Piccolomini's black riders pistoled him in the back, and another did for him once and for all. Still, his army did not break."

"The cause was Bernard, of Saxe-Weimar. He will succeed you all."

"I succeeded, shook the musket-balls from my cloak, and rode on."

"And such glory afterward. You beheaded fourteen of your officers."

"And seven more broken on the scaffold besides. They failed us all. You forgot my rewards."

"These things moved your men to fight. Think if they fought for themselves, their families, a state beloved for its reason and virtue."

"They would have fought no better or worse. Your countermarchers, whatever they fought for, would have won or lost as they did. I drilled my musketeers just as your precious Maurice drilled his. No reason but fortune moved my soldiers. All our states today are too weak to ask for more than this. You say your Roman virtue is the better reason? I have heard all that before. I have seen reason twisted to any purpose or method, and the wreckage of war is the same for all of it. You would have war be virtuous. I say war is only the highest form of commerce: it is both lender and borrower, one and the same."

"And I say we will never see your kind of war again. Europe can no longer tolerate your kind of warrior, Wallenstein."

"War will be a pretty dull business, then."

"We will return Mars to his orbit, Wallenstein, to his old Roman stations."

"I say we can use the Roman ways without the Romans' reasons. My old soldiers were right when they complained of their drills: one can teach a dog to dance. He will keep time, and he will keep time if you beat him or if you feed him. It matters not. Don't you see, Lipsius? Armies are like the whores who follow them with the baggage trains. They will fight well or they will fight badly for any cause at all. They have so done. Only remember: your precious legions were a nightmare for their Caesars, just as my armies were for my emperor . . . "

"Yet your wars were engines of disaster . . . "

"What war is not? You would have disaster become noble, yet be a disaster all the same. How innocent you were, dreaming all those years of your fine purposes, Lipsius. Do not forget, my scholarly friend, that it was my kind of war that followed yours."

"Your payment was assassination. The world will repudiate your ways, Wallenstein."

"Could it be, Lipsius, that we are both fated to be robbed of our satisfactions? Will history forget us?"

"It may be true, Wallenstein. We are come to a bad end, after all."

5

LA NOCHE TRISTE

In which modern imperialism invades the New World to ignite a war between cultures and a revolution in the culture of war, as a singular imperialista *might have recalled in her memoirs.*

The fragmented manuscript that follows was discovered several years ago in the *Archivo General de Indias* of Seville. The surviving manuscript was well preserved, save for the folds in which the paper was quartered, in a wine cask, between sheaves of tax rolls from various *municipales* of Spain's Extremadura region. The ancient hand in which it is written—not that of the true author, we may surmise—was blessed with an artistic flair unknown to old Castile. If the manuscript is genuine, it is of great significance to the history it purports to describe.

The manuscript is in the form of a memoir by one Maria de Estrada, once of Seville, who was one of only eight *Castillanas* to have accompanied Hernan Cortés in his campaign of conquest against the Aztec empire of Montezuma. She is the only Castilian woman named by Bernal Diaz del Castillo in his own memoir of those events from 1519, when the Cortés expedition landed near present-day Vera Cruz, and the destruction two years later of Montezuma's capital at Tenochtitlan.

Estrada may have begun this campaign as a camp follower in

Cuba, barely distinguishable from the mass of female *indigenes* that the conquistadors always seemed to have on hand. But she did not remain so, for the chronicler Bernal Diaz showed her fighting alongside her *companeros* during the great crisis of the Cortés expedition; and later, when the conquistadors celebrated their victory over the Aztec empire, Diaz pointedly named her with other notable—and raucous—celebrants. By then, she was certainly no camp follower but a *conquistadora*.

The rest of the story is hers to tell.

In New Spain today there reside many men whom the passage of time has allowed a certain freedom to recount all manner of fictitious deeds from the earliest days of the conquest of this land. They recline in the comfort of their estates or in the plazas of their towns and tell stories of what they did in this time or that at the side of the great Captain Cortés when he took this land in the name of his God and the Emperor Charles. When these stories make their way to my ears, I nod and say nothing and only pretend to be interested. I know these stories are not true, for I was myself with Hernan Cortés and his companeros from the very day he slashed the tree three times with his sword and laid claim to all before him, and all that could be, besides.

Now, so long after these great events happened, many accounts of this time have been written down by impostors or, to say the same, *historiadors,* who with their pen have tried to conquer what they could not by sword. And also, some of my old companeros, wanting to profit still more by their deeds than they have already done, have written their own stories that they can give to lawyers in Spain who lay claims against the memory and fortune of Cortés, now that he is dead.

Because I am an old woman, some will wonder that I presume to write down my own story. They will say this is not the way any woman should serve her men, and anyway who will listen to *cuentos de viejas?* How could a woman know of these things that happened in those days? Those who say such things are ignorant, or dishonest, and lie to themselves as well as to others. I know their stories will live on to lie to the innocent. I look at my great-grand-children, playing about me here on the tiles of my house, and I wonder if the truth of those days will ever find them.

That is why I must write down these things. I am eighty-four years old and have come to the end of my adventures, which began so long ago and so many leagues away from this place. I have no need of money. I am well provided for by the estates of my several husbands and my children. Nor do I yearn for fame. I do not care to be remembered except by my family. But I would have them know of my own story, and how I came to be here in the cool mornings of Jalapa, alongside the high mountains I crossed over many times with Cortés himself, sometimes in triumph and victory, sometimes in wretched fear and despair. They will see that the stories they will hear elsewhere are not my stories, and they will be able to judge for themselves what their *nana* has done for them and the lands in which they live. And they will see that it is a most wonderful story, indeed.

I was born Maria de Estrada, eighty-four years ago, as I have already said. Because of the life I have led, many have supposed that I was a natural child, but I was not. My father, Francisco Maria Hernandez de Estrada, was a craftsman of fine houses and sometime soldier. He fought in Italy and against the Turks and, later, against the Moors, but his wounds in the last war brought an end to his soldiering, and he returned to Seville with his honors and married my mother, Anna, in his twenty-ninth year. I was born the following year, and when I was five the pestilence took both my father and mother from me and I was left an orphan. My father's estate, such as it was, passed to his brother, Pedro, who kept his own family, which was very large, in a fine house near the center of the city. My father's estate was meant to contribute to my welfare and upbringing, but my uncle took it as his own. I was regarded in his family as more a housemaid than a relative. I was kept in the servants' quarters and ate with them and slept with them and did the chores of the household and was never to hear a kind word from my uncle's family, although his servants treated me as one of their own.

In my uncle's house there was a vast library, and even before one of the servants taught me to read I would steal into this room and gaze upon the many books it contained. The books were arranged along two shelves like so many soldiers going into battle, side by side, with armor made of leather, and so I came to think of them as my little soldiers. After many secret visits to this room, I took one of the little soldiers with me to my bed and with a little candle lay awake all night, running my fingers over the beautiful words and the wonderful pictures that framed each page. The other servants warned me that I was not to enter this room and that if I were caught by anyone in my uncle's family it would go very badly for me; but I was beginning to be headstrong and refused to listen. As they predicted, my little soldiers did cause me trouble, for one night when I thought my uncle had gone out he returned unexpectedly and caught me on the ladder, reaching for a thick volume on the top shelf. He used his cane on me for a long time, but I do not know how long. When he was finished, he summoned his manservant and told him to take me away. He said that I could stay in the house so long as he never saw me again, but that if he ever did see me again, I was to be cast out in the street.

So it came to be that the servants protected me by keeping me away from the house as much as they could, working in the stables and helping them on market day when they went to obtain goods for my uncle's table and other necessities for the house. I much preferred my new duties. I did not have to traffic with my uncle or his ugly family, and when I finished helping the stable boys with their chores they permitted me to ride the horses if no one was looking. In this way I learned all about horses, which was a very unusual thing for a girl in those days and times, for I learned about horses as a boy learned about horses: how to care for them in stable and field, how to fit their saddles and bridles, how to train them, how to load them if necessary, how to work the leather on the saddles, and many other things. But I refused to beat the horses and treat them as the stable boys did, and for that reason I was able to ride the wilder horses that the stable boys would not go near. These wild horses would permit me to mount them without saddle or bridle or spur and ride them as I pleased. One of the stupid stable boys put it about that I was a witch who used special powers on these animals, but I hit him on the nose and told him to quit spreading such ugly words.

On quiet days when the family was gone, I could creep into the library and continue my reading. As time went by, I read many wonderful books and learned many things of which my fellow servants were unaware. When we were resting I would sometimes try to teach them what I knew, or tell them of the stories I had read, but they were afraid I would be discovered again and that my uncle would blame them for not keeping me where he had set me. So after a while I stopped trying to tell them what I knew, for I understood their fears. I could be brave on my own account, but some of them had families to care for, and without my uncle's patronage they would have all become beggars. They knew as I did that my uncle was capable of becoming very angry and flinging them into the streets.

When I was a few years older, because I was such a horseman and could read the list of goods for purchase that had been written by the head servant, I was allowed to take a horse and cart to the market days by myself. I had loved the market days since my first visit as a little girl. I enjoyed these days because I could see all manner of people moving about, and I laughed heartily at the merchants when they bargained with their customers, and even insulted them or threw clods of dirt at them, even though they all might have known one another for years. Always, there was much noise, and every time someone would start singing and someone else would start dancing and soon many of the customers would forget their duties to their households and join in the merriment. In such times I too forgot about my duties and often stayed too long at market, singing and dancing and arguing with the merchants and trading insults.

Already by this time I was becoming a woman. In my life I had never attended much to my appearance except to be as clean as I could from time to time. Thus I believed I could present myself anywhere in the world. This of course was a stupid thing to believe, but all the same I saw that men looked at me differently than they looked at other women in the market. Naturally, there had been brutes at market day since my first visit who never seemed to change, who seemed only to think of lifting any skirt whose hem was within reach, no matter how they felt about these women. These were the most numerous of their kind, but other men seemed as though they did not care about such things, while still others could be very kind. Some were not unpleasant to look at, I found. Such a one became my first husband, and I was fortunate that he attended market on one particular day, for otherwise my life would have been far different than the one I have had.

One of the kitchen servants, who was also named Maria, came to me early one morning, all flushes and excitement and worry on her face. She told me that while she was helping to serve dinner the night before she heard my uncle and his stupid wife talking about someone named Maria. Thinking they were calling her, the servant went into the dining room, but my uncle shooed her away, saying, "We are not talking about you, silly little goose." Still, the servant girl was curious now and managed to hear the rest of what they were saying.

Uncle complained that he was growing weary of supporting me, and that whenever he asked the servants about my welfare they responded sullenly, as though he was to be blamed for the beating he had given me, whereas he had been the offended party. My uncle said that he thought I had turned the servants against the family, and that the servants surely loved me far more than they loved him. The whole affair was intolerable. He said that as long as I was a little girl, I could be kept out of the way and was of no trouble and did not eat much. But now, as I was surely a woman, albeit still a very young one, men were beginning to make trouble about me and my antics at market days. None of this would matter, he said, but for a letter he had received recently from an old friend of my father and mother. This friend, whose name I did not remember, said that by his reckoning I had come of age and that he would be willing to support me at his estate until such time as I found a husband. But my uncle said he had no wish for my happiness or prosperity. He would give me to the Church instead.

From that moment I knew I would never serve my uncle again nor would I serve the Church, for I was already an unbeliever in my heart. While I was still young, I tried praying very hard for many nights, asking God to return my parents or only to turn my uncle's heart back toward me. As my life went on much as before, whether I prayed or not, I decided that I would no longer defraud myself by believing in a Church that permitted a life like mine. And now, so many years later, I am comforted by the knowledge that my decision was right. For a young woman such as I was then, headstrong and independent, there was only one road, and this returns me to my first husband.

Perhaps it is best that I do not give his name, for his family was a prosperous one and remains so today, with powerful friends at court. I was told long ago that my union with this frail young man would never be acknowledged by his family, who blame me for turning his head and taking him away to his death in a savage new land. The truth is that I had no plan at all but to escape from my uncle, but for that, if it proved necessary, I would have traveled to hell itself. So it mattered not to me when he proposed that we take ship for the New World and seek out our fortune there.

When I learned of my uncle's plans for me, I sought out my

young man and told him of what I had heard. Without further talk he said we would run away to the New World and make our way there, heedless of what our families might say or do, and that when he had made our fortune we would return to Spain and take our place in society.

After a few days we made our way to Sanlucas de Barrameda, where the Guadalquivir emptied into the sea, to join a company about to sail for Hispaniola, and that is how I came to cross the great ocean sea in a ship of one hundred tons.

Before we were at Hispaniola a year, a new expedition under Diego Velázquez was organized to go to the island of Cuba where it was said that great hoards of gold and other riches were to be had. Our life in Hispaniola was so bad that I thought any new life must be better than this and so we went to Cuba as soon as we could. But I was wrong, for no sooner had we arrived at Santiago de Cuba and settled on our little farm than my husband cut his leg with an axe and bled to death while I and other settlers sat powerless to prevent his suffering. We buried him, and Fray Oviedo said a mass for him and others who had recently been taken by a fever. Nor did I ever see any gold, although I heard others had found a few grains of it.

Perhaps this was why the Castilians could not seem to rest. No sooner would they arrive at a place than they would begin to dream of other places they had heard of that were to be found across the sea. Whenever I went to market days, I heard all manner of schemes and plans and rumors of new lands elsewhere, opening around me like a great flower. Fantastic tales arrived with each ship that put in to our ports. Sailors told of mermaids and monsters they had seen during their travels, and people with beaks and two heads, and cities made of gold. But where? I would ask. To the north, one would say, in Terra Florida. To the south, would say another, across the Great Southern Sea, beyond which lay the riches of Cathay. One other even told of a great race of Amazons, fierce tribes of all women whose skills in combat would best those of the Cid himself. And, then, still darker were the tales of heathen cannibals who fed only on the hearts of men.

But everyone knew that sailors were the greatest liars of all. I heard so many strange things I grew impatient with these tales. One falsifier grew so angry with me one day that he drew his sword and threatened to beat me with the flat of it until I stabbed him with my husband's old dagger that I always carried with me then. I did not hurt him very much, but his pride at being bested by a mere woman hurt him more, and he called out to his friends to set upon me until a small and pale but fierce-looking gentleman stepped between us. He placed his hand upon the hilt of his sword and pledged to use it in my defense against any man who sought to abuse me. "Doña Maria is from this time under my protection," he said. This was the first time anyone had referred to me in this way, and it was the first time I met the one fame now knows as Hernan Cortés.

Don Hernan turned his back contemptuously upon my would-be assailants and inquired of me whether I was in need of anything and whether I might do him and his wife the favor of dining at his estate whenever I was in the vicinity. I thanked him for his offer of hospitality, and I said that I wanted for nothing, although this was a lie. I remember that when all this happened I was faint from lack of food and living on what the Indians would bring me from the forest. As for visiting his wife, Catalina, whom I did not know, I felt no particular need of the companionship of other women. Most of them complained bitterly all the time and anyway would die from the hardship of the place, and this would only make me sad. Too, I heard later that this wife of Cortés was illiterate, stupid, and lazy besides, and I am none of these things.

Soon one of these ruffians came back to me. His name was Rodrigo Lares and was called Lares the fine horseman because there were other men on the island named Lares who did not have his way with horses. Lares said to me that I was brave to stand my ground that way and that I was fortunate to have Don Hernan as a patron, for he was an educated and important gentleman in the service of the governor, Don Diego Velázquez, which I did not know at the time.

By then, everyone knew that two expeditions had been sent to the south and there had found more islands with many natives who, unlike the Caribs, were very warlike and fought bravely. Some of the men who came back from these expeditions thought they were bird-people, but others said they seemed so because they wore cloaks and headpieces made of beautiful feathers. Others said they were cannibals who ate their own people. Before long, word came that Don Diego was mounting a new expedition to these lands under a new captain, for at this time the fever in Cuba was very bad and Don Diego did not think it was right for him to leave the island. I had decided that I would try to join this expedition, even if I had to go by myself, but it happened that several other Castilian women on the island wished to go as well and offered to cook and wash and nurse the sick if they were allowed. But Lares the fine horseman said I could go with him if I wished to do so, and that he would treat me not as a servant but as a sister if I would work as the other women did, and I agreed with this arrangement.

It came to pass that Lares and other horsemen were instructed to gather up as many horses as they could find and drive them overland to the old port of Havana, which was where the new expedition was to gather. The *hidalgo* Pedro de Alvarado was in charge of this march, which was to recruit as many settlers along the way as would consent to go on the expedition. As the fever was very bad everywhere, many settlers left their farms behind, and some left families as well.

Of course, some of those who agreed would never have made farmers in even the best of seasons and with no sickness or accident. They were adventurers, and their interest was in a life without labor or care. They fancied themselves great fighters, but most of them had no way of knowing whether or not they were because they had never been in a war. They were mostly great talkers, idlers, gamblers, complainers, and skirt-lifters. I had no respect for such men, and said so, and some of them had words with Lares the fine horseman, who said to them: "If you must complain about Doña Maria, complain to her personally if you will, but I would not do it if I valued my health. As for myself, I will treat her with respect, and I would advise you to do the same. Who knows what trials we will meet on this expedition? Every hand must have a value."

Only when we arrived in Havana did I learn who Don Diego had selected as captain general of the expedition. One day as I was helping Lares the fine horseman prepare mangers for the horses on board one of the ships, Don Hernan himself came aboard. "Why Doña Maria," he called out, laughing, "I mistook you for a sailor because you were working as well as any, and better than most!" Perhaps some women would have been insulted by such familiarity, but then Cortés followed his speech with a deep bow and a sweep of his hat to me. "I am very happy you have decided to come on this voyage, Doña Maria. You will be of great value, I know. Great honor and fame await us, for we sail in the name of God and His Majesty."

I thought that was a fine thing for him to say, even if it wasn't true. He was, I thought, discontented like the rest of us, seeking adventure and freedom. If he believed he made God happy doing so, all the better for him. And as for His Majesty, so far as I was concerned he might as well have been talking about a mermaid. I had never seen one and anyway did not care if they existed or not.

As Lares the fine horseman and I had joined with Pedro de Alvarado in the drive to Havana, he claimed us for his company when Cortés named him one of the captains, and of course Cortés agreed to this because Alvarado was a gentleman of a distinguished family and his closest friend in the Indies. He had accompanied one of the earlier expeditions under Don Diego's nephew, Don Juan de

Grijalva, and was an excellent horseman. Or so Lares said, but I think Lares was as impressed by Captain Alvarado's fine appearance and winning ways as much as anything. Sometimes people were at first misled by how the captain dressed and his golden necklace and rings and the white cloak with the red cross that he wore. They derided him as *el comendador* because the cloak had belonged to his uncle who was a knight in the Order of Santiago, and the captain was not. But no one ever said this directly to the captain because he was also very brave and very quick with his sword, and because even though he smiled all the time and had a hearty word for everyone, he could be very cruel, as we were to learn. This was in February, in the year of Our Lord, as is always said, 1519.

Although the captain general's commission from Don Diego Velázquez required him only to explore, or so it was said before we left, I suspected from the first that this expedition was to go to war against whomever we might find if they would not submit peacefully to our command. I had never known of any expedition to have so many ships, or so fully fitted with all manner of the implements of war and the men to use them. Counting the sailors, who it is true were not so good for fighting, we had more than five hundred men. Of these, thirty-two were crossbowmen and thirteen were arquebusiers, and more than once in the months ahead these men were to prove themselves worth more than anything else we carried, save of course for the sixteen horses that we had.

Some of these horses were not very good, such as Baena's roan, which was as empty-headed as its rider. Ortiz's dark horse, which we called El Arriero, was a brave and strong animal, and of course Lares the fine horseman rode his chestnut, which was sleek and fast and a beautiful dancer. Captain Cortés's chestnut horse was very difficult, of high spirits, and one that few could ride, although I was to ride him without trouble in the days ahead. He died later at San Juan de Ulua. Alonzo Puertocarrero's horse, a fast silver-gray mare, was bought for him by Cortés himself, who had used the golden tassels from his cloak to buy the animal for him because Puertocarrero had no money.

In addition to the crossbowmen and the arquebusiers, we had ten brass guns and some falconets and some lombards from the ships. I was fascinated by the guns, which could fire balls or stones of two or three pounds if they were correctly handled. A veteran of the wars in Italy, Francisco de Orozco, was named captain of artillery, and as he and I became friendly he would sometimes allow me to work these guns. They were very light pieces and could be moved without much trouble, and we later built carts that would allow us to carry them more easily, and as the gunners spent so much time with their weapons they gave them names such as Santiago and Juan Ponce and so forth.

By the middle of March we had doubled the headland beyond Isla de Mujeres and held fast to the coast, passing the place where the Indians had attacked Hernandez de Cordoba so fiercely, and finally dropped our anchors at the mouth of the Tabasco River, where, as we learned, the Indian town was called Potonchan. All along the way, the *naturales* came out to watch us. They showed no fear of us, and indeed in several places they beat their drums and shook their weapons in our direction. Cortés, on whose *nao* I was then, pretended not to notice their behavior. Anyway, when we arrived at Potonchan, someone said this was where Grijalva had met friendly Indians during his expedition the year before. Potonchan was the largest town we had seen, with perhaps 20,000 buildings made of adobe. At the center of the town were three large pyramids with temples on top that we called *cues*. This was where their priests sacrificed their victims to their hideous gods.

On the morrow, the Mayas offered up eight turkeys and several baskets of maize. Cortés told them he wanted more food, and water, and gold besides. The Mayas said there was no gold, no more food, and that if water was wanted Cortés could have his men dig for it. Cortés said that the water was salty. The Mayas said that he should dig elsewhere, but not there, for if Cortés and his men remained where they were, they would all be killed.

The Mayas made Cortés remain in his boats in the middle of the river for four days. From time to time, they would bring a few more turkeys and some more maize, but finally they said there was no more food for Cortés and that he and his vassals should leave. Cortés replied that he was required to see their town and speak with their chiefs, whom they called *caciques,* so that he might obey his king's orders. The Indians said that the town could not be visited, that there were no longer any people there because they had run away. The Indians said they did not want presumptuous barbarians who smelled so badly in their houses and that they had their own king and did not need another, although I do not think Aguilar translated these insults exactly. Cortés said he must have gold as well, to satisfy his king. The Indians said they had no desire to give him anything, especially since he had sent men without permission the night before into the town and beyond. Cortés said they had no right to starve his men, and that if they allowed all his men to come into the town he would tell them more about his king and his God and give them advice. The Indians said they did not want his advice, and that they had their own gods, and then they attacked briefly with their arrows, stones, and spears, which they hurled with a device they called *atlatl,* a kind of sling that increases the distance of a spear or dart.

Every time they refused Cortés a request, he would ask for more, never agreeing to anything the naturales said. It was as if he was not listening to them at all, although I know he was. This was his habit throughout our campaigns. Nor did he seem to care that there were many thousands of Indians and not so many of us. I never heard him lament our lack of strength. Instead, he always said, "Fortune favors the brave," which was all the more impressive because he said it in Latin.

So now, even while the Indians beat their drums and formed for battle, painted and dressed in great plumes of feathers with fear-some designs, Cortés called upon the royal notary, Diego de Godoy, to read the royal requirement that the Mayas submit themselves to the rule of our king. But this seemed to enrage the Indians, for as soon as Aguilar finished interpreting what Don Diego had said, they attacked even more fiercely than before. As there were so many Indians, attacking from all directions, Cortés could not allow a boat to remove me and others from combat. I was allowed to remain, provided I keep myself close to the guns. One of the men, an arquebusier whose name I cannot recall, drew his sword and handed it to me, and said, "God go with you, Doña Maria." I saluted him with the sword and turned toward the Indians, who were becoming more numerous all the time and were drawing closer to us.

We could not remain with our boats in the shallows or along the bank because the mud was so thick we could not move. Cortés understood this right away, so he called upon the whole company to advance with him, and so we did. The Indians gave way reluctantly, but they were strong fighters and brave, too. Never did they turn their backs to us that day, but fought us face to face, although many of their number were killed by our muskets and swords. But our soldiers were wounded, too, by the many arrows and the swords they faced, both of which were armed with obsidian points and edges and were very sharp. It was during this first fight that we learned the Indians were trying to capture us so they could sacrifice us to their gods. Instead of killing us, they wanted us for their idols, and many of them died trying to take us from our formation, which we kept whole even in the worst moments.

At first I tried to remain with the guns as I was told, but seeing several Indians lay hands on Lares the fine horseman I made my way to him and fought with the sword by his side. Everyone was too excited to notice that a woman was among them, and in truth I forgot about all else except keeping the Indians away from me and Lares. Then Lares and I were joined by an old expeditionary named

Bernal Diaz, whom I had only briefly spoken to before. Diaz already had been wounded in the thigh by an arrow, but he fought on anyway, and very bravely. He did not retire with the other wounded but made a friend withdraw the arrow from his leg and bound up his wound and continued as before. Finally, the company made its way into the town square to the three *cues,* and here Cortés called a halt. That was when Cortés drew three strokes with the sword on the old *cieba* tree and claimed the land for the king. And so that all of us should hear, he shouted that no one would move him from this spot if God so pleased. At the end of the day, I took a breastplate and helmet that one of the wounded had left behind and fell asleep with the rest in the great court of the three temples.

And so my companeros and I fought for the next two days. On the very next morning, after mass, Cortés ordered two companies into the forest to find a way behind the Indians, who were sure to attack us again, as they said they would. Cortés remained to guard the wounded, and before long the Indians assailed us once more, just as bravely as before and as numerous. Our other two companies, commanded by Francisco de Luga and Pedro de Alvarado, fought with a very large group of Indians and were made to retreat toward the town. Cortés once again showed his bravery by leading a small band to assist de Luga's company and returned to the town in good order.

During the second night Cortés had ordered that the guns be brought forward, and also that the horses be brought ashore as well, in preparation for the next day's fighting. Of course our guns frightened the Indians and killed very many of them, but still they came forward to give combat as before. However, when we sallied out to the savanna where de Lugo had been attacked on the day before, thirteen of our horsemen made their way around behind the Indians and charged into them with great ferocity. Then the Indians broke and ran for fear of the horses, which they told us later they thought were dragons and that the men and the horses they rode were one and the same. The horses and the guns together killed very many this day. Some said eight hundred Indians died on the savanna. I did not fight much this day but remained behind with our many wounded and tried to help them as best I could. As we had no other means of succor, we used the fat of a dead Indian to sear the wounds. Some we could not help. One of our soldiers had been struck by an arrow in his ear, and another in his throat.

As for myself, I had not even been scratched in the fighting, and afterward several of my companeros came to me and thanked me for my assistance in the fighting and said how they would fight at my side any day, and so in some way I was regarded afterward as a soldier. I did not feel badly about killing Indians, for in truth I had no choice if I wished to live, but if the Indians had treated us peacefully I would have treated them the same. Still and all, I kept my sword and my breastplate and my helmet with me always, and no one ever asked me to return these things. Perhaps my benefactors were dead by then.

After these battles, some caciques came and made peace with Cortés and provided food and lodging for us. Cortés and the priests were very busy, treating with the Indians, who accepted God and the king and allowed us to tear down their idols and replace them with images of the Virgin Mary, who they called *tececiguatas,* which meant "great lady" in their language. Cortés asked these chiefs where they obtained their gold, and they pointed westward and said "Culua" and "Mexico," words that we did not know at the time. But when I heard what the caciques had said, I knew Cortés would take us in that direction sooner or later.

Once we had defeated the naturales, Cortés told them that they need only return to their homes to have peace, and not one day had passed before the whole town came to life once more. One of Cortés's captains, who like Cortés was from Extremadura, stood by me to listen while Cortés and the preachers explained to the naturales about our God and why he was the only true God. Sandoval grinned in a devilish way and said to me, "These naturales are telling Cortés what he wishes to hear, and the interpreter Aguilar is playing false with how he renders their speeches. One need only look at his face to see that he has trouble himself comprehending what Omedo the preacher and Cortés are saying. This seems to me like having a wolf talk to a chicken: the wolf says I will eat you if you do not obey me, so the chicken agrees so long as the wolf allows a little pecking here and there." I understood what Sandoval was saying in his blasphemous way.

We also had in our company now many women given to us by the caciques, among whom was Doña Marina, the daughter of one of them. Because of the rough way that soldiers usually treat women I expected trouble in the company, but there was very little, and I think the reason was that Fray Olmedo preached to these women right away and told them of the demands our religion made upon women and made them into Christians. And so one might say that their new religion protected these women somewhat. All the same, Cortés gave these women into the care of his officers, and Marina at first went to Puertocarrero because he was Cortés's favorite and she was pretty and intelligent. When Puertocarrero left, Marina went back to Cortés, but from the beginning Marina was first among these women because she learned Spanish very quickly and could translate for us with the Mexica when we encountered them so that we did not have to depend so much upon Aguilar. As she was never very far from Cortés's side, she did not have to do the chores required of the other women. But because she was also quite modest and of stately bearing, no one resented her either. So on the whole I was happy for the arrival of these women because it was in this way I was able to learn some of their customs and their language, which they called *coatzacoalcos*.

Besides these women, some other naturales came with us, and from then on it always seemed to me that there were far more of them than there were of us. We taught them how to do our chores, and they found game and cooked for us and carried our loads, so that even the rudest soldiers had two or three Indians to look after him. One might think that with so many servants our soldiers would grow soft and quarrelsome. However, our quarrels did not grow from softness but from greed, for it was here at San Juan de Ulua that the followers of Velázquez grew so restive that Cortés was forced to imprison some of them and hang some others to prevent the grumblers from taking flight back to Cuba. That is why Cortés had the ships run to ground and taken apart. I have heard it said since that Cortés burned the ships, but that would have been foolish indeed. He had the pilots and their shipwrights take the boats apart very carefully so that if required they could be put together at his command.

And anyway, just burning the ships would not have caused the grumblers to change their minds and cease spreading poison against Cortés in the company. For that, he had to meet the complainers head-on, which he did, and after that there was little difficulty. If he had not succeeded in suppressing his detractors in the company, we would have not been a company but only a mob, and our unity was essential if we were to succeed. Cortés was fond of the old passage from the Bible which said that a house divided cannot stand. It was a phrase he spoke many times during our trials in New Spain, but I believe he first learned the truth of it here in San Juan de Ulua.

Furthermore, this truth was no less important to Montezuma than it was to us, perhaps even more so, as we were to learn before long, for it was here at San Juan de Ulua that we obtained our first knowledge of the great king of the Aztecs himself. We did not learn until later that from our first appearances along the coast, Montezuma's spies had been watching our movements and reporting them every day to their king in his capital of Tenochtitlan. And everything we did was rendered into picture books, painted on their paper that they called *amal*. In this way, Montezuma knew how we appeared and what we were doing, but he could not know what we were or what we intended. Montezuma and his *papas* sacrificed many of their own kind every day in their usual way, cutting open their chests and offering their victims' hearts and blood to their god of war, Huitchilopochtli, in hopes of receiving divine guidance. But there was none, and Montezuma began to despair that we strangers had been sent by a rival god, Quetzalcoatl, as his legends had foretold.

Montezuma's suspicions did not prevent him from learning as much as he could about us even though we were still many leagues away from him. So we had not been long at San Juan de Ulua before two of Montezuma's governors and their retinues arrived to take the measure of us. The most important of these two caciques was Tendile, and it was with him that Cortés preferred to speak because it was clear that he had Montezuma's confidence. While Cortés was speaking with Tendile, his artists moved freely about our camp, drawing and painting as much as they could, and counting us too. This made me so nervous that I spoke with Sandoval and Olid and asked how we could allow our enemies such an advantage. Cristobal de Olid laughed and said, "Why, Doña Maria, you have your hand on your sword already before the naturales have shown they will fight! Perhaps they will not, seeing the strength given us by our Holy Mother." To this, Sandoval replied, "You may be wishing for your Holy Mother if one of the papas lays hands on you like a bloody spider to tear out your heart! I think Doña Maria is right to be watchful, and so should we all. If we are watchful now, perhaps we will not have to be brave later."

At first Tendile ordered that Cortés and the whole company be attended with food and drink and presents of gold and feather cloaks and shelter and many other things besides. One of Tendile's warriors, not understanding that I was a woman since I was wearing my breastplate and carrying a sword like the rest, gave to me a little statue with golden eyes that showed one of their priests doing rude things to another of his kind. When Lares the fine horseman made this warrior understand that I was a woman he tried to take it back from me. But I would not let it go, and after all these years I have it with me still. When I look at it, I think life would be better for women if more men had just contented themselves in this way and left us alone.

Montezuma was the greatest of all kings in this world, and his power reached many leagues in all directions from his capital, as we would learn, where many hundreds of thousands lived under his rule. Cities and towns far distant from him had been defeated by his armies and made to swear allegiance and to pay tribute to his throne, which they did every year, bringing to Tenochtitlan many *cargas* of cloth and feathers and game and jewels. And on special days, these cities would be required to offer up to his priests many victims for sacrifice to his hideous and blood-splattered gods. Woe be it to those who defied Montezuma's rule, for his armies were strong and always on hand to march against those towns that resisted him, and so it was by virtue of his violent power that his kingdom lived.

Naturally, some of Montezuma's cities wished to be free of his terrible rule and so, as we were to learn to our benefit, their resentment could be depended upon. Cortés's priests believed that we won allies because of the strength of our God, but I think they were wrong. I think that even if we had not arrived, this kingdom would have crumbled before long. It was our good fortune, therefore, to have come when we did and to have discovered how fragile was Montezuma's power. And this happened very soon because Tendile had just left us when emissaries from the city of Cempoal came to us and bade us join them there, which Cortés agreed to do right away.

At Cempoal and the other hill towns where we marched, Cortés took pains to win as many allies as he could. He was very successful because he knew it was not enough merely to sympathize with their hostility toward Montezuma; Cortés had to show them that we could help them win their freedom from Montezuma, but he had to ensure that they would become loyal to us and remain so in the times ahead. Perhaps the naturales did not see how they were exchanging one master for another, but Cortés played upon their fear of our weapons and horses and success in war and made sure of our allies by acting the friend one moment and harsh master another, so they were never certain how he might use his power.

But Cortés demanded as a return for our friendship that the naturales replace their gods with ours and put an end to their human sacrifices because this was a sin against the one true God. Nor would Cortés allow our allies to loot and plunder the new towns we happened upon during our marches, so that the new towns would rejoice at our arrival and join us to fight Montezuma as the Cempoallans themselves had done. By these means we gathered several thousands about us as we made our way through the towns of Jalapa, where I now write, and Zocotlan and Xacalingo and many other lesser villages and so, eventually, we came upon Tlaxcala, the great city whose people were to be our most important allies of all.

By this time, which was near the end of August in the year of Our Lord 1519, as they say, I had come to spend less time with the women and more time with my companeros. Perhaps because of my rude upbringing, those things that upset the women, including even those among the naturales, did not bother me so much. I took my meals and slept among the soldiers rather than with one of the officers or with the followers of the camp. And I kept my sword and other arms about me in the manner of the other expeditionaries. Now Rodrigo Lares, Cristobal de Olid, and Mesa the old gunner reckoned that we were under threat of attack from the Indians all the time.

Except for some grumblers and skirt-lifters, my companeros kept their spirits high. Sometimes Rodrigo Lares and I shared a blanket just to keep one another warm at night, but he never failed to behave in a proper way toward me. Once I said to him, "Rodrigo, why is it that neither you nor the others have ever made any advances toward me? Am I not worthy of attention?" To which he replied, "Bah. I may satisfy myself well enough among the women the naturales have given us, and it is the same with the other soldiers. As you are a Christian woman, well-born and with much dignity and a fine fighter besides, we have come to think of you as one of us. We have decided that we should treat you as one of our family. Once our campaigns are over, perhaps we will think differently, but now, amidst great danger, we must have a care for our unity, for if we do not keep our quarrels quiet, we none of us will survive this expedition."

Some of what Rodrigo said was no doubt true. It seemed to me now that nothing would prevent Cortés from leading us on to "enjoy the company of the great Montezuma," as he jovially put it. Of course, since Cortés was never excitable, even in the greatest danger, one could never be sure what he was really thinking. All we knew was that he meant to go forward, and for this our unity and bravery was of the utmost importance, as he often said. As for Rodrigo's God, if he had ever been in this place he had long since abandoned it to the blood-clotted priests who enslaved their own people with their superstitions. I told Sandoval that we should burn all these papas at the stake and their bloody temples too, whereupon he laughed and said, "Ah, my little soldier, you would fight all the way to Cathay by yourself, leaving your companeros with nothing at all to fight for. But as we are here despite all that has happened, I propose we fight together in a measured way until we discover what our destiny might be." With this, I readily agreed. This was my way of thinking at the beginning of our journey to Tenochtitlan.

Cortés had at last decided upon the men he wanted as captains of his companies: of course, there was Pedro de Alvarado, impetuous and cheerful and loyal, but also very hard; and then Avila, whom I did not know well but who was said to be as humorless as a monk; and Velázquez de Leon of a noble and enterprising family; and I was happy to hear that Olid and Sandoval had been chosen as well. Although Gonzalo de Sandoval was young and untried, Olid said he had a soldier's heart, a judgment that proved to be true. Cortés gave each of these about fifty men, and for the companies we also had 40 crossbowmen, 20 arquebusiers, about 350 men in all. To these were added 150 Cubans who were no good for fighting but useful as servants. The Cempoallans, true to their word, provided a band of 800, who were led by their own headman, named Mamexi.

Finally, we turned south toward the mountains and after crossing over the pass we now call La Lena we gradually made our way to the city of Zautla, where we were greeted by the chief, who was called Olintecle, and his people. We were made comfortable and given food and shelter and allowed to rest and repair our arms. Zautla was a very great city, as great as Cempoal, and with more people and houses and with more of their dreaded temples as well. And as we learned, Montezuma held Zautla with a very large garrison, at least one *xiquiple* of 8,000 warriors. So while the people of Zautla did not fight us, neither were they as generous to us as the other naturales had been elsewhere. When Cortés asked Olintecle for gold as a sign of his good will, Olintecle replied that he thought he would not provide gold, nor much else, unless his lord Montezuma so ordered.

Nor, when Cortés in his customary way demanded that Olintecle and his people call an end to human sacrifices, did the Zautlanos agree. On the contrary, as if to challenge Cortés face to face, they held a festival in which fifty victims were sacrificed upon the dreadful *penol* as we all watched. But Cortés did not meet this challenge in the way Olintecle may have thought he would. Instead, Cortés told Olintecle that his great lord would soon be a vassal to our own king, and that he should consider what that meant to the future of Zautla. If necessary, Cortés said to Olintecle, we would kill them all. When I heard Doña Marina tell me of this conversation, I thought that this kind of talk was very brave and wondered if Olintecle believed it at all.

If we had not been treated badly by Olintecle, neither were we treated so well as we had wished, and so after several days we marched toward Tlaxcala, the greatest of all the cities under Montezuma's hand. Our cool greeting in Zautla, and our certainty that we were no longer in lands that could be made friendly to us without a fight, filled me with foreboding. Not long after I happened to speak with one of the leaders of the naturales with us who was named Teuch. He said he had been to Montezuma's capital when he was a child and spoke of how the great city floated upon a great lake. I asked Teuch whether we would prevail if it came to war between us and the Mexica. Without waiting or even looking up from his path, he replied, "You will all be killed and eaten by the Hummingbird." For some days thereafter, I felt as though we were in a strange kind of sea, coming upon a great storm. This is how I felt as we approached the great city of Tlaxcala.

Once we had refreshed ourselves at Zautla, we set out for Tlaxcala, which was the way Mamexi had advised us to go. Olintecle had told us to go to Cholula, but Mamexi warned that he was playing false with us because the Tlaxcalans hated Montezuma very much and were an independent city, whereas the Cholulans were loyal to him. Mamexi said the Tlaxcalans would be friendly toward us and become our allies as the Cempoallans had done, all of which was true in the end. But first we would have to fight them, as we were to learn. Some leagues beyond Tlaxcala we came upon a great fortress wall that stretched from one side of the valley to another, but it was undefended and so we passed through without mishap. However, not far beyond this wall our mounted scouts came upon a small band of warriors who fled as we approached. When our horsemen pursued them, a great army rose up with wild cries of war and attacked our riders, who defended themselves with great skill. Seeing the fighting break out in front of us, Olid and the other horsemen rode forward and attacked the Indians, while the rest of us hurried forward too. The Indians had painted themselves for war and put on their headdresses and feather wings and skins and presented a fearsome sight, but they did not stand their ground before us. Mesa and some other of the gunners fired right at the Indians and killed very many of them, and though they retreated they did so in good order, never failing to carry away their dead and wounded. When the skirmish ended, we found that the Indians had killed two of our horses and wounded some others. One was Olid's fine little bay, for the Indians had dismounted Olid and would have carried him away too if Cortés and Sandoval had not come to his aid.

Olid was said to be a crude man, without fear but also without fine feelings, but later as we sat by our night fire he shivered when he said to me that he had felt the grasping fingers of the devil himself that day. I gave him a bowl of *pulque* and he finally went to sleep. I would wager that few of my companeros slept without the comforts of drink or a crucifix that night. Caring for no comforts such as these, I tended first to the wounded horses and then to our wounded men.

On the very next day the storm broke over us. We marched out at sunrise along our trail. On the night before, Cortés had met with his captains and other officers and arranged the order in which we would fight. He decided that our horsemen should go first in full force of arms, not *a la jineta* as our scouts usually did, and that the crossbowmen and arquebusiers would follow them. Then would come the guns, which we would not form in line until their captain gave the signal. Our soldiers would advance into the fight as fast as they could, taking care to protect the crossbowmen and gun men so they could do their work. Cortés told us to kill as many of the enemy as we could, because he was sure they would not be so easily driven away as before, and once again Cortés was right.

Not far along an army of Indians stood in our way, bedecked in red and white war dress, dancing and shaking their weapons at us. Cortés rode forward to make a speech as usual, to tell them of our peaceful intentions and desire for friendship. But the Indians replied to all of this by hurling all manner of things at us: spears, arrows, rocks, even bits of wood fitted with the sharp obsidian flints we had already met. All this did no harm except to Cortés's pride, for then he ordered us to attack, and so we did, and all about me I heard the old war cry, "Santiago, y cierra Espana!" I too shouted the cry and took my sword and buckler forward to be with my companeros, for I was too frightened to be left behind.

My memory cannot contain all the events of the great combats that followed for days afterward, for the enemy came at us in numbers beyond counting, and I was barely sensible, being overcome with the noise and fear and fatigue as I fought alongside my companeros. I felt as though I was inside a great whirlwind where thousands of fighters screamed and pushed and stabbed at one another. The very air around me was filled with stones and spears and arrows and swords so that one did not have the feeling of fighting one single combat but many at the same time. I remember once, when several hands reached for me out of the dust, a great sword flashed by me, cutting them off to fall at my feet. I can see in my mind even now Alvarado, grinning furiously, astride his great horse, cutting his way so neatly through the enemy, as if he was harvesting a farmer's crop. I see Olid, covered with blood and screaming, running by me and straight into an enemy warrior and cutting off his head with one sweep of the sword. Once I remembered my girlhood days at market, dancing until I was exhausted with joy, and thinking that this was how I felt now. And once I remember killing a warrior who had my uncle's face.

And then, as quickly as the storm had come, it passed. Those wounded who could not take themselves off remained upon the ground, like so many red and white birds dashed from the sky by some terrible god. Now a gentle wind blew across this field of birds, moving their feathers to and fro, keeping time with the low moans of those who suffered. I walked among the misery, and I cried because I was so tired.

We learned that these brave warriors mostly belonged to the great young Lord Xicotenga, who had defied his elders and insisted upon giving battle against us. He had boasted that his ten thousand would dine upon our flesh once he had defeated us, and he had convinced his fellow lords to follow him against us. But after these several days of fighting, the great elders of Tlaxcala saw that as they could not resist us and that as we were not allies of Montezuma, as we had said, they would do well to join us, and this they did. And from this time forward the Tlaxcalans served us very well.

And so it was that we passed, numbering less than four hundred companeros, into the district of the great city itself, in the early part of November, in the year of Our Lord, as it is said, 1519.

My first sight of Tenochtitlan came just before we reached a small causeway across Lake Xochimilco, one of the five lakes in the district of Mexico. We were still several leagues away, and yet I could already see the great *cues* against the sky, and if I looked carefully I could see the greatest of the lakes, Texcoco, and saw that it was filled with all manner of boats, though none bore sail as far as I could tell. Now with every step we encountered more and more people so that from this moment on I could say that we were never completely alone or beyond the gaze of the Indians, and therefore we were never safe thereafter. And on every side were many villages and towns full of houses made of fine materials and gardens and orchards and well-tended fields wherever the ground would allow.

Here, too, we were met by the lord of Texcoco, who was Montezuma's nephew, a great prince of much grandeur and stately bearing who was adorned with a cloak and headdress of many colored feathers. He came to us on a much-bejeweled litter, born by eight of his own caciques, and when he dismounted they swept the ground as he came forward to greet Cortés. Lord Texcoco bowed grandly and kissed the ground in the usual way. He had been sent by Montezuma himself to offer us every comfort and hospitality and to conduct us on our way to the city. Perhaps by now Cortés was accustomed to

Montezuma's ways, for he showed no surprise when Lord Texcoco announced his purpose and appeared to me to have no care in the world. Thus escorted, we marched across the causeway and found our rest in the city of Ixtapalapa, which guarded the southern approach to a greater causeway over Lake Texcoco to Tenochtitlan. Now I permitted myself a bath and a little of the many dishes of food the Indians brought us, and fell asleep on the bed of feathers they had made for us, but my sword was always within my reach.

On the very next day we arranged our march across the causeway to Tenochtitlan proper. The causeway was very large, wide enough to ride our horses twenty abreast if we had had that many. We formed our horses as well as we could, then the crossbowmen and arquebusiers followed, and then the rest of the soldiers with their swords drawn and held upright. The companeros had taken much care with their weapons; polished so, they glistened in the sun. And then came Cortés himself with some other horsemen and all the banners we could fashion, but Cortés's banner was foremost and the bearer kept it in motion, swinging it to and fro in a fine way.

Of course, news of our arrival had swept throughout the district, and the causeway and the houses along it were crowded with Indians in company with their chiefs, each one of whom was dressed in the colors of his own clan. So it was when Montezuma himself approached on his royal litter, preceded and borne by other lords, who were dressed in an even grander manner. These, indeed, were the rulers of the great city and its surroundings. Green feathers, adorned with gold and precious stones, a fine tall headdress, ear plugs of turquoise, and an ornament on his lower lip completed Montezuma's outfit, which he bore with much dignity and fine bearing. He was spare of frame, and his hair was fine and wavy. I thought he seemed tall, sitting there in his litter. His face bore a benign gaze, calm and without fear of all of us, who must have seemed very strange to him. All who accompanied the great king held their heads toward the ground so as to avoid meeting his royal gaze.

He descended from his litter and approached Cortés, who spoke in courteous words to his majesty, asking first, "Is it he, the great Montezuma?" And it seemed to me that the great king merely answered, "It is I." He then welcomed Cortés and all of us and bade us follow him into the city and then resumed his place on the litter. Although no signal was given, now the many Indians moved aside and allowed us to pass into the city. This was, I think, on the eighth day of November, 1519.

Upon the king's orders we were installed in a grand palace near his own, in the very center of the city, from which only three causeways were available to us for escape if that proved necessary. My companeros made sport of me when I spoke of my forebodings. "Maria de Estrada, you would pull a cloak over the sun if you could," one of them said to me. But while I still had doubts about our safety, I also reminded myself that here I enjoyed an easier life than I had known since leaving Seville, and so even I began to relax my guard.

After my morning meal I often betook myself about the city. The whole place was divided into *barrios* by the largest avenues, which themselves were sometimes divided by canals. Each barrio had its own *cue,* and smaller neighborhoods possessed their own temple as well, which meant of course that each division had its own cacique and its own priest, much as do our own cities. The many people were constantly in movement, but the streets of the city were so well laid out, even though many of them were very narrow, many thousands were never halted in their business. And it was so in the many canals as well, where boats full of goods trafficked without mishap.

It was in this way that I gradually learned about the city and its people. Several times I proposed to go alone on these wanderings among the commoners, or *macehualtin,* as they called themselves. But my companeros were horrified when I said I intended to do this, and so it seemed were our hosts, all of whom said my safety could not be ensured, especially as I did not know the language well enough yet. I protested that with the few words I had already learned and by using my hands I could make my wishes known, but they all said this was not enough, and besides what would happen if harm befell me?

The old soldier Bernal Diaz, when he heard about my desires, absolutely forbade me to go out alone. I shouted back at him, "You are not my commander. By what power do you order me, you old *bobo?*" He replied in a reasonable voice that he had been bodyguard to Cortés every time the *caudillo* visited the *Tecpan*, Montezuma's palace, and that the king was never of one mind for very long. One moment he was courteous and accommodating and the next he resisted all of Cortés's entreaties, so that our safety was not reliable. No one knew what might upset the king from agreeing to become our own king's vassal, which Cortés wanted him to do. Diaz said it was bad enough to have an unruly woman in the company. "You abuse the men with your sharp tongue and best them with your mind, and you kick them in the shins when they try to restrain you from hitting one of your companeros," he said. "I ask whether a woman of your station should treat our poor men in such a way? And if you took such behavior among the naturales, who knows how they might respond to your rough ways? You are much trouble, Doña Maria. Please do not make trouble with the naturales, for while Cortés seems confident of success, I am not, nor should we any of us be until these matters are settled once and for all."

In the end these arguments were of no moment because Cortés said I would not go about the city without a troop of the Jaguar knights at my very side, and I was forced to consent. And so it happened that every morning when I left my quarters, the troop of knights, the bravest of the brave among the Mexica armies, stood waiting for me outside no matter how early I departed, and even when I decided to remain in my quarters the troop waited for me in the street below. And on cool mornings I took to wearing a cloak of cotton of the sort favored by the commoners, brightly colored, loose and very comfortable. One particular morning when I came out for my walk the captain of the Jaguar knights, having greeted me in the usual way, produced a new cloak for me which was much the same as his own, bearing the colors of his troop and of a much finer weave. Never did I have a suitor as attentive as these fierce warriors, and because of this the macehualtin sometimes called me "the Jaguar woman," even though they came to know my name very well. Before long it seemed that no matter where I went in the city the people knew of my coming and called out to me in a very friendly way.

Soon after we arrived Cortés and his captains were taken to see the great marketplace at Tlatelolco, which with Tenochtitlan made up the whole city of Mexico. The stories they brought back were so wondrous that I made up my mind to go and see it for myself, and one morning I bade my Jaguars take me there, a request that seemed to please them well enough. My old market in Seville could have fit inside this one many times over. If I attempted to name all the things the merchants sold there I would have to go on many pages. As usual, this place was well arranged to accommodate the comings and goings of many thousands of people at any time as they traded with one another for various foods and also many finely crafted goods which had been made from one corner of the empire to another, and even beyond. Slaves were sold here too, kept in cages or on a long rein at the end of a pole. I suspected that some of these poor people would be purchased for sacrifice, and in one corner of the market flats of human skin had been laid out for all to examine and purchase if they wish, and none of this seemed to trouble those who passed by. Certainly my haughty Jaguars seemed not to notice these wares at all.

One day, my Jaguar captain asked why I did not demand gifts, as my chief, meaning Cortés, seemed to do all the time of Montezuma.

I replied that my life and contentment were gift enough, and that what most pleased me was seeing the people go on with their business, for by then my presence no longer excited much interest. Then the Jaguar captain asked why I did not speak of my gods as much as the other Spaniards did, and why on our days of worship I did not fall down on my knees and make the various signs with my hands, like my companeros. Not wishing to cause Cortés difficulty, I merely said that my needs were simple and that I wished neither harm nor favor from any quarter and so I was not obliged to speak to the gods as much as the others. The Jaguar captain, whom I had given the fanciful name Fidelio, wondered then how I might protect myself from misfortune without the aid of the gods. I tried to say that my gods had not much troubled me and that most of my troubles had come from people, and that I had found that I could deal with these matters as they presented themselves to me. Then Fidelio smiled and said that my way was wise, for life seemed to him the same way, although because of his rank he had to make a show of worship. For himself, he said, he would place his own faith in his sword-arm, and that would be enough. After this conversation, I found that the people were even more welcoming to me and would even sit and drink pulque with me until darkness fell and the braziers were set alight against the evening cool. So while Cortés sat with Montezuma, I sat with Fidelio and the others, drinking at the market, and this was how I began to learn their language. In this way I passed the winter at Tenochtitlan.

I do not mean to say that my time in Tenochtitlan was without event, for that was by no means true. I only mean to say that I had come to spend my days without much thought of the future and was not so interested in great affairs as were others. It often happened that on a particular day I would hear rumors from the macehualtin only to return to my quarters to hear a different version of the same stories, so that I would worry my mind with wondering which side told the truth. Throughout the troubles that followed, I was never threatened or treated rudely by either the macehualtin or even by Fidelio and his knights.

But one morning toward the end of November as I left my quarters to see Fidelio and his troop waiting for me in the usual way, I quickly saw that his manner was much changed, as if a dark cloud hung over him. When I asked him the matter, Fidelio said that I should know because last night the Spaniards had sacked Montezuma's palace and taken him and some of the lords under guard to Cortés's quarters. I had heard nothing of this, but I wondered then why I had allowed myself to think that Cortés would be satisfied by all he had done and gained already. By now, Cortés and his captains had collected many thousands of pesos' worth of gold and other goods, more than anyone should ever want. But having heard this news I went to Cortés's quarters and there spoke with Bernal Diaz, who I thought should know the truth of things if anyone did.

Bernal Diaz said that Montezuma had angered Cortés by ordering an attack on Captain Escalante and the other men we had left behind at Villa Rica de la Vera Cruz, the news of which Cortés had just learned. Escalante and several of his men had been killed in the fighting, and as soon as he heard this Cortés had dispatched a column to right the upset among the naturales at the coast. "There will be more trouble from this, you will see, Doña Maria," Diaz said. "The Mexica who bring us food and serve us act more rudely with every passing day. Have you not noticed their behavior? I and some of the others say that this is because Montezuma is still playing false with us, as he has always done." I said that I had noticed nothing new in particular, but that I would be more attentive when I went to the market and listened to the commoners. "Have a care, Doña Maria," Diaz warned, "and do not wander so freely or far from our quarters, so that you may hear if we sound our call for assembly. And if once the naturales believe you come among them to spy, I fear for your safety. Even your Jaguars would turn upon you if they were so ordered by their commanders."

I do believe now that the greatest danger to us was the poisonous greed that had grown up among us. Cortés himself was the king of greed, if of nothing else. All through the winter Cortés spoke daily with Montezuma, and each time the captain seemed to return with attendants carrying all manner of riches that the king had given him, and so he found a special room for his treasure, just as Montezuma had done before him.

Besides Cortés, the other captains imitated our leader by gathering up as much as they could threaten the naturales into giving them. Around and about each of them there grew hoards of treasured things, close by their beds, for there was so much there was no other place in our quarters to keep it. Too, because there was so much, the companeros really could not remember all the things they had taken, so at night after the companeros drank themselves to sleep, the Indians would steal back the most precious things that had been taken and return them to their owners or to the *cues* that had been plundered.

This was the state of affairs when in May of the year of Our Lord 1520 messengers arrived from the coast with news of a threat from a different quarter. A strong expedition from Cuba captained by Don Panfilo de Nárvaez had arrived under orders from the governor of Cuba to arrest Cortés. Without a moment's thought Cortés chose 80 men and marched straightaway out of Tenochtitlan, leaving Captain Alvarado and 120 men in command until his return. I remained behind in Tenochtitlan as well, for I did not relish a forced march back to the coast. Also, I was sure Cortés would not accept arrest and therefore that there would be much fighting. I had hoped that my own fighting days were over, but this was not to be, much to my sorrow.

The unavoidable departure of Cortés was in so many ways unfortunate that even now tears come to my eyes when I remember it. Although Cortés had many faults, as we all do, I believe events would have been far different had he stayed. But life is never so obliging as to provide an easy choice for us, for if he had remained, who knows how much poison de Nárvaez would have spread against us at the coast and here in the city? So Cortés went away and made the short work of de Nárvaez that we all know of now, wounding him mortally and taking most of his men under our banner. But while Cortés was away, evil work was afoot, not only among the Indians, as we might have imagined, but among Alvarado and his captains as well. One day not long after Cortés marched off, our servants stopped coming to Axayacatl, the palace where we were quartered, and the next morning one of the women who attended to our wash was found hanged outside. Nor did Fidelio and his Jaguar knights appear beside the gate to patiently escort me to market, as they had done so many times. I know now that this was because Alvarado had refused Montezuma permission to ready the Great Pyramid for the fiesta of Toxcatl by returning an image of the Great Hummingbird to its rightful place. No longer did food come to us in its many pots and bowls with fine napkins to keep it warm, nor were we given water either. Minute by minute, Captain Alvarado became angrier and angrier.

Since we had been so well served by the Indians, we had come to pay little attention to our supplies, and thus we quickly found our meals so short that we had to find another way to feed ourselves. Captain Alvarado ordered Juan Álvarez to take a company to the market every day to buy what could be had, and because I knew the market so well I went along as well. How very different were these visits to the market from those that had gone before. Upon our approach now the Indians would sullenly withdraw from us, uttering sneering words that I could not understand but whose hateful meanings were clear enough. Not long after we began these expeditions we passed by the courtyard of the Great Pyramid, where I saw canopies of cloth spread over the yard and many stakes that I had not seen before. Before Álvarez could stop me, I went inside and with signs and my few words of their language asked the Indians what all this was for. With a grim smile, one of them told me that the stakes were for us, and that when we had been sacrificed we would be cooked with chocolate to disguise the bitter taste of our flesh. "There is even a stake for you, Jaguar woman," he said. When I told Álvarez what had been said to me, his face grew white and he trembled as one might in a cold wind. He hurried us all back to the palace so he could tell Captain Alvarado of what we had learned.

As much as I wanted to see the fiesta, I knew it was out of the question now, for hatred hung in the air about us. I collected up my arms and saw to their readiness.

The fiesta was four days old when I went to the market again with Álvarez and his men. We loaded our carts with as much as could be carried, and our Tlaxcalans also each carried a *carga* of goods, and then as quickly as we could we made our usual way back to our palace past the district of the Great Pyramid. This was where the climax of the celebration was to be held, and we had learned in the market that all the leading lords were to participate in a great dance that was meant to satisfy the god of rain.

As we came upon the court of the Great Pyramid we could see the fighting. Hundreds of Indians, perhaps thousands, fleeing this way and that from the walls that enclosed the district. From within the shrieks and cries of anguish and pain could be heard, and even this did not obscure the sound of arms at play. Finally the doors of the courtyard were flung open and from within there issued still more Indians making their escape. Some had no hands or arms. Still others bore terrible sword wounds all over their bodies. Neither women nor children had been spared: mothers, mortally wounded themselves, covered with blood, struggled to carry their infants from the terror inside. Nor were the warrior knights able to protect themselves, so completely had they been taken off their guard, for I recognized members of each of the great clans among the many wounded, running as fast as they could manage. Slowly I found it easier to move forward, for as I did the most terribly wounded recoiled from me, some crawling away with their entrails following them like a tortured snake.

The paving stones were slick with blood and flesh and covered with bodies, some on top of others, some still moving, some completely still. No part of the courtyard was unsoiled by the carnage. Standing in the midst of the terror was Captain Alvarado and several companies of his men and perhaps a hundred or more of the Tlaxcalans. A stone had struck Captain Alvarado on the head, and he too was bleeding profusely. Few of our men bore any signs of struggle at all. They all had the eyes of fiends, and they stood there wildly looking about, arms and hands covered with blood. I saw Vasquez de Tapia, one of the captains. His mouth was covered with froth.

For some reason I do not know even now, I attacked Captain Alvarado with a great anger taking me over, dagger in hand, only to be knocked to the ground by one of his escorts. He lifted me up with shining eyes and his ferocious grin. "Don't be mistaken, Doña Maria," he laughed, "for today I have ensured our safety. We have seized our opportunity to crush our enemies' hatred before it overtook us. Cortés would have done the same." I do not remember what I said to him. Perhaps I was screaming. Later, my companeros said my speech made no sense to them.

This massacre, I learned later, had been the subject of Alvarado's late-night councils with the captains. Resolved to strike a blow to forestall the treachery of Montezuma's nobles, Alvarado saw the great dance as his opportunity. He knew that several hundreds of them could be contained within the courtyard, and that their dance would pack them so closely upon one another they could not easily defend themselves as he and his men moved among them with their swords. Hacking any way at all, they were sure their swords would find a target, and so they did. I also learned that one young warrior was chosen as the first to dance before all others as the leader of the celebration, and that he was the one Captain Alvarado chose to begin the slaughter with. So it was that my Jaguar captain, Fidelio, was the first to be struck down.

Captain Alvarado had been right to hurry us back to our defenses, for before darkness fell we were attacked from all sides. So began our virtual imprisonment by those whom Alvarado thought he had defeated. That night, and indeed, for some time afterward, we could hear the sorrowful cries of mourning from all quarters of the city. In one barrio the cries would be very loud and numerous for a while, and then they would be taken up in another, almost as if the districts of the city were competing with one another in their grief. The sounds made me think of waves on the vast ocean, some heaving stormily for a time while others were calm, and then the tumult moving to another part of the deep.

We were awakened by drums and conch shells, sounding the call to arms for the inhabitants of the city. After a watchful night, we were all undone by the ferocity of the noise. Quickly the avenues outside the palace filled with warriors in full regalia for battle, and on the rooftops beyond us archers and slingers took their places to fight. Their call to arms served as our own, and I ran to my armor, which old Álvarez helped me with. When I was done up properly, he turned me about and looked me over in a kindly way and asked his Lord to protect me. I thanked him with a sisterly kiss and told him that he was an old skirt-lifter who sorely tested his god with needless requests. Then I made myself laugh very loud so that he would too, and then some of the others laughed as well, and then someone raised his sword and offered our old war cry, "Santiago, y cierra Espana!" and then we ran to our places at the ramparts we had built in front of the gates.

We fought all day. Our gates, which the Indians almost immediately set ablaze, were most zealously defended by our guns and crossbowmen. When several times the Indians threatened a breach, we retired behind the guns to let them do their work; in truth so many Indians gathered in front of our guns, the greatest difficulty was in protecting them until they could be fired. But they did so fire, and often, into hundreds of the fine warriors who fought as though they had been entranced by their hatred of us. They were not easily turned away. Bravely, they came on, again and again, as though their victory was only a sword-arm away from their reach.

Above those of us in the courtyard, others fought in the skies, it seemed, along the battlements on the rooftops, which was more dangerous because there were no gates there, nor anything to protect them from the arrows and stones and spears hurled at them. And we had managed the night before to lift only a few of the lighter guns to assist our defenses. Everyone who fought in the combat on the rooftops was wounded in some way, and although the numbers there were not so great as below, still this part of the palace had to be as stoutly defended as the courtyard. The battle could have been won or lost at either place.

Once, late in the day, our big gun at the main gate failed to fire when touched off, but then the gun smoldered and finally set itself off, as though it was fighting for us all by itself. By then, we were so exhausted I do not think we could have prevented our enemies from charging through us into the courtyard. Then we surely would have been doomed. Now, nearly all the companeros had been wounded, because although our armor served us well enough, the enemy's weapons eventually found a mark as we fought so long. Sometime during the fighting my leg had been cut just above my boot top, but this was nothing. My armor was scarred and dented from numerous blows, and so too my helmet, but I was unharmed except for the constant fear which made me very tired. That night we saw to our defenses and our arms and treated our wounded. Again we tried to sleep, but as we had no food and little water to comfort us, and as we were so afraid, our sleep was fitful and of little good. In the darkness, I listened to the weeping of my companeros. I did not hear much praying. Perhaps now they believed themselves beyond the protection of their god.

As soon as the fighting began, Alvarado went straightaway to Montezuma and cursed him and put him and all his attendant lords in irons. Even now the great king behaved with much dignity, telling Alvarado that he had brought these miseries upon himself, but this only made Alvarado angrier, so that he hurled the vilest oaths at the emperor and called him a traitor against us and a liar who had pretended friendship only to rebel against us. Sometime in the afternoon Alvarado took Montezuma from his prison onto the rooftop and demanded that the king order his subjects to cease fighting. Montezuma did as he was charged, and slowly the fighting did slacken. I heard from Vazquez de Tapia, who was there when this happened, that some of the Indians scorned their king and threw stones and insults at him. Montezuma's powers may not have been so great now as before, but his subjects obeyed him all the same, even if they showed him disrespect.

As for us, the Indians neither respected nor feared us. Our guns, though deadly, no longer made the Indians shriek and flee in astonishment, and they fought us magnificently, without regard for their safety. "We have planned special meals that we will make of you for our tigers and snakes," they cried. "We have tasted your flesh now and know you are no good to eat, even with chocolate or garlic, so our animals will eat you for us." Upon hearing enough of such defiance, one of the companeros called out in full, strong voice that no quarter was to be asked or given and invited anyone in the avenue to trial by single combat. I think he had been drinking pulque for the pain from his many wounds, for his friends easily dragged him off to bed, but still and all his defiance of the danger gave me hope. I did not know then that Montezuma had spoken to his people, and I still expected to fight again on the morrow.

So the fighting subsided for a time, but the mourning did not. Finally, our hunger drove us out of our fortress. Old Álvarez and I resumed our trips to the market, which was then still open, under heavy mounted guard, which was dangerous all the same. Every street was deserted. All the Indians concealed themselves as we passed, but every step we took was watched by eyes filled with hate. Now the bridges over the canals on the causeways had been taken up. Barricades had been thrown across some of the great avenues as well. When we returned, Alvarado questioned us closely on what we had seen. Then he said to me, "Well, little companera, we are conquistadors no longer. Shall we become so again?" To this I replied that we would so when the caudillo returned from the coast. Alvarado turned away, his scarlet cloak whirling angrily about him. One of the others, Bernardino de Tapia as I recall, shouted at me, "How do you dare to speak to our captain so disrespectfully? First you assault him with your nasty little dagger and now with your evil tongue. No one is above his command, and if you do not have a care in your manner he will order you in irons for your insults." I said that when the caudillo returned, Alvarado would be the one in irons, for he had murdered those thousands without cause and that by following his command we had murdered many thousands as well, and what had we got for it in the end? Now we were prisoners of the hatred we had created for ourselves.

To this very moment I do not see why Cortés did not arrest Alvarado for wrecking all his plans so cruelly. It is true that Alvarado was the best of our fighters and commanders. No one was braver, not even Cortés himself. Perhaps Cortés thought he could not imprison such a man at the time. When Cortés returned from his triumph over de Nárvaez, bearing so much equipment and supplies and with so many more soldiers than we had left, he of course had already heard what had happened in his absence. Instead of arresting Alvarado, he accosted Montezuma, who was heartsick with grief and did not seem to bother defending himself against the charges Alvarado made against him. Cortés pretended to be angry with the king and said that Alvarado had been right to put down this

rebellion, as he would do with any subjects of our king. He also accused Montezuma of permitting human sacrifices and said that if
reason could not bring these barbaric rituals to an end, the sword
surely would, and that Our Lord would demand, in his anger, that
we kill everyone in the city if necessary.

Word had reached us by then that the market had been closed.
Cortés demanded that Montezuma tell his people to open it again,
but the king answered that no decree of his would be honored. He
thought that if Cortés were to free his brother Cuitlahuac that this
might be done, and so Cortés permitted this. As it happened, Cortés
was wrong to have given Cuitlahuac his freedom, for on the very
next day he began preparing his city to fight us again. Several messengers Cortés attempted to send out from the city were attacked
and driven back to us, and so there was no doubt that our imprisonment had not been relaxed as a consequence of Cortés's good deed.
As if he did not yet understand how matters really stood with us,
Cortés sent out Diego de Ordaz and 300 men to patrol the immediate district around our palace, but they too were promptly driven
back, and the palace was again set on fire. Thirty of our men were
wounded in this fighting, including Cortés himself, who suffered a
serious cut on his left hand. It was said that Cuitlahuac himself was
seen directing the warriors in their assaults on us.

Montezuma and his attendant lords had been kept in irons all this
while. On the day of the fiesta, some of these lords had been killed
by their guards, but I do not know how many, and none of my
companeros would ever speak to me of these murders. Perhaps they
were ashamed of killing men in chains. Now there were no more
than twenty of these in the king's chamber, along with all their servants.

Cortés still seemed to think that the fighting could be stopped on
Montezuma's word, so he spoke gently to the king and bade several

of the other captains who got on well with him to do the same. I believe Fray Olmedo also did what he could to convince the king that he held peace in his hands. By these means, Montezuma was finally persuaded to return to the rooftop of the palace to speak to his people. Cristobal de Olid, Captain de Cervantes, and Francisco Aguilar, along with some others, took him to the roof. But the result was the same as before, or should I say even worse, because as soon as the king showed himself our enemies loosed a hail of arrows and stones at him.

I have heard it said since that Montezuma was struck several times by the stones and that this was why he died the next day, but I do not believe it because first of all I have never known anyone to be killed by a few stones. Next, I do not believe this story because soon after this the rest of Montezuma's attendant lords were killed by their guards, and this was something no one but Cortés could have ordered. Not even Alvarado would have been so bold as to kill Montezuma in defiance of Cortés's wishes. But of course there were many in the company who thought that Montezuma should have been put to the sword long before in payment for his treachery and only waited because Cortés would not permit it. When the time came, only a word or a nod from the caudillo would have been sufficient to cause the murder.

Now, however, the blood of the great king was on our hands, and no matter what the truth of it was, we were to blame. Once he had died, Montezuma's body was pushed outside on a cart so that his people could care for their dead king in their customary way. Instead, he was merely placed on a funeral pyre as the commonest citizen of the city might have been. So the great Montezuma, emperor of the Mexica, came to his inglorious end, despised by his captors and his subjects alike. How fragile is greatness!

Fortune now spun her eternal wheel. The Mexica lords had told Cortés that the war would continue until all of us were dead, even if a thousand warriors had to die to bring down each one of us. Only if we left their land, they said, could we hope to live much longer. Cortés said we would not leave, and he repeated what he had told Montezuma: that we would kill all the Mexica if they did not quit this war against us. And as if to prove that he was not dismayed by their threats, Cortés took a strong patrol against the Great Pyramid itself and there destroyed what remained of the temple rooms and the great statue gods.

But his demonstration was not without cost. Hundreds of Indians died defending their temple, and we lost twenty killed and more wounded in the combat. Cortés just escaped being killed himself. I met the company as they filed through our gate into the courtyard. Bernal Diaz del Castillo came in first and saw my questioning eyes. "Was there ever a fight like that?" he said, shaking his head. Young Gonzalo Ponce de Leon came by then. "Was it not a day to be in bed?" he asked. Cortés, bleeding from his old wound, followed them and without pause ordered all his captains to assemble. From this moment, we were to set preparations in motion to escape our imprisonment. So welcome was this news, no man remained at ease but immediately attended to what had to be done. Even some of the wounded, fearing perhaps that they would be left behind, steeled themselves with pulque and joined in as vigorously as they could.

Because we knew that most of the bridges over the canals had been taken up, we set about ripping down the great wooden beams that decorated our palace, so as to fashion a bridge that could be carried from place to place. Francisco Margarino was given 60 men to attend to this important task, and his company was to be in the van of our guard. Sandoval, who was to captain part of the vanguard as well, took the remaining wooden beams in case they were needed along the way. One might suppose that the soldiers would see to their arms, for it was clear to me that much fighting awaited us. But the vast treasure that we had collected was uppermost in their minds, and Cortés was not unlike these men himself. Once he had given orders for our preparations, he and his personal attendants saw to the loading of his treasure, which was now cast into flat bars, onto one of our mares. So loaded she could hardly walk, this mare was placed in the care of one of his attendants, poor Alonzo de Escobar, a tremulous man with the eyes of a mouse. Some said later that this treasure must have been worth 300,000 pesos if not much more. Then Cortés told the rest of us that we could have what was left. I feared the soldiers, being what they were, would begin fighting among themselves over the leavings of this treasure, but in truth there was so much of it no one grew anxious that he would not receive a proper share.

As for me, I wanted none of it. I had made a small leather pouch that could hang about my neck. In it I placed my little statue of the priests with the golden eyes doing dirty things to one another that had been given me by Tendile's warrior so long ago. Next to it I placed the tiny jade hummingbird with gold inlaid along its feathers that my poor Jaguar captain Fidelio had given to me one day at the market. Then I turned to my arms, which I burnished and sharpened as I had been taught by Rojas the Greek. I made sure of my wound, to see that it was well cleaned and protected, and for this I used pulque instead of the filthy water that we still had. The sting of the cleaning was worse than when I received the wound, so I thought I must have been doing the right thing. Then I put on my cotton armor and over it the breastplate and placed my gauntlets inside my boots and went to my bed under my cloak and tried to rest. I ate a little chicken and some tortillas and drank some of the pulque I had left and went to sleep right away. One could hear the thunder and lightning of a storm in the distance.

When I awoke a few hours later, I went straightaway to where my old friend Lares the fine horseman attended to the animals. His manner was very quiet as he led me to my mount, and I was surprised to see that he had made El Arriero, the Mule Driver, ready for me. Despite his homely name, he was one of the finest and strongest war horses we still had among us. Lares was still riding his fancy and very beautiful chestnut, which he now called La Fleche, the Arrow. When I looked at his face, Lares lowered his eyes and spoke in a whisper to me. "Doña Maria, you must take this strong horse, for only the strongest of horses and men will survive this night. As I cannot leave my Arrow, I must ride him to take care of him, but I do not think he is the kind of horse best made for a night like this. And if fortune turns against us, you must dig your spurs into the Mule Driver with no mercy. He will move heaven and earth for you if you command him, and do not look for me, Doña Maria, for I will ride with Captain Alvarado as I have done so often." Lares had never said this much to me at any time, and never with this much feeling, so that I was surprised by the sorrow in his voice. I put my arms about him and held him against me and stroked his long hair, but I could say nothing. Then I took the reins and led my big war horse away.

Cortés and his captains had decided that it was best to leave at midnight, because the Mexica did not like to fight then. Neither Cortés nor anyone else believed that we would be able to leave the city without a fight. The only question was how far we might go before the alarms sounded throughout the city. Now Cortés and his captains had also decided the order in which we would march. In the vanguard with Captain Sandoval were five other captains and the strongest, youngest men among us. Ordaz and Tapia and Lugo were all to captain there, as were Acevedo and a new one, Antonio de Quinones. With the van, Cortés ordered all the mistresses and the two priests, Olmedo and Diaz. Here I rode also.

Then came Cortés with the main body and the gold as well: about a thousand of our soldiers and some few Tlaxcalans who were still with us. With Cortés in command there were Cristobal de Olid and Alphonso de Avila. After Cortés came the rest of the Tlaxcalans, perhaps 200 in all, together with the remaining prisoners, including one of Montezuma's sons and two of his daughters. Finally, to guard the rear, came Captain Alvarado and Velázquez de Leon with 60 horsemen, one of whom was my own Lares. All this came about at midnight of the first day of July, in the year of Our Lord, as it is said, 1520.

At the appointed hour, we marched out of the palace of Axayacatl toward the causeway leading to Tacuba, the shortest of the three. A light rain fell upon us and made me so cold that I pulled my Jaguar cloak about me tightly. Then one of the companeros, perhaps Bernal Diaz, called out to me that, should we come to fight, I should cast my cloak aside, for the Mexica would surely try to unhorse me by pulling me off by it. I courteously thanked him for his advice and wished him well and moved ahead to keep good order. Our horses' hooves were not muffled, and no one had ordered a silent march, but all the same I could hear no talking from the ranks. Even the arquebusiers, who were always rowdy, seemed to keep their silence. The pace seemed slow to me, almost as in a stately parade, but as the streets were so narrow we could do little else, and so we passed through the city at night. Even the dogs were not to be heard. Thus, we crossed four canals and found the edge of the city where the causeway began without mishap.

Then we came to the first of the three large canals that cut the causeway. Here at Tepantzingo, as the canal was called, the crossing had been destroyed, and the company halted to lay the bridge we had brought with us. That was when the alarms were sounded. I removed my Jaguar cloak and drew my sword. I could feel my hands sweating inside my gauntlets.

They came at us from all sides. In the water along the causeway, and from the front and behind, thousands of torches grew closer from the darkness. It was as if a storm of fire burned toward us. Their war cries reached out for us from the fire. At first, they seemed a lowing groan, and then we could hear high-pitched screams of hatred. The storm seemed to crash into us all at once, and then we were at blows, face to face with our enemies. "Do not stand," our officers yelled to all who could hear. "Move forward, move forward!" I dug my spurs cruelly into my Mule Driver, and he leapt forward powerfully, pitching against the pressing bodies. I struck with my sword right and left without aim, and each time I felt the sword against yielding flesh. My horse ran down and trampled all who could not move away, and he twisted and whirled his way around and about the causeway. A spear flew out of the darkness and careened from my breastplate, and a stone caught my arm and caused the reins to drop from my hand. As I reached for my reins again, a warrior rushed at me from the other side, sword in hand, but a companero struck him down with a murderous blow across his neck. Blood splashed my boot top.

Time itself seemed to slow, as if an unseen hand stayed the clock. Figures floated in and out of my sight dreamily, first a companero, then a band of Eagle knights, then another horseman with his lance buried deep into a warrior's chest. Now I could hear nothing, nor did I grow tired from the fighting. I felt as though I could fight forever. Off to my side I saw another horseman, his animal sliding slowly into the lake while warriors attacked him all around. I saw his sword fly from his hand, and from among the warriors a hand seized his and dragged him from his mount. He disappeared from my sight as the warriors closed over him. I turned and struck again at an Eagle warrior and hit him in the face, and he was followed by two more. Now my horse fought for himself, and turned against the one while I parried the blow of the other's lance, cutting it in two. Then someone ran him through from behind, and then my savior too was felled by a club. I rode over his assailant and cut him down.

Now I had let my reins fall altogether and took my sword in both hands like a Moor, and still my old war horse pushed his way on through the confusion. As we went, Diaz the priest took hold of my saddle so that the horse would carry him forward too. Beyond him, I saw old Álvarez, my companion from our dangerous trips to the market, also wielding his sword two-handed style, walking calmly ahead, protecting the priest from the spears and swords. I imagined him a farmer, scything grain at harvest. Ahead, in the dim light of the torches, I saw the second crossing on the causeway, the Toltec canal, and then many warriors closed in front of us. "Doña Maria!" a voice called out. I turned and saw Cortés and several horsemen pressing forward. "We must fight our way through. Join us and we will go forward together!"

I asked my war horse for more speed, and he replied with such a jolt I nearly fell from my saddle. Cortés took his own charger in front of me, cutting his way ahead mercilessly. Then Cristobal de Olid did the same, and he was followed by Captain de Avila, and I understood how we would maneuver, and so I imitated them and hurried my own horse ahead of them all, cutting and thrusting all the while in all directions, and thus we repeated this fighting method again and again until we came to the canal itself.

When I looked into Toltec canal I believed I had seen the mouth of hell. There in the water were canoes and horses, many dead and many living, and warriors and our soldiers struggling with one another in the flickering light of the torches. Pieces of the old bridge were scattered about, and many wounded were clinging to them. The water was alive with misery. At first my war horse hesitated, so I put my spurs to him again and we plunged down into the chaos below. My old Mule Driver must have been as terrified as I was, for he somehow found a footing and crossed to the far side. To this day I do not know how this could have been done. Perhaps he took wings all of a sudden. Just beyond the canal, I looked for Cortés and the other horsemen. Some had come across, and some were still fighting on the other side while our soldiers fought their own way on foot past them. Then I saw Cortés unhorsed in the water below. But he did not lose his sword, and even though the water was at his waist, still he fought with great skill against all who would come at him. Then the old fighter Cristobal de Olid drove his way toward the caudillo and snatched him up from the water onto the back of his horse, and so was Cortés saved again.

Ahead of us, Sandoval and the vanguard had crossed the Pelacalco canal and reached the mainland, where they drew themselves into formation to protect the landing. Cortés and I reached this place at the same time. Sandoval gave him a horse, saying, "You will not return to the causeway again, captain?" This confused me at the time, and I did not understand until later, when someone told me he had already been there and then returned to the fight after he saw to Doña Marina's safety. Cortés simply stared back toward the causeway and said, "Alvarado is still there." But he did not move his horse. Nor did I myself.

I think only half of our horsemen survived the fight. Only a while later did I see Captain Alvarado himself come forward into the light. Cristobal Martin de Gamboa, the master of the horse and a good friend of Lares the fine horseman, had saved Alvarado at the Toltec canal by riding over several attackers and pulling him out of the water. Cortés rushed to him, asking, "Where are those in your charge?" Alvarado replied that those who could come had done so already. The rest were dead or wounded or simply had disappeared into the lake. Nor was there any trace of Cortés's treasure-laden mare.

Someone, perhaps Cortés himself, said we lost 500 men this night. I saw Bernal Diaz, wounded again, for as usual he had been in the thickest of the fighting. Rojas the Greek, wounded also but cheerful, greeted me with a wild embrace and a kiss. Many of the old skirt-lifters we had come ashore with so long ago had fought their way through, but very many of the new men Cortés had taken from de Nárvaez were lost in the darkness behind us. My old market companion, Juan Álvarez, was among those.

Years later I heard from an old Indian woman who herself was at the causeway that many of our soldiers had been defeated and turned back at the very first canal, and that many hundreds of our men had been left behind at the palace who had not been told when we began our march. She said these joined together and held out in the palace for several days before they were overrun. To a man, they had been sacrificed on the Great Pyramid. Their remains were thrown to the animals in the royal zoo, who fed upon them for many days thereafter. Even so many years later, the old woman smiled as she remembered this story.

Our victories had made us prisoners. Now our defeat had given us freedom.

Cortés refused to be downhearted, or so it seemed. In the morning's light we reformed ourselves as best we could. Only 400 of us remained. Nearly everyone was wounded, and most of our horses had been hurt in some way too. My good old Mule Driver seemed as strong as ever, but when I left him to the grass he would not stay and followed and nuzzled me wherever I walked, as if he were afraid I would abandon him to the terrors of the night before.

After we had marched for five days beyond the lakes, the ground began to rise toward the high pass in front of Otumba. For three days we had found neither water nor food, and our poverty affected our wounded most cruelly. Several died each day, no matter how carefully we watched over them. Only the horses seemed to recover from the trials on the causeway, for the grasses were plentiful. Once, my Mule Driver and I ate grass together, but while this made me sick to my stomach, he was happy and strong. On occasion I would ride along with Cortés, who talked almost all the time about how we might take back what we had lost.

Our Tlaxcalan scouts had told us that Cuitlahuac's army was approaching with a quickened pace for the past several days, and so it was on the seventh day that our tormentors drew themselves up for battle in a large clearing near Otumba. When I saw the many thousands arrayed all in their battle gear, fiercely painted and dressed like a sky full of rainbows, I wondered at first how we could combat them. But this army looked like a Mexican army of old. In the city, our fighting had forced them to act in battle as they had never acted before, in violation of their many customs. Then, they wanted more than anything merely to kill us, and they did not seem to care about their formations or their discipline. Every warrior seemed to fight for himself alone, instead of fighting together as we did. They did not fight at night, but our escape forced them to respond in the night, and they became very dangerous. This, and our own inexperienced soldiers, explained why we had lost so many on the causeway.

One might have thought that the causeway was more dangerous to us than to our attackers, but in truth there were so many of them they prevented their whole number from combating us at once, so that at any time we were fighting only a portion of them. Their numbers, which one might think conferred great power upon them, were a disadvantage to them unless they were fighting an army of their own kind. As for the old style under which they fought before we came to this land, we knew already that we could win against it, for we had done so quite often. My doubts came to me now because we were so weak of body and spirit. But then the two sides joined for combat and I no longer had time to think.

Of all my battles, I remember Otumba as the most tiring. I never felt in danger, because the Mexica did indeed fight in their old way, trying less to kill us than take us prisoner, no doubt to crown the Great Pyramid with sacrifices for their new emperor. And so one or two ranks might rush ahead to meet us while the great body of their warriors could not bring their weapons to bear. Their own warriors acted as shields for us while we combated them. But the fighting that began early in the morning lasted until the sun was very high, and our strength began to wane. Once I looked about to see several of our soldiers fall to the ground when there were no more Indians close by them. One even looked as though he fell asleep, there in the middle of the battle. I myself could have joined him easily enough. I could feel our soldiers growing weaker and weaker.

I could see Cortés calling other horsemen to his banner. Sandoval came there. So did the brave Olid and the terrible Alvarado and another horseman I did not know. My Mule Driver felt my spurs, and I rode to join them, pulling up as Cortés spoke. "Do you see their commander?" he asked as he pointed to a small group on a rise just beyond the mass of warriors. The commander and his attendants wore the most fabulous regalia, black and white feathers reaching upward from their backs, protected by their gold shields and brightly colored cotton armor. "We shall attack them," Cortés said, and then he told how we would ride, one slightly behind another, as if we were a wedge. "Doña Maria," he said, "you will ride to my left, and then Sandoval. And on my right comes Alvarado and so on. This way we will move their warriors aside easily enough if we ride quickly." Everyone was out of breath from the hard fighting, but we all knew if we did not do something the enemy would wear us down by their great numbers alone. We all moved our horses where Cortés wanted, and at his signal we fixed our lances on our stirrups and drove our spurs deeply.

So we went like the wind across the field, my old war horse and I so fast that we nearly outpaced the others. But as we reached the full gallop we recovered our formation so that we took exactly the shape Cortés had described to us and then we rode as one together against the foremost lines of our enemies. So fixed was I upon our enemies, I did not notice right away that Cortés and the others had leveled their lances, so that I was almost on the Indians before I brought my lance down under my arm and pushed its point as far forward as I could. I shifted deeply in my saddle so that my whole body leaned ahead, almost touching the Mule Driver's neck, which rose and fell as we hurtled on.

Now we were riding as fast as I had ever done, but once again, as on the causeway, the clock moved slowly so that I could see with completest clarity how the Indians began to pause and then jostle one another in fear. I could hear the others yelling as we closed with the enemy. And then, as if by magic, the clock began to move very rapidly, so that we crashed through the line and up the rise toward Cuitlahuac's splendid commander and his entourage. The horseman whose name I did not know drove his spear right through the commander and caught the army's standard in one motion and held it high in the air. My own lance I drove through a knight and left it there, and I brought my horse around to protect Cortés's flank and drew my sword in time to catch yet another warrior under his chin. I saw his face fall away from his brilliant headdress. In just this moment, all of their chiefs lay on the ground, dead and dying. Far away I could hear our soldiers as they too rushed the Indians with a great frenzy. The cries of the fighting were terrible.

My throat was so parched I could not speak above a whisper. The Indians fled in every direction, and our soldiers pursued them, striking them down from behind, until they could no longer catch them in their flight. The field was covered with many hundreds of dead and wounded, beautiful birds unable to fly. I dismounted and sat upon the grass for longer than I can remember. My faithful Mule Driver stayed close by my side, his flanks rising and falling, covered with lather and blood.

After some time, the other horsemen rode up and dismounted beside me. Cortés's left hand was bleeding mightily and hung by his side, the drops of blood falling slowly into the grass. I tore away part of my cotton armor, thinking I would staunch the bleeding, but he looked at me queerly. "First you must see to yourself, Doña Maria. Look to your arm." Only then did I see that I had been wounded on my right arm. There, below my elbow I saw a great and deep gash, with the reddest blood issuing forth, and it seemed that I could not completely open my hand. My fingers would only go so far and no more. Then young Sandoval came forward and wrapped his scarf tightly about my arm and bade me to sit down once more. Captain Alvarado placed a flagon of water in my good hand. "I am sorry it is not pulque, Doña Maria," he said, grinning his awful smile. I looked at Alvarado. Somehow, I cannot say how, he seemed different to me. "My captain," I said, "will you forgive me for my disrespect?" I do not know how he replied, for then I fell asleep.

When I awoke I saw that I had been carried to a cool glade of trees, and that a fire and a small shelter had been made for my comfort. Several Tlaxcalans were there, and Rojas the Greek as well. I felt much refreshed. The day was quiet and sunny. "At last you are awake, Doña Maria," Rojas said. "I wondered if you would sleep forever. No, our company has gone on to Tlaxcala, and I am under orders from the caudillo to bring you along when you can travel. These Tlaxcalanos will guide us. They saw you fighting and believe you are a great hero." I shifted on my pallet and saw the Mule Driver, close to me as usual. He looked rested and strong, and someone had brushed him nicely. I was naked and clean underneath my Jaguar cloak. When Rojas noticed my surprise, he said quickly, "Do not take offense, Doña Maria, for Captain Cortés himself saw to your wounds and watched over us as we cleaned you, for there was much blood to be washed away, but not all of it yours." Rojas was still speaking, but I fell asleep once more.

After several days, my small company made its way into Tlaxcala, where Cortés and the rest had been comforted. I was given spacious quarters all to myself, away from the other women, whose company I had never sought. A courtyard off these quarters provided me with a quiet cool place in which to rest after the evening meal, and as I grew stronger I began to walk about the city, which was unchanged since we had marched through the year before. From time to time I would visit those of my companeros whose wounds still kept them in bed, or I would walk with others who could move about now. My wound began to heal itself, although I could no longer open my hand completely. Slowly, I watched our little army regain its strength.

One evening as I sat with my pulque in the courtyard, Cortés came to see me. He courteously inquired how I fared and seemed happy when I said well enough. Then he said, "Doña Maria. You have been at my side since Cuba, and few can have been more loyal to me than you have been. No soldier has marched longer or fought harder than you have done. I shall be in your debt forever, yet this will not prevent me from making payment on this debt of gratitude. Before long, we march again, back to retrieve what we have lost. Will you return with me, or will you remain here where I can guarantee your safety?"

"My captain," I replied, "I follow your orders. Where you would have me be, there I shall be." He said this was the answer he expected. He then proposed that I remain in the safety of Tlaxcala under the protection of old Lord Xicotenga and the other elders of the city, "unless," he added, "you wish to return to Cuba, or even to Spain? You could be of great assistance to our cause in Court." His proposal startled me, for until that moment I could not remember when I had last thought of Cuba or Spain. That is when I knew for a certainty that New Spain was my home, come what may, forevermore.

A few days later Cortés and our companeros, now rested and refitted with arms, and with a new army of 10,000 Tlaxcalans, marched away. Alvarado rode with him, and Sandoval and Olid, and Ordaz and Bernardino de Tapia. Then the gunmen went chattering by, as usual. There was the royal notary, whose name I have forgotten, and the priests as well, Olmedo and Diaz, who held so fast to my saddle at Toltec canal. I wished with all my heart that I could see Lares again, and old Álvarez. I watched Cortés take his leave of the city elders and assume his place under his banner at the head of the army. As he rode by, he removed his cap to me and bowed deeply. I never saw him again.

Now everyone knows that Cortés succeeded in what he intended, as he usually did. Eventually, he laid siege to the great city and brought it to its knees, destroying most of it in the end. Hundreds of thousands more perished in the war. These days, the great lakes are turning into salt flats, and the people who remain are leaving this valley of destruction. For his deeds, Cortés was much honored by our king, being known from that time on as the Marquis de Valle, and he was said to be the richest man in all of New Spain and perhaps much of the rest of the world besides. Although, as he said, I had marched and fought side by side with him many times, I cannot say that I knew this man, nor, I would venture, did any of those who claimed to be his friend. To me, the caudillo will always be as mysterious as the old Hummingbird.

It has been said in Neuva Espana and even at court that Cortés was only victorious in the end because of our horses and guns, but I am here to say that these were not the things that were important. I have read the writings of the father, Peter Martyr, who presumes to say that our God gave us victory, as though we ourselves had nothing to do with the matter, and then all the same disapproves of our actions. But I say that our spirit gave us victory, and not whether we were right or wrong, and perhaps as well the fortune that Cortés always spoke of when he talked with the companeros. And I say I am right, for I was there during these great days, and I say that when my grandchildren read of the history of this land, the right and the wrong of it all will have faded into the dust that the historiadores content themselves with. I am as well read as they are, and besides I know the course of things that happened, as I have shown.

Someday we will see clearly what we have done to this land, for in truth we have only conquered this place by force of arms and by our cleverness and good fortune. We have said, as Cortés has done so often since, that we took this land to save it for our king and for our God. I see how our king may be grateful for our service, but as for God I wonder how he could take pleasure from what we have done here. I wonder how much we have changed here at all. Sometimes at night, deep in the forest and far from Spanish eyes, the naturales still pray secretly to their old gods and ask them to deliver Mexico from our power. Their gods have fallen silent and have abandoned them. Some day their prayers may be answered.

Of course, Cortés is long since dead, as indeed are nearly all the rest of the companeros. Rojas the Greek stayed with me in Tlaxcala, and we became man and wife after a few years. But he broke his neck in a fall from a horse. We had two children, who still live and have their own farms and families. After Rojas died, the old master of the horse, de Gamboa, and I took up with one another, and we had two more children, one of whom died. The other, whose name was Martin, grew into a fine but restless young man. He was in Honduras, the last I heard. Then de Gamboa died of some nameless fever. At about this time, my old war horse, who had been so faithful to me for so many years, finally died. I buried him with my own hands and sat by his grave for several days, turning over in my mind our times together.

Now many people come from Spain and elsewhere to seek out their fortunes in this new land. From time to time, they have passed through this town, and seek an audience with me to learn of this place. Some of them bring books with them, and in return for my conversation I ask them for a book. In this way, I have gathered my little soldiers about me once more, since my old soldiers are all of them dead by now. The little soldiers speak to me as they did when I was a girl in Seville, and I sit and read them and smell the japonica when it blooms. As I have those who attend my horses and my fields, I can fall asleep in the afternoon sun, and then I take my supper on the veranda and take myself to an early bed.

And so now I sit in my courtyard, sipping pulque, and remembering what I have done and wondering how my grandchildren's children will regard me. I look at my little statues from time to time and remember the fabulous city and its market, and my poor Fidelio, and Lares, who was an even finer man than he was a horseman. And from an old chest, I remove a little note that Captain Cortés had sent along with his messenger who carried the news to me of the *encomienda* he awarded me. The note is in his own hand, and it reads: "Fortune favors the brave."

6

GALEN'S PROOF

Too soon after his disastrous Russian campaign, Napoleon fires another army eastward. His army is new, brittle, fragile, and uncertain; his commanders are battle-worn. His enemies are no longer intimidated. Can this army survive? A Napoleonic surgeon journeys through battle's human landscapes for the first time, where courage and cowardice fight side by side.

IN THE FIELD NEAR BAUTZEN, JUNE 22, 1813
General Headquarters, The Imperial Guard
Most Confidential

Having conducted a most arduous investigation into the charges of cowardice made against the soldiers of the Army of the Elbe during the recent campaign, and having promptly reported my findings to the emperor and general-in-chief, Napoleon, I am compelled while time permits to record a more complete account of this affair. I do so because the course of the campaign in Saxony has excited the most intense feelings among several of our generals, feelings that have been aimed at me directly.

I have no assurance that this year's campaigns will conclude satisfactorily for France; indeed, no one can be so assured at the moment, for the Allied powers arrayed against us appear more intent than ever upon our destruction, notwithstanding the armistice recently agreed upon. However, if France does succeed, the assault upon my reputation and service to our soldiers may resume with even greater vigor than at present, for the substance of my report may be seen, however mistakenly, as an affront to some of our most influential officers. Only my service and our general-in-chief's friendship may stay their hands against me, but not even he can sustain the degree of vigilance my safety may require. Rather than surrender myself to fortune, I must at least assist my own case by stating the complete truth of this affair as it is known to me.

Thus I have determined upon this course, so that having composed this document at the actual time of the controversy—or as close to events as the press of my business will permit—I will have in hand a contemporary document available for my subsequent defense, should it prove necessary. Because of the sensitivity of the subjects touched upon herein, however, I intend to preserve its security among my private papers. I do hope and trust that such a necessity may not arise, and that if this *aide memoire* should ever fall under the eyes of another, so many years will have passed that the controversy that brought it forth will have subsided in intensity so that it may be viewed as only a curious artifact of an unhappy time in the history of our empire.

To these important reasons, sufficient alone though they may be, I must add another. This affair, which not only threatened the lives and impugned the honor of thousands of our soldiers through ignorance and neglect of reason, contains within itself questions bearing upon the nature and conduct of war, questions that to my certain knowledge have hardly been touched upon in the course of history. The unfortunate character of the recent campaign has moved me to consider these questions in a fresh light, or at least in a manner that the soldiers themselves have not employed. Nonetheless, I believe my observations touch upon the very fabric of our armies.

Therefore, it is necessary to recount in some detail events which

in retrospect seem inevitably to have led to these charges of cowardice among so many of our brave young soldiers. I hope this pream-
ble will of itself do much to explain these regrettable accusations
and what we may learn from this affair if we are wise. Further, I
hope that even my most fervent detractors will come to understand
that throughout this affair I had uppermost in my mind only the welfare and continued success of our army.

To begin, then: our campaign in Russia had not long since concluded before I was once more called to service as surgeon-in-chief
to the Imperial Guards. For me, this marked the beginning of Napoleon's grand mobilization for this year. In truth, however, I myself
felt only the briefest pause in my activities, for I had recovered in-
completely from the exhaustions and the typhus I contracted toward
the end of last year. Nevertheless, I had recovered sufficiently to
know my duty, as I have always known it: the present campaign
marks my twentieth in the field with our armies.

In my capacity as surgeon I have now served with Napoleon from
the Nile to the gates of Moscow. My general-in-chief has seen sufficient merit in my conduct to have been a true and faithful patron of
my work. Indeed, his patronage has been essential. This is evident
when one understands—as, alas, few do—that surgeons and their
assistants and indeed all who attend to the health of our army are not
themselves privileged to bear rank or preferment of any kind; rather,
we are made to labor at the sufferance of the generals in whose
commands we are placed. Only the manifest need and salubrious effects of our labors protect us from the whims of certain superior
officers who might easily inhibit our effectiveness.

For example, it is well known that for many years certain officers,
entrusted with monies meant to pay for the care and treatment of
soldiers in their charge, have instead chosen to keep their medical
allowances for themselves, regarding these monies as merely another emolument for their own important services. Thus, while our
poor wounded may regard us with the utmost favor, certain com-

manders accuse us of interfering with their prerogatives, cloaking their accusations against our work in high-minded language, as if their own conduct were animated only by the finest feelings.

Perhaps the persistence of such manners in our commanders over the years gradually and insidiously played a role in our present circumstances. Despite their constant appeals to our soldiers to remember that they sacrifice themselves for France alone, they do not hesitate to waste the sons of our republic by discarding them without a thought if they are wounded, and resent any attempt to save our soldiers so that they may serve France still more. After so many years of war, our citizens understand how our soldiers have been used and have become rather more wary of appeals to patriotic necessity. From the first, therefore, our general-in-chief met the greatest difficulty in raising a sufficient number of troops to replace the disastrous losses we had suffered in Russia. Our losses were felt in every category of necessity: not only men but equipment, and horses perhaps above all.

These deficiencies were now to place an indelible stamp upon the character and course of the present campaign. Not even I could claim to have greeted news of this campaign with enthusiasm. How, then, might one expect those who were called to service for the first time to regard the raising of this new army? Napoleon wanted 656,000 soldiers at his disposal, for no lesser number was thought sufficient to combat the forces the Allies were assembling to fight us. Already last autumn Napoleon had summoned the class of 1813, and he had seen to the embodiment of 80,000 more from the National Guard into the army proper. In February he called for the class of 1814 well ahead of its time. But still our strength was insufficient. To all these were added a further demand of 100,000 from earlier classes whose service had been forgiven on one ground or another, such as age or family necessity. Finally, twenty-four more battalions were found by drawing from the ranks of our navy. These were ordinary seamen as well as very valuable gunners.

One may see immediately the consequences for an army thus raised. The insult to our effectiveness was profound, for if our numbers were barely equal to the campaign at hand, our skills were not. Napoleon resorted to every expedient whereby this deficiency might be ameliorated. Several regiments of the Imperial Guard then posted in Spain were ordered to join our army. The most experienced non-commissioned officers were taken from their old regiments and apportioned among those newly made. As even by these measures the skills of the newest soldiers could not be improved upon without more time, Napoleon insisted upon a greater number of artillery pieces to accompany the divisions than would otherwise have been thought necessary for success. Now every workshop in France, it seemed, was required to produce a certain quantity of the equipment necessary to arm us, so that eventually one might sit by the roads to our assembly points and watch in perfect amazement for hours as these goods joined us. Even so, I might observe in passing that the supplies necessary for my own work and that of my colleagues were anything but adequate. No sooner had we reached the River Saale than we were forced to content ourselves with half-measures of all sorts to care for our wounded. We were fortunate that the light combat gave us only a few casualties at any one time.

Of all our army's deficiencies, one in particular seemed beyond redress. Our cavalry, which had performed so bravely and suffered so much in Russia, was now in the most complete disrepair. Neither horses nor cavalrymen can be made overnight, and thus far our strategic movements have been seriously impaired for want of both. Thus, our movements have been less well-informed and the communications between our several corps have not been as reliable and productive as we would wish. It is to be hoped that our difficulties will be made to yield in the face of our general-in-chief's genius. Failing that, we may only hope that the coalition that opposes us will permit their own interests to sabotage their common goal, as they have in other campaigns.

Notwithstanding the impediments mentioned thus far, we advanced rapidly against light opposition toward the points the general-in-chief had fixed for our assembly, near the towns of Naumberg and Merseburg that guarded crossings of the Saale. Toward the end of April, our advanced units began to skirmish rather more intensely. We now know the enemy had decided to oppose us just beyond the river, at Lützen, the better to protect the approaches to Leipzig itself. So as we moved to complete our crossing of the river, our enemies—mainly Prussians under Wittgenstein and Blücher—moved forward to engage us.

The enemy held fine positions on a low crest before us, Gross Görschen as it is known, well assembled and prepared to receive us. General Bertrand's IV Corps came up smartly to complete our arrangements on the right. But on the left, where Marshal Ney was to advance, matters were rather less satisfactory. He was still some distance to the north and at some confusion as to what he was to do. Now the most severe engagement ensued, opened by the enemy's employment of his numerous guns. These, sited most expertly, forestalled any further advance and gave us many hundreds of casualties, despite which no move was made by any of Bertrand's or Oudinot's divisions to withdraw to safety. As they stood fast in their suffering, Napoleon came onto the field, having been attracted by the enormous commotions of the artillery in this vicinity. Exposing himself to the greatest personal danger, he placed himself at the head of Oudinot's III Corps and led them forward. I was some distance to the rear, advancing with the Guards, when I heard cries of "Vive l'Empereur!" going up ahead of me. There was a general advance, and our lines became desperately entangled with those of the enemy. For the rest of the day only hard fighting remained. From my own vantage point I could remark upon the surging back and forth of the engagement, and before long my attentions were wholly occupied by the increasing numbers of wounded, the greater part of them being from Bertrand's redoubtable IV Corps.

The wounds suffered during the fighting for Lützen were unremarkable to me, bespeaking clearly the heavy volume of artillery fire. I saw numerous cases of gross traumatic amputations as well as the great disarrangements of tissue common to solid cannon shot. The rest were merely gunshot wounds of various sorts. On that day, May 2, my surgeons and I saw to the needs of several thousand wounded, treating several hundred of the most dangerous promptly and then the rest by the degrees of their severity. I performed eighteen amputations, none of which presented any difficulty. Only four of these have died from various infections since. By working through the night, we had attended to those most in need of us and sheltered the remainder in the houses and hospitals of the district. Then, I saw to the proper rearrangement of our field ambulances among the several corps, which were still in movement until the next midday.

The battle had more seriously disrupted our formations than experience had led us to expect. The Prussians had managed to extricate themselves from our grasp, moving rearward toward Leipzig. No organized pursuit was attempted by our general-in-chief, which I know must have been a disappointment to him, for it was his habit after a general engagement to continue fighting until the enemy army was completely destroyed. Later in the day, I heard several staff officers from the imperial household say that Napoleon was most displeased with Marshal Ney's failure to grasp and act upon our general's instructions. They believed Ney's dilatory attack permitted Blücher's forces time to withdraw in good order.

Lützen gave us 20,000 casualties. The enemy suffered a like number. My colleagues and I were therefore obliged to remain in the vicinity for several days before we found it possible to reform our ambulances and set out to find our army, which was moving directly upon the city of Dresden. The enemy was still in good order and withdrew deliberately, still posing no small danger to anyone who would contest them. Only a few leagues beyond Leipzig, at Colditz,

Prince Eugene's Army of the Elbe, which then acted as our vanguard, engaged the enemy's rear guard, Russian troops under General Miloradovitch, and fought a very sharp action. The wounded given us by this engagement of course prevented myself and my colleagues from pressing on, and it was some two more days before we rejoined the main army, which then was already across the Elbe at Dresden.

As Napoleon had reached Dresden, on about the 10th of May, he set about rearranging the army as he customarily did before closing in the general engagement. The bridges across the Elbe wanted immediate repair before he could continue, so this delay permitted Napoleon to attend to his new arrangements for command. This was all the more necessary, for our intelligence told of Wittgenstein's reinforcement by Barclay de Tolly together with 13,000 more Russian troops, thus almost making good the losses the Allies had suffered at Lützen. For his part, Napoleon combined Prince Eugene's army with his own, enabling him to dispatch Eugene to Italy, there to command an army of observation against the Austrians. Thus, on the eve of his movement across the Elbe, Napoleon had arranged our army, the whole now being designated the Army of the Elbe, in the following way. To our north, and already across the Elbe, Marshal Ney commanded with 79,500 infantry and 4500 horse. With Napoleon commanding the main body of the army were 110,000 infantry and 12,000 cavalry. Marshal MacDonald served as Napoleon's second-in-command. As usual, Napoleon kept his Imperial Guard close at hand, and so it was to these regiments that I came as fast as I could manage. On the 12th of May, Napoleon had ordered Marshal MacDonald forward with several corps in a strong reconnaissance. Four days later our forwardmost troops made contact with the enemy, who had established outworks behind the River Spree at Bautzen. Determined not to allow the Allies to escape as they had at Lützen, Napoleon composed his orders and hastened to concentrate the army. He also called upon Marshal Ney to move toward the northernmost positions of the enemy in the hills beyond the river.

During these preparations, I visited the medical establishments close by, as was my habit. I was particularly interested to see the Saxon techniques for amputation and found them most unsatisfactory, so that deadly infections, not to say the most terrible discomforts, were certain to ensue. I remonstrated with the local surgeons and even taught them my simpler—and safer—technique, but they were unconvinced at first, insisting that these infections were of a transient nature. So they were, I fear, for the greater part of their patients died within a fortnight. I do believe now, however, that they have taken up my technique, which does not so encumber the flesh remaining at the site of the amputation and allows it to heal without dangerous constrictions. Even so, the skills of one and all, refined or crude as they may be, were already sorely tested by the great numbers of wounded from all sides. From Dresden to Leipzig and every place between and for leagues on either flank of our line of march there lay in unheeded squalor the human destruction of our armies. Only the kindness and care of the Saxons themselves prevented the deaths of thousands of wounded soldiers my colleagues and I had no hope of reaching. Saxony had already been made into a charnel house, and yet even now another battle was promised. As I moved among our patients, I was impressed by their demeanor despite their desperate circumstances. I was impressed, too, that by far the greater burdens of this campaign were being borne by the young only just called to service. For all that, they suffered their pains as well as any veteran ever would. So long as France may call upon their kind, our marshals should be content.

I left Dresden with my ambulances on the 19th of May some hours after the departure of Headquarters and the Imperial Guard. As we approached the town of Bautzen on the following day, the skirmishing which had been almost continuous since we crossed the Elbe now blended insensibly into a continuous though relatively light engagement. Only the weather, which was turning to heavy rain and storms, impeded our progress. But it was clear enough to me that the enemy was not far ahead. Almost as if I were aboard my old ship *Vigilante,* I felt the army gliding ever more slowly to its anchorage below the low range of ridges that reached out to us from the mountains of Bohemia beyond. At noon on the 20th, our guns took the enemy's positions across the Spree under intense fire while our engineers built bridges for our infantry. Slowly the army arrayed itself thusly: Bertrand's corps held the left flank, Marmont and Mac-Donald the center, and Oudinot moved up to take the right of the line. The Imperial Guard as usual acted as reserve, while Napoleon kept himself free to direct the battle.

Our general-in-chief's plan was to fix the enemy in his place while Marshal Ney marched his several corps behind the immediate battle so that the enemy might be trapped. The decision that Napoleon had wanted at Lützen might finally be achieved here. That done, France might gain at least a respite from her trials. Because Napoleon wished to allow more time for Marshal Ney to bring his forces into play, however, our general-in-chief decided to delay the general engagement until the next day. But that did not mean we would remain idle. As if to occupy the enemy's full attention, at 3 o'clock in the afternoon Oudinot's infantry was ordered forward across the Spree against the enemy's first lines. This was done in such a manner as to convince the Allies that the weight of our attack would issue from our right, with the aim of severing any possible communication with the Austrians to the southeast, should they decide to join the Coalition. Of course, this impression was precisely the opposite of Napoleon's intentions, which were to interrupt the Allies' lines of communication with their Prussian bases. Once Ney found his proper place, Napoleon expected, the whole of the Allied army would be at our mercy. Thus, our infantry, principally our IVth, VIth, and XIth corps, forced their way into the town of Bautzen and beyond. As darkness fell, the enemy's first lines were in our hands. A heavy rain then intervened, so that those of the enemy who survived retired to Würchen Heights and the redoubts that their commanders had prepared beforehand.

Already the wounded were struggling back across the Spree toward our reserve positions, and toward midnight, after I had toured the other ambulances, I betook myself across the river with a number of our field ambulances to attend to those who had been left on the battlefield. Here we worked until the approach of dawn. I was standing amid the wounded of Oudinot's corps when an officer from our general-in-chief's *maison* rode up and bade me to return to my position with the guards. "Sire," he said to me, "our emperor desires that you should withdraw yourself to safety. Knowing you, he said, he was sure you would remain here though you understand full well that as soon as dawn breaks this field will be swept with the enemy's fire." I accepted these instructions with sorrow, for I knew also that this same fire would fall among our wounded and those of the enemy as well. Regretting these orders as I might, I directed the retirement of our ambulances with as many of the wounded as they could carry and organized those who could manage to walk so that they might help those who could not. I sent my horse to the rear and walked back with the wounded, stopping as necessary when their wounds demanded attention. The staff officer had been right, for it seemed to me that no sooner had the dawn broken than the most vicious cannonade opened up from all sides, the most terrible effects of which fell where we had been the night before. I imagined that from time to time, as the artillery fire abated slightly, I could hear the cries of the wounded we had left behind.

The Allies' defenses reached nearly seven miles along the river and were punctuated by heights quite favorable to their own design and disadvantageous to our own. Our troops were thus obliged everywhere to make their assaults uphill against fixed positions. Here, the enemy had placed his strength in the center and to the left of his line, thinking the greatest danger from us lay in these directions. But of course Napoleon would not oblige the enemy by attacking where he was strongest if he could find success elsewhere, and for this Marshal Ney's arrival far to the enemy's right was of the utmost importance.

Except from time to time as I moved between our ambulances I had little opportunity to observe our maneuvers. Everyone who listened with an experienced ear could understand very well how the battle progressed. Our center, under Marshal Marmont, and our right, under the intrepid Oudinot, resumed their attacks, coming up to support the advances made the day before by Marshal MacDonald at the head of the XIth Corps. It seemed to me that our soldiers made no progress for the longest time. First the tumult would be greatest near Oudinot, and then Marmont's poor VIth Corps would produce a din that overtook all else, for they had met the fury of the enemy's most heavily concentrated artillery on the heights. About noontime, Bertrand's IVth Corps, which thus far had not been committed, advanced in good order across the Spree and aimed for General Blücher's defenses on the heights above. Sixty more of our guns were brought up to assist in this attack and promptly took Blücher's positions under fire. Marshal Soult, who had been given supervision of this part of the front, pressed the troops forward most gallantly. Looking across the river I could see our soldiers between the clouds of smoke and fire. Never in all my campaigns did I see such persistence and bravery. The sons of France sacrificed themselves upon the enemy's defenses. Here and there, cheers rose over the battle's noise. But I wondered at our lack of progress, for it seemed to me that the IVth Corps, and indeed our entire assault was held hostage to the moment of Marshal Ney's arrival. Only an attack from his columns, I thought, might provide relief from the slaughter here. Napoleon must himself have despaired of assistance from Ney, for early in the afternoon he called for the Young Guards to advance to support Soult and Bertrand. Only this addition to our weight enabled Marmont's IVth Corps to finally reach the heights. Even at that, our center could do no more, for having achieved its goal, General Blücher's defenses held on stubbornly. Finally, from the north we could hear the sounds of Ney's forwardmost troops coming into action, and in the center the commotions of the battle seemed to subside ever so slightly. Then, to my south, I heard cheers go up from Oudinot's troops as well. At that very moment, Napoleon sent the Imperial Guard forward against Blücher's left. These positions had been defended gallantly by the Prussians, but our fresh troops were too much for them to bear. As darkness approached, Blücher, seeing that he was assailed from two directions at once and in danger of being cut off from escape, began to withdraw eastward. So too did Miloradovitch's Russians opposing Oudinot. The fighting continued well into the night as the Allies extricated themselves once more from our grasp. Our pursuit continued until the most violent thunderstorm interrupted our maneuvers. This was, I recall, about 10 o'clock in the evening.

The pursuit resumed the next morning, but in the most dilatory fashion, owing to our lack of cavalry and the exhaustion of our infantry. In truth, our army merely followed the enemy as he retreated, although a very sharp action that was fought at Reichenbach convinced us that the Allied army was still very dangerous. My old comrade Marshal Duroc, the chief of Napoleon's imperial household, was grievously wounded in this action when a cannon shot carried away his stomach. Having been summoned from some distance away, I was only able to hold his hand in his last moments as his life slipped away in terrible pain. It was said that Napoleon, who regarded Duroc as one of his closest friends, was overcome by his grief and retired for some hours to take his own anguish in solitude.

Still, the armies advanced, skirmishing fiercely as they marched. In this way, rather like two wolves snarling at each other, we reached Breslau on the Oder River, some forty leagues distant. It was here, on the 1st of June, that the Allies agreed to a brief armistice, although on the following day it was agreed that this might be extended until August. It seemed to me that the armistice was agreed less for reasons of state than for the simple reason that our armies had completely spent their energies. From Breslau, rearward through Bautzen, to Dresden and even as far as Leipzig itself, our armies had left a trail of human wreckage. Saxony seemed to be a vast graveyard.

Every variety of wound rose up to meet my colleagues and me, for though the armies rested, their pains did not. We were beset by shortages of all the most important articles for our ambulances, but even had we enjoyed a wealth of linen and lint, we could not hope of attending more than a fraction of our wounded. Bautzen had given us 20,000 casualties of our own and the Allies a further 20,000 of theirs, now abandoned and made prisoners of their miseries. These we treated without regard to whether they were friend or foe. Indeed, given the pitiable state to which our medical stores had been reduced, all were made to suffer alike. Like our own wounds, theirs carried none but the bloody flag of combat. Once the fighting subsided, the local people came forward to comfort the wounded as best they could and employed their carts to carry the most desperately ill back to Bautzen. One of my assistant surgeons said he had counted 150 of these little carts, carrying their bloody cargoes down the gently sloping road toward the River Spree.

After the armistice, Napoleon reestablished his headquarters at Dresden. His imperial household settled into the routines and intrigues of peace. This was where, for the first time, on the 5th or 6th of June, I heard rumors of the bitterest recriminations against our troops. It was said that during the recent battles many of our soldiers had willfully wounded themselves so that they might escape their duty in battle. Further, it was held that the number of these cowards was so great that their behavior had quickly and easily communicated itself among our several corps. Thus, our whole army performed as might a man who was afflicted by a febrile disease: with a most pronounced lassitude, indeed of a profundity heretofore unknown in the armies of France. For these reasons, many of our highest-ranking officers believed our army had not succeeded when another would have triumphed. The result, so said these traducers, worked an effect not different from mutiny or even treason. Although no one alleged conspiracies of any sort, still no provocateur could have hoped for a better success. The charge was that each soldier who had wounded himself contributed to the sum of our travails and so had participated in a collective treason against his comrades, against his army, and indeed against the glory of France itself.

These slanders prepared the way, no doubt, for the moment when Marshal Soult made his report to our general-in-chief. No doubt, too, the impression of Soult's report was all the more profound at this time, when our general could not have avoided reflecting upon the unfavorable course of our campaign thus far, for we all knew he was never satisfied with any outcome short of decisive and complete success. Soult reported to him that nearly 3,000 soldiers had been confined under suspicion. Their wounds, he argued, were of such a similar character as to suggest that they could not have been suffered in action. Upon hearing this, Napoleon reacted most violently and demanded an order be published which required the execution of two soldiers from each of our twelve corps. Upon receipt of this order, however, our provost marshal amended it further so that four, not two, soldiers from each corps be made to suffer punishment. Thus, by the conclusion of these transactions, nearly fifty of our brave soldiers stood to lose their lives to ignorance. Their executions would absolve our ranking officers of any responsibility for their own shortcomings.

Preparations were set in motion, therefore, for what I was certain could only result in the most egregious injustice. I was certain, moreover, that the soldiers of France had been slandered, their honor, integrity, and service impugned. I had myself seen them furiously press their attacks. The only foreseeable effect of the accusations would have been a stain upon our cause. I certainly did not hold our general-in-chief to blame. Indeed, as I turned these matters over in my mind I came to believe that he himself would ultimately be made a victim in this affair. Were the executions carried out as ordered, no end of harm would be done to those who continued to serve. Their spirits, already low, would be done down by the fate of their unfortunate comrades. Too, those who had inspired these charges would revel in their success. Who knew to what lengths their success might drive them next? Should it become the custom in the armies of France that their marshals could revenge their disappointments upon the very men who fought for our nation? Such things were very much on my mind when I was summoned to the presence of my general-in-chief.

He greeted me most cordially. "Ah, my dear Larrey," he said, "I am glad you are here. I have need of you. You know, I presume, of the grand collection of cowards our provosts have made since the engagement at Bautzen?"

"I do, Sire."

"And you know as well that I have ordered the most outrageous of these to be punished, so that my army may see that a soldier may not escape his duty by shooting himself? I would have you, Larrey, examine the accused so that we might say to the provost which two cases in each corps are the most flagrant examples of cowardice."

This was too much for me to bear. Now I was to participate in the travesty. One who had sworn to do no harm was to be an agent in the death of nearly fifty men.

"Sire," I replied excitedly, "I would beg you to stay these executions. I fear that you have been badly advised in this business. No one can say with certainty, merely by inspecting a wound, whether it was self-inflicted. I am suspicious of these charges. They seem too facile an answer. We cannot allow mere supposition to condemn these men. We want more proof than what we have."

"Brave men, you say!" Napoleon fairly exploded at my impertinence. "My order has been published, Larrey. All that is wanted
from you is to see from these soldiers' wounds who is the more
cowardly among them."

"Permit me to explain if I may, Sire? May I inquire if you know
the name of Galen?"

"I do not. Is he one of my officers?"

"No, Sire. Galen was a Greek physician who served the great em-
perors of Rome. He may be said to be the very father of medicine,
greater even than Hippocrates himself. He was the keenest of ob-
servers and experimenters and showed by prodigious example how
it is so unwise to accept the outward appearance of things, how we
must always subject our impressions to a precise test, to discover a
proof, as it were. Only in this way might we learn the truth of what
we see. Otherwise, we might be led along a false path, guided only
by our prejudices. This is as true in war as it is in medicine, Sire.
And I believe you do not need me to tell you so, Sire. I have seen often enough how you have disputed with Corvisart and other of your
household physicians in a good-natured way when they have prescribed medicines for your own complaints. Without fail, you have
demanded to know precisely how they arrived at their diagnoses. I
must say that your demands have not only assisted in their treatment
of you but have made them better physicians as well. Indeed, I have
observed that in all practical matters you have demanded proof, just
as Galen did himself. All I ask now, Sire, is that you permit me to
follow the course laid down not only by Galen but yourself as well.
Once we discover our proof, we will see the true way of proceed-
ing."

"By God, Larrey," the emperor shouted. "If Corvisart had had
you by his side, I warrant I may never have won an argument. Now
you would have me oppose one of my own marshals, would you?
You go too far."

"Sire, perhaps our marshal cannot bear to be disappointed in himself; perhaps he seeks the source of his disappointments elsewhere, even if he can offer you no proof of what may have been claimed. Allow me to conduct an investigation. Perhaps the combatants themselves may tell us what we need to know. Do not permit our disappointments to drive us toward dishonor."

Napoleon fixed a terrible gaze upon me. "You are on dangerous ground, Larrey. You have placed yourself in opposition to a marshal of France. Have you considered the consequences if you fail?"

"Sire, there may be consequences even if I succeed, but as long as I suffer them in your service I have no alternative."

"Very well then," Napoleon replied at last. "I would have your proof, or Galen's, if you like. I will allow you time but not too much of it. Be gone with you."

I took my leave in haste, knowing that my general would grow impatient if my investigation took too long. Once he had decided upon a course, he did not like to question it, nor did he often need to, so great was his confidence in his powers of discernment. And though it is true that his powers are very great indeed, on occasion they have led him to mistake his certainty for the truth. Thus his subordinates must possess great presence of mind themselves if they make so bold as to gainsay him. Sadly, he enjoys the services of only a few such men, and I am not, I fear, among them. But the circumstances in the present case were such that despite my great reluctance to question his orders, something moved me against all hazards to propose a course contrary to his. The consequences for my own fortunes were very dangerous, for if I failed to satisfy him I feared I might forfeit his confidence in me, but the danger to our men was far greater. I think this was what drove me to importune my general so.

Without delay I called for as many surgeons as could be spared from their duties. Baron Desgenettes, the physician-in-chief, came straightaway. So did Dr. Yvan, who had attended poor Lannes when he died at Lobau, and several others. When I explained our orders, they were aghast. "You must give up this folly, Larrey," Desgenettes remonstrated in the most confidential tones. "You have placed yourself in opposition to the most powerful men in the army. Soult will be outraged by what you have done, and he will not forget your interference. He will find a way to revenge himself upon you. And as for Napoleon, I need only remind you of our time at the Nile when he ordered me to put to death all our wounded before we evacuated. He will not be denied. I have never regained his favor for refusing him then. He has been cool toward me ever since."

"Yet here you are, Desgenettes," I argued. "And the affair at the Nile was quite different. Napoleon feared the torture of our wounded when they fell into the hands of the Turks. We all knew what they did to their captives. He could not bear to think of it. He knows your great value very well, no matter his disappointments."

Desgenettes shrugged off my reply, "He did not want to burden his transports. They were few enough after Nelson had done with us. To our brave generals, the wounded were merely an encumbrance. I have not your high opinion of our generals' motives, Larrey."

Dr. Yvan was no less alarmed: "I pray you, Larrey, not to press this business further. Even now the provost marshal has designated his officers to keep the closest surveillance of our activities. We ourselves are but a few steps away from being accused of thwarting the emperor's wishes. Do listen to Baron Desgenettes."

I told my colleagues that they need have no fear and that our skills would protect us. If we could conduct our investigation with the most careful attention, no one could attach any blame to us. The acuity of our observations would speak for itself, and everyone would see that our only interest was justice to the honor of our army.

"My friends, we must go on," I pleaded. "Even now several thousand men have been collected in bivouac near Bautzen. We need only examine these promptly, to see what these men and their wounds may tell us. Then we will assemble our findings and make our report. Nothing could be more straightforward." Though I could see that my colleagues were extremely reluctant even yet, we nevertheless agreed to begin promptly, for we all knew there was precious little time.

When we arrived at the bivouac, my colleagues and I bade the provosts to arrange the wounded according to the various corps in which they fought. As this was being accomplished we decided that we must take a statement from each of the accused soldiers so as to discover the circumstances in which the wounds had been suffered. And as the provost officers had been ordered to record their own observations, I enlisted their assistance in recording ours as well. Since common purpose would be served, they readily agreed to my request. I might also observe that by so doing, some of the provosts altered their opinions as well and considered ours with a good deal more sympathy than they otherwise might have done.

Upon each inspection, therefore, I insisted that we must all pose the same questions of each wounded man: in what corps, division, and regiment did he serve? What was the length of his service and had he fought elsewhere? At what time of the day and precisely where was his wound suffered? At which part of the formation was the man when he was wounded? Was he immediately disabled by the wound, or was he able to fight on? And so on, these questions were posed as each of us closely inspected each particular wound, and as the provost officer wrote down their answers, along with notes of our own physical observations.

Our inspections had no sooner begun than we recognized a surprising sameness to the wounds we saw. Far the greater number of these soldiers had been wounded more than once. But, always, one of these wounds had been suffered along the right side of the body, and most commonly above the waist, and, still more commonly yet, on their shoulders, upper arms, elbows or hands. Almost all the wounds were initiated from behind the body, and in very many cases the flesh surrounding the wound bore signs of severe scorching. So great had been the velocities with which they had been struck, the balls had passed through the mass of tissue and bone without much pause. Their fiery passages had cauterized the insulted tissue so that even now one could detect the earliest signs of the body's repairing itself without further care. Even in cases where several fingers had been shot away, little or no infection could be discerned.

None of these features attended the additional wounds. These betrayed the usual variety of location, condition, and infection. We inspected the soldiers' clothing as well, and in very many cases we recorded tears which could only have been made by musketry, so neat and round in appearance were they. And when we asked these soldiers to say their precise location in the battle, we learned that most of them fought in the first or second rank of their battalions. Not wishing to prejudge our findings, we worked without further remarking upon these coincidences, preferring to wait until we had collected all the information that could be had.

For nine days we conducted our investigation. On occasion we would return to this soldier or that to pose more questions so that we might clarify a point. At the conclusion of each day, we collected the soldiers' statements from the provosts and gathered them together with our own notes. The whole was arranged according to the order of the battle in which the soldiers had fought, and further divided by the time of day in which the wound had occurred. This I insisted on doing myself at the end of our day's labors, spreading the various reports about my quarters. The picture of this affair was gradually forming in my mind, but I did not reveal my own reservations to Desgenettes or my other colleagues for fear that I might unduly influence their next day's findings. By these means, we examined in all 2,632 wounded soldiers.

I confess that I worried what my colleagues might make of our findings, for even before we had begun several of them pronounced themselves satisfied by what they had already heard. To them, the close proximity of the weapon to the wound was more than enough proof that these soldiers had contrived to shoot themselves, and indeed their experience could permit them to think of no other cause. We all had known of soldiers inflicting wounds upon themselves by various stratagems, some quite fantastic, for indeed the ingenuity of cowards is often not to be believed. Dr. Yvan, in particular, wondered whether we had merely postponed these poor men's executions, which he regarded as completely inevitable, no matter what our jury found. Yvan suspected that either Napoleon himself would refuse to believe us, or else be accosted by Soult, who naturally would protest that he must by his rights as a marshal of France be supported by the emperor against the claims of mere physicians, who after all held no commissions whatever. I could not agree with Yvan, for if I did, the result would surely follow his dire predictions. While there was the merest chance to reveal the truth, I insisted we were honor-bound to continue.

Once we had completed our work at the bivouac, I remained in my quarters for a time, attempting to learn all I could from the documents we had gathered. Still I felt that I could not form a true and complete picture of what had actually happened. Our investigations revealed that far the greatest number of the suspicious wounds came from among the formations in Bertrand's IV Corps on the second day of our engagement at Bautzen. Quite often, our soldiers could recall with fair precision the moment when they were first wounded but not when, or even where, they had suffered their second wound, and the second wound was almost always the more suspicious of the two. One poor fellow had even been wounded four times, but after a bullet struck him a glancing blow along his left temporal lobe, he could not recall receiving the other three, although one of these had carried away the two middle digits of his right hand. At some moment, he knew not when, he had fallen. Only much later he had awakened on the ground among several other of his comrades who had already died.

As these and other mysteries presented themselves, I grew less confident of our documents. They recorded with great precision the physical details of the wounds and as much as we could learn from their victims. But I could not envision the exact circumstance that would have brought about such an incidence of wounds at very nearly the same time. My colleagues remonstrated with me, urged me not to torture myself with questions that could not be answered, and argued that every source of proof had been called upon already. What more was to be done?

Quite without knowing why, I felt compelled to make my way to Bertrand's encampment to search out officers who had themselves fought at Bautzen. It was in my mind to ask these officers to accompany me to the old battlefield and to answer such questions as might arise from a close inspection of the ground itself. Armed with such authority as I enjoyed, I found a gathering of officers easily enough, but to a man, save one, they spurned my requests. "Leave us be," one cried, "We have no wish to revisit such miseries. The war is not over. We will have no shortage of battles for you to investigate! We will see you again when you come for us with your amputation knives."

But then one young *chef de brigade* came forward, introduced himself as Colonel Moreau, proclaimed himself at my service, and promised to show me what I wished. Glancing backward as we left the division officers' quarters, Moreau whispered, "Pay them no mind, my dear Baron. They have drunk without pause these many days since Bautzen. It was the first real battle for most of them. They are slowly drinking away their terror so that they might acquit themselves honorably the next time."

Very perceptively, he saw my question forming. "Oh, I have done drinking of my own in my younger days, I assure you, and I had much to forget. In my own first engagement I soiled myself so badly one would have thought me the merest babe-in-arms. Happily, so many of my brethren had done the same, none of us dared speak of it to the other. Since then I have observed the same accidents, so to speak, many times over, although I have never embarrassed myself again. It has nothing to do at all, I find, with whether one is honorable or courageous. The senses will rebel if they are sufficiently insulted, don't you agree, M. Larrey?" I swore that I did agree, most completely, and I congratulated myself on having found such an enlightened companion in my quest for the truth.

Colonel Moreau's brigade served in Division Carnot, which along with several others made up Bertrand's IV Corps. The IVth, along with the corps of Marmont, had effected *le coup de foudre* against the center of the Allies' positions. As my companion and I made our way across the river, momentarily forgetting the utmost confidentiality of my task, I wondered aloud why so many of the accused should have come from the IVth. Before I realized what I had said, Moreau drew up his horse and looked at me intently. "M. Le Baron, I hope you do not think me forward, but I think you are not merely indulging your curiosity, as I had first supposed. You appear to have deeper purposes."

"Indeed, I confess I do, my colonel," I said, and then recounted so much of what I then knew, the true nature of my interests, my fears, and my intentions. To my surprise, he excitedly grasped my sleeve. "My dear Larrey! Of course I knew already of your devotion to our army. Everyone knows, too, the love and regard our soldiers have for you. We all know how last year you were rescued from death during the retreat over the Berezina, how the soldiers passed you across the crumbling bridge, hand to hand, until you were safe. Had I not heard of this fabulous adventure with my own ears from several of those who were there, I would have dismissed the story as an old soldier's tale. Now that I understand what you are about, sir, I can only repeat with the utmost enthusiasm my pledge to offer you any assistance I may."

"And yet, my dear colonel," I answered, "I fear I may have unintentionally placed you at some risk. Are you not concerned lest my folly, as some of my colleagues regard my project, will threaten your own interests?"

No, he said, he feared no retribution from such a noble cause, for he had seen the provosts take away some of his own men under these charges. He believed the accusations against them were wholly without foundation and swore he had never been more satisfied with the conduct of troops under his command. "When we assaulted Blücher's redoubt, M. le Baron, you should have seen them. They fought like lions. Not even the Imperial Guard itself could have done more," he said. But when the provosts had informed him of Napoleon's order of the day, he had no basis upon which to argue for his men. Now, he said, he saw a chance to put their case so that they might be treated justly, as any soldier of France must be. And as for his reputation, he said he cared nothing for it, because he had labored under a cloud since he was a cadet. I replied that the cloud must have been thin indeed, for he appeared to have grown into a most gallant and successful officer.

"Do not be deceived, Baron," he replied. "The name of Moreau casts a shadow still."

Then I saw his meaning. "Could it be that you are connected in some way to the family of General Moreau, the victor of Hohenlinden?"

"My father, the same," Moreau said quietly.

"What a battle it was! Snow, rain, freezing mud. And the Austrians completely encircled. What a day for France!"

"It was, too," Moreau agreed. "My father told me of it, and together we traced the armies' movements with finger and caliper, measuring the distance, calculating the speed with which his men moved to the attack." While Moreau spoke, his memories seemed to soften his face, making it younger, less careworn than the veteran I had met only a while before.

But his former mood returned presently. "I fear father's fortunes have declined since then. Victor of Hohenlinden, yes; but also accused as a conspirator in Cadoudal's plot to assassinate the emperor."

Yes, I did remember, I said, but General Moreau was exonerated, I had thought.

"Hardly exonerated," he said. "Napoleon's police agents raided our house in the city, and not finding him there, raced along the road to our country estate at Grosbois until they found him. Of course you know he was once regarded as a rival to Napoleon himself for the affections of the Republic, though no one dares speak of it today. And during father's trial, Napoleon was said to have been much chagrined to hear that court sentries presented arms whenever father arrived. Under the circumstances, only banishment was possible. Father was too popular with the army. The duc d'Enghien was not so fortunate. Father went to America, but the duc was kidnapped and executed."

"Is your father still in America, after all this time?" I asked.

"He is still there after these ten years in all. I am deputized to act on his behalf in France, seeing to the affairs of the family and such. Of course, now his name is anathema. Indeed, ever since I have worn this uniform, when someone speaks my name they do so *sotto voce,* as if the very mention of it would resurrect my father's rivalry with the emperor. I have learned to live with the unpleasantry."

I said that I could easily imagine all this to be so. But surely his own career had not suffered so: a *chef de brigade* at his young age? Yes, he said, he had been more fortunately advanced than he supposed possible. But he clearly believed he would not survive to become a general, and to serve France so, which was his dearest wish. He had two sons and a wife he hoped he might see once more, before he met his end, but he did not think it possible now. The Allies had learned enough to be dangerous, not only to himself, but to the whole army, perhaps even France herself.

With that, we returned to the matter at hand. He proposed that we retrace the steps of IV Corps. Perhaps we might observe some physical feature of the battlefield that bore upon the case. Having no better plan than this, I readily agreed. The fields were abandoned now, but the crops had by no means recovered their vitality. Here we could easily detect the course of the various battalions as they met at their crossing points over the river. We knew that the corps had remained here peacefully in the forenoon and that, indeed, its eventual passage across the bridges had been unnoticed by the enemy. Once we were across the river, I realized immediately why the corps had even then been unmolested, for Marshal Soult had ingeniously seen to the throwing up of a huge earthen wall that protected the corps from observation as it reformed itself on the enemy's side. Although the enemy occupied the heights beyond, this demilune obscured the enemy's view of our preparations for the assault.

But it was likewise true that IV Corps could not have known what awaited them advanced beyond their fortunate protection. I attempted to imagine myself in the place of a young and untried soldier, as most of them were, filled with dread of the unknown, awaiting my signal to advance, for though the sights were obscured, no doubt he could have heard the tumult from all sides. These furious sounds could only have intensified his foreboding.

"Look there," Moreau called out as we made our way past Soult's earthwork, pointing to the low hill ahead. At first, I did not understand what had attracted his attention so, for the ground before us was a perfect hell of ruin. Bodies were still to be seen everywhere, frozen in awful death, and the carcasses of bloated horses punctuated the putrescent heaps of flesh. Gun carriages were overturned throughout the scene, some so thoroughly destroyed one had difficulty imagining what they originally had been. Nor was the ground itself undisturbed, for great masses of earth had been upturned by thousands of feet, and hooves, and wheels and cannon fire. Here and there, furrows as straight as might have been made by a diligent farmer were to be seen. I thought these must have been made by the passage of shot, striking the ground at the perfect angle. All this impressed Moreau but little. He was pointing to the hill in front of us. At its apex, one could see a hint of the forwardmost battlements of Blücher's redoubt, guarding the crest.

"The redoubt: that is what we all aimed for," Moreau said quietly. "Now it does not seem so far. Then, it might as well have been a thousand leagues. Every step wanted the energy of a pilgrimage. We seemed to struggle against the winds of a great storm. Even on the best ground, keeping to a column of battalions, one directly after another, is not easy. The slightest irregularity will distract them from their line of advance, but on this . . . Old Marshal de Saxe called this kind of formation 'wretched work,' and nothing truer has ever been said. Not even firewood ought to be stacked this way, still less soldiers. No, a column of battalions is only a good formation for the weight it carries, and often it is made to suffer even for that meager benefit. But of course our superiors do not know de Saxe from Blücher, and anyway decide how we must arrange ourselves. Whenever the opportunity allows, I send ahead as many skirmishers as I dare. At least the *tiralleurs* protect us for a while."

"Your allusion to stormy winds seems apt to me," I said, "for I have observed how under fire our soldiers seem to bend forward, as though some unseen hand stayed their progress."

Moreau thought for a moment. "It is of course the enemy's fire they are shrinking from. They will do it, no matter how well drilled they are. Among poorly trained troops it is even worse. One would think they proposed to disappear altogether. Were it not for the formation, I should think no force could prevent their complete disarrangement. The battalion itself contains them, along with a few good sergeants, else they would fly apart once they suffered the enemy's first volleys. As it is, anyone who wishes to flee quickly learns what a prison our battalions are. But if one should make good his escape, he will learn too that the battlefield offers no other refuge. Dangerous though it may be within the ranks, there is more danger beyond them."

"I remember this place," he continued. "Here is where we stopped. I must have been afoot. I remember these folds in the ground quite clearly. M. le Baron, look here: a piece of my *cartouche,* shot away from my belt. I had stooped to assist a fellow officer. I thought he had missed his footing in this rough ground, for he seemed to fall very slowly. Indeed, every movement about me seemed infernally slow. But the poor fellow had been struck by several bullets at once. As I lifted him up, his insides fell from his wounds. That was when I felt a sharp blow myself and saw that my case had been carried away. Strange to say, it did not occur to me to wonder why I had not been hit myself. Men all around me were falling. I heard everything, and yet none of it seemed really to be happening. It was like a dream to me."

"The Prussians had all their guns on us now. We could not withdraw, for our way was barred by the thousands who followed us. To either flank, even greater numbers prevented any maneuver whatever, even had I been disposed to so order."

"Were you not?" I exclaimed. "Would you have your men be slaughtered without a chance of defense?" But I perceived immediately that I had so lost myself in his account that I had gone too far. Colonel Moreau examined me sharply. Evidently satisfying himself that I meant him no reproach, he smiled as if to forgive my outburst. "My dear Baron," he said slowly, "our only salvation was to advance; the way to relief lay through the enemy himself. Our very suffering and terror would move us forward if we were to move at all. To have turned our backs on the Prussians would have invited certain disaster. They might well have taken heart at our retreat, perhaps even sallied forth, protected by their own fire when we could produce none to oppose them. We would have been swept down the hill like so many leaves. The panic would have compounded itself, and then again as we would have disrupted the battalions to the rear. When a battalion breaks, you see, my dear Baron, it breaks for good. Not even the threat of death itself can repair it. Surely you remember your Thucydides?"

I wondered whether I had heard him correctly.

He laughed, "Thucydides, on the great war between the Athenians and the Spartans. I was made to recite him by my tutor, at the insistence of my father. I have come, finally, to understand why my father was so unyielding, despite my childish pleas."

My surprise was not to be denied. "You had Greek?" I asked. "Had not your father decided that you would follow him into the army?"

"Oh, he had, and no other argument would be heard," Moreau said. "When I protested that a good soldier need only be brave, he laughed at me and said it was far better to know when to be brave and what to be brave about, instead of dashing about like some brainless hussar who would give up his life in a trice, so long as it could be done in a stylish manner. He said war was changing, that the better mind was needed now . . . But, I forget myself. I was thinking about the awful massacre of the Athenians at Syracuse, when in the darkness they fell prey to their fears, became confused, and killed each other in the panic of the night. The Syracusans had no need to press their attack at all, the Athenians killed themselves so well."

"But if their commanders had only controlled their fears, surely they need not have suffered this calamity." Yet, even as I said this, I knew somehow that I had not grasped the truth of the matter.

"No, Larrey," said Moreau, forgetting his usual formality. "We commanders may do only so much. We do not control men so much as hope for what they may accomplish. We profess to know so much about war, but every combat reveals our true ignorance. The shape of a campaign or even a battle can be comprehended easily enough. When the fighting begins, our knowledge melts away. One can feel it slipping through one's fingers. We know nothing of the secret lives men live in combat, how the trials of battle work upon one's intelligence, mind, or even the spirit itself. We are like children in the presence of these mysteries. Against the storms of combat, our hopes seem very fragile indeed. Even for myself, hope seems as brittle as a fine crystal in the face of such power. You see the result all around you, do you not? What power has hope given these poor souls? Surely you are no stranger to scenes like this."

"Indeed, I am not, Colonel," I replied. "But until this moment, I believe I did not perceive what I have seen these many years. My dullness of mind fills me with shame. Battlefields have been the arenas for my own passion. I was blind to the carnage of the human spirit I see now. During my interview with the emperor, I was so seized with anxiety I babbled on about Galen. He must have thought me daft. But the ancient Galen, whose name was first in medicine for over a thousand years, must have spoken through me. He suspected that man's spirit dominated his intellect, that in extremity the spirit of man controlled the mind of man, no matter what he intended. How else could the behavior of our soldiers, who only wanted to fight bravely and with honor, be accounted for?"

"His answer lies here, my dear Baron," Moreau said. "Look how this hill is formed, rounded on the top. If everyone made for the top as did my own battalions, toward the redoubt, we naturally would have converged. Our numbers were very great at this place. Our rank and file were so closely packed they could scarcely move."

"Yet you did answer the enemy's fire, even then?" I asked.

"So we did, for nearly an hour before an interruption from our right caused the fire against us to subside momentarily," Moreau answered.

"How would those in the following ranks contribute? Did they not withhold their fire in favor of those in front?"

"Oh, no, indeed not. Everyone fired as he could," Moreau said.

"Why, then," I said, "the only avenue for the fire of those in the following ranks was along the open spaces of their own battalion, down the files?"

"I do see," cried Moreau. "So crowded were we, one could hardly avoid striking those in front of him. And from here you can readily see that all were firing upwards, toward the crest."

"So our own fire must have been striking our soldiers, do you agree?" I asked.

"It must have been so," he said after a moment. "Our lads lost their composure and acted in the only manner left open to them. They could do no other to relieve their suffering than discharge their pieces at will. Since they could see nothing at which to fire, only the act of loading and firing must have occupied them, without thought of the rest. That was the only way they could take their minds off the death that was all around them."

"Alas," I said, "There was no lack of it that day."

We both stood alone in our own silence for a very long time. Finally, Moreau sat himself on a ruined gun carriage. His head sank into his hands. I could see his hands tremble as he began to sob into them. "My poor boys," he cried softly. I could only stand at his side, stupidly looking about. I placed my hand on his shoulder, but his suffering was too great to be consoled. "My dear Colonel Moreau," I said as solemnly as I could, "the soldiers of France owe you a great debt. I salute you."

There was no more to be said. I picked my way alone down the slope to my horse. Once I had mounted, I looked up the hill. Moreau remained as I had left him. Later, I found myself at my quarters, insensible of having ridden at all. All that night, my mind was most restless and prevented sleep.

On the morrow, I called for my colleagues and described my adventure. Even Desgenettes proclaimed himself in favor of my conclusions. "It only proves," he said, "that one does not create an army with the snap of one's fingers. A new army cannot be handled in any old way. These are different men today. A great cause alone is no protection against the enemy's fire. Somehow, I feel as though we are participating in a great crime against all our soldiers." With very little more discussion, we decided what shape my report to the emperor should take.

Knowing that the emperor would be anxious for my return, I begged for an audience with him straightaway.

"So, Larrey, you've come to me again, and none too soon," said the emperor as I was conducted into his quarters. "Soult grows more impatient with me by the moment."

As concisely as I was able, I recounted our investigation, the methods we had employed, the records kept, and what were our conclusions. I told him of my visit to the hill, but I did not mention my companion's name for fear of harming his interests.

"Well, sir," Napoleon said after I had finished my presentation, "you persist in your opinion, then? The soldiers of the succeeding ranks in their excitement unwittingly struck their own comrades ahead of them?"

"I do, Sire," I answered. "And thus I beg you most earnestly to release these soldiers from arrest so that they might rejoin their regiments, to be among the brave soldiers of our beloved France."

"So be it, Larrey," he said promptly. Standing up from his desk, he came around and fastened his hands on my shoulders. "No sovereign could be more fortunate than me, to have such a man at his side, Larrey. You are a faithful and worthy friend. Go now, and with my gratitude, M. le Baron."

As I left his quarters I was overcome by both sadness and profound elation. I had helped to save the lives of forty-eight soldiers, who had been slandered because of the vanity and ignorance of their commander. I think this must have been the best day of my life. I expect no better.

This morning, having finished my usual rounds among our wounded, I called for my horse with the intention of seeking out Colonel Moreau and telling him of our general-in-chief's decision in the hopes of comforting him. By chance I saw one of the young officers of the division whom I had met that day in their quarters. I gave him a hello and greeting.

"Good day to you, Baron," he said. "It is my pleasure to see you on an otherwise sad day." When I inquired as to the reason for its sadness, he looked toward the ground: "I have come to headquarters in order to beg permission for leave so that I might perform a sorrowful duty. Have you not heard? Yesterday, poor Moreau's horse fell and carried him down the riverbank. His neck was broken. He was dead when we found him some hours later, poor fellow. And as he was a most gallant officer, everywhere admired for his skill and his care of his soldiers, we have decided that his body must be returned to his family seat. There are too many French graves in Saxony already, do you not agree, M. le Baron?"

I was overcome with his news. As soon as could be done with sympathy and courtesy, I took my leave and returned to my quarters, where I turned to writing down as quickly as I could this account of the whole affair. Toward evening, I received a staff officer from Napoleon's household. With much dignity, he drew himself up stiffly and presented me with a package, saying only, "By order of the emperor." The package contained an exquisite miniature portrait of the emperor himself in a frame encrusted with diamonds. It was accompanied by an imperial warrant for an annual gratuity of 3,000 livres.

I hastily wrapped up the portrait again and pressed it into the hands of the staff officer. I bade him ride after Moreau's body as fast as he could go. He was to instruct Moreau's escort to place the package into the hands of Moreau's family and say to them that this small token accompanied the profoundest thanks of Moreau's brigade, the Army of the Elbe, and all of France. After swearing the staff officer to secrecy as to the true source of this gift, I saw him ride off as swiftly as his horse could carry him.

And I returned to my rightful place, among the wounded.

7

IN WINTER QUARTERS

As smoke pours from the factories of the West and Napoleon's memory fades into history, the foremost interpreter of his style of war defends himself and his ideas against the encroachments of obsolescence, old age, and the new style of war. But even a modern civil war on the battlefields of America may not be enough to kill old ideas and the old men who cling to them.

I thought, for the merest moment, the old man had been stricken by one of his infirmities. "My god, Lecomte, it is he. I have seen his ghost!" So crying, he pointed excitedly across the great vault of the sepulcher, his aged finger describing an enfeebled orbit.

I looked in the direction he pointed. "No, general, it is only a man you see, nothing else. Look closely." But I did not have to say this, for his excitement had changed itself to curiosity. He was leaning forward on his cane quite precariously, however, squinting intensely. He had so completely abandoned himself to his inspection I feared he might lose his balance and pitch headfirst into the vault itself. As gently as I could, I took his arm in mine. He seemed not to notice my intervention at all.

Of course, one should never be surprised at the curious turns of a mind that had by then labored nearly eighty years, nor at the frailties of a once-robust frame, battered by the great excitements of the age.

159

Determination, consistency over logic, these have ever been his watchwords, the sources of his long success. Once he fixes his mind upon a course, he will not be dissuaded by any power. His temper, or should I say temperament, has not to this day deserted him; it is still as demanding as if he were a newborn. He cannot suffer being denied in any way.

I looked again at the man who had so arrested the general's attention. He was young, perhaps no older than I myself, and powerfully formed so far as I could see. Not even the very fine cloak, which I thought then he held about himself in the manner of a Roman senator, could conceal his physical strength. Not so tall as to be called so, but not short; the same height, about, as my excitable companion. The sun had browned his face very darkly. With his moustaches, one might mistake him for a Turkoman, except that his demeanor marked him with the character of a civilized man. A man of country estates, perhaps? Not a metropolitan, to be sure. No idle hours strolling the grand boulevards or the Bois, nor lounging in the cafés, surely. Not, in any case, a Frenchman. Who?

Quite before I had finished my speculations, I felt the general's hand on my elbow, guiding me toward the man. Dragged this way and that have I been these many years since I was first presented to him in Lausanne. As we approached, the young man lifted his gaze from Napoleon's tomb and stared at us quite directly and openly. What a curiosity we must have seemed, an animal of two distinct parts, one incapable of moving without the other!

"Forgive the intrusion, young sir. From afar you struck me as someone I once knew, many years ago. Now I see it could not be, but just the same, you held yourself so . . . "

"No apologies are required, my dear sir. I fear I do not have the pleasure of your acquaintance."

No. Not a Frenchman. A Frenchman would merely have shrugged us away. But of what nation? His French was academic, correct but without confidence, as if he were exercising in a school-room. Then, where?

"Allow me to present myself," he offered with a genteel smile, drawing himself up to full height. "I am George Brinton McClellan, captain, United States Army, 1st Cavalry Regiment. I am at your service." All this, accompanied by a courtly bow.

"A soldier! At least in this I was not mistaken," the old man exclaimed. "Yes, it was your carriage that struck me as familiar. I am a soldier myself, as is my young friend here. May I present Major Ferdinand Lecomte of the Federal Army of Switzerland?" I thought I felt a slight pressure from his hand on my arm. A certain electricity transmitted itself.

So. American, then. I had little experience of them yet, though I have since come to know them as well as one could say. One never knew all about the Americans. They seemed then only to send their best abroad, and those were few. Only after my recent visit did I come to understand there is no such beast as an ordinary American. This captain seemed a cut above at the time, and I do not believe my subsequent association with him in America has distorted my memory of him during our first meeting.

Captain McClellan bowed politely toward me, gathering his cloak about him. He knew our formalities well enough and waited for the general to compose himself. I wondered how the old man would reveal himself. I did not doubt he was savoring the next act in our polite little play. He was not often allowed to draw upon this skill in these times. Here in Paris the mention of his name alone was sufficient to produce gushes of obsequiousness, especially among the courtiers of the crude new monarch. Perhaps this was true even in all of Europe. He certainly would have preferred to believe so. But had his fame traveled to America?

The old general finally worked himself up to his advertisement. "As for myself, I am the Baron Jomini, once of the Swiss Army and then for some time in the service of the Grand Army of . . . " He paused and then delicately swept his hand toward the tomb, "of His Majesty, the Emperor Napoleon. Presently, I have the honor of being on detached service from the Army of Russia as military advisor to the Tsar. I have done some small amount of writing on the subject of strategy. I wonder if perhaps you might have . . . read any of my work? Does it come to America in any form?"

Yes, I recall how adroitly it was done, the desired effect achieved straightaway. Ney, Alexander, even Napoleon himself, all at one time or another had fallen under the sway of the old man's delicate pauses. The captain's eyebrows arched ever so slightly. Good. No fawning, at least. In Lausanne, everyone had been insufferably deferential. The old man had got what he had wanted with only the smallest deployment of his courtier's talents.

McClellan's voice was warmth itself. "My dear Baron, is this not the happiest of coincidences? I am just returned from the Crimea and of course I could not delay visiting this remarkable monument, but I had determined to seek an audience with you on the morrow. And yet it seems our mentor has brought us together in his own presence, as it were."

Oh my, I thought.

"Our, our mentor? Why, young sir, I do not take your meaning."

"I mean Napoleon himself, Baron. Here he reposes in great splendor, and even now he moves us mortals to do his bidding."

Had the captain's enthusiasm departed reason altogether, I wondered? Could he not see the old man screwing up his face? I confess I suppressed my amusement at seeing Jomini so discomfited. As he has struggled his entire life to advertise his particular genius for war, he has in old age grown resentful of any slight toward the reputation he has so painstakingly created. McClellan seemed rather humorless, all too like my companion, and so I surmised his *lese majeste* was not a bit of drollery. If my memory of this encounter has not been corrupted since my recent sojourn in America, I believe I wondered even then whether a jest had ever passed through McClellan's brain. I thought not, and nothing that has happened since encourages me to change my opinion.

Jomini chose not to take offense at McClellan's forwardness. What a strain this forbearance must have placed upon his true feelings! Never in my presence has he behaved so circumspectly. Indeed, as I labored upon my study of Jomini's life—happily now concluded and set to print—I saw the most innocent remarks throw him into a sputtering tantrum from which he could be disentangled only by the loyal and self-effacing Madame Jomini. The catalog of references that might so excite him was very large indeed, at the head of which stood Marshal Bertier. Even an oblique mention of his *bête noire* would launch him into paroxysms of vituperation, and there were many more such names, all of which were united in their failure to recognize his unique gifts of mind and special aptitude for war. A lifetime of vainglory has won him as many detractors as sycophants. Even now I would say only that I stand uneasily between the two sorts.

So it was to my surprise on this occasion that, far from being offended, Jomini actually attempted a *bon mot.*

"Then, Captain, I believe the emperor's work is done for today. Shall we venture outside to walk along in the fine air?"

We abandoned the emperor to his solitude and passed outside to the Place Vauban. Surgeon Larrey's statue, erected a few years ago by his loving son Hippolyte, watched our procession go by. The air, I remember, was in no manner fine. I hoped we might turn toward the Palais de Chaillot so that we might reach the promenade along the river. But Jomini guided us toward the Champ de Mars, that great mud bog which our newest Napoleon had pledged to transform along with the rest of Paris. His agent, the Baron Haussmann, has set in motion so many projects of reclamation as to keep the city nearly everywhere in disrepair. A pall of dust seems to have become a permanent feature of city life, so much so that any family of substance has fled toward the new western suburbs. On windless days such as this one, a lace of destruction covers everything and everyone. Now I have learned to go abroad only after dusk and dew have fallen, when it is possible to ignore the noxious smells given birth by sewer gas and blasting powder.

Both men so thoroughly fixed their attention on one another, the city might have disappeared altogether. McClellan submitted happily to Jomini's interrogation, which at first turned upon his journey to the seat of the recent war. McClellan confided that his mission was an official one. Although junior in rank to the other two officers in his delegation, whose names he did not disclose, he gave the impression that he was the real leader by virtue of his superior military knowledge and his facility in French, German, and Russian. His secretary of war had directed him to conduct a tour of investigation among the warring states and to observe their field armies in actual operations if possible. By such means, it was hoped, America might profit from contemplating the present state of the practice of war in its most expert manifestations without actually suffering its indignities. McClellan thought his mission had been quite successful. He praised the English for the courtesies they had extended to his delegation, in marked contrast, he feared to say, to the very unhelpful officials he had called upon in Paris on his way to the Crimea.

McClellan related how these officials had refused any sort of permission or accreditation to him or his colleagues, and how upon inquiring the reason for the Ministry of War's obstinacy, he was told merely that such things were not done. Hearing this, Jomini's face darkened. He stopped momentarily and gazed ahead, as if looking into a past he knew too well. "Such men, petty in every degree, must have always and everywhere existed," he said. "They enjoy no power except not to act. But it is France's misfortune that here they have raised such practices to a high art. No: it is always no, it is 'not done.' They are the enemies of progress of any kind, and the world finds too many uses for them now."

"Yet able men must always oppose them," McClellan replied. "I believe God has invested some men with the moral strength and superiority of character to triumph if they will not lose heart. Above all, able men must not submit to their will."

Jomini agreed that this was so, and that history would not be misled. Wisdom would in the end be confirmed by events. A heavy blanket of self-satisfaction settled over the two men, and we walked along in silence for a few minutes before McClellan resumed his narrative.

McClellan's lack of success in official Paris persuaded him and his companions to attempt a different approach to the war, by way of Berlin and St. Petersburg, where they obtained permission to travel on to Constantinople. Upon their arrival, they learned that the final and most dramatic feat of the war had already occurred, for only a few days before the Allies had successfully stormed the fortress of Sebastopol that had so long thwarted their siege. Now the Allies had the ruined city in hand, and the war was effectively finished but for desultory operations in the Caucasus.

English officials in Constantinople, as obliging there as in London, issued McClellan's company with passes to visit Balaclava, where they were allowed to billet upon General Simpson's 4th Division and enjoy the amenities of the officers' messes. From this vantage, McClellan and his colleagues were given leave to examine the detritus of the various battlefields and to interview such Allied officers as they pleased. This last, to McClellan's way of thinking, was far more rewarding than negotiating the human and material litter of the battlegrounds, for, as he averred to Jomini, he was more interested in the conception and execution of the war's strategic designs.

Moreover, he said frankly, he had an aversion to gazing upon the dead (of whom there was a plenitude still unburied)—so much so that the sight actually sickened him. He had discovered this aversion, he said, during his own field service in his country's war against Mexico some years before. He had long since concluded anyway that strategy was the only dimension of war worthy of the notice of the truly scientific mind, and that it was in the strategic realm that wars were finally lost or won. All the other parts of war, mostly drudgery or gore, were significant only in the degree to which they contributed to the achievement of the general's strategic aims. In a tone both embarrassed and coy, he said that his views had been shaped by an assiduous study of Napoleon's campaigns which he had undertaken while still a student at West Point, and that above all he had been guided in his discipline by the works of none other than Jomini himself. Indeed, he gave it as his opinion that virtually all of the students in the academy, then and since, learned what they knew of Napoleon in the very same fashion. So far as McClellan could say, Jomini had the field to himself alone.

No other confession could have been better calculated to win Jomini's affections. The old man fairly beamed with pleasure. He mumbled that Captain McClellan was far too kind, but it is unlikely that Jomini thought any such thing. Rather, he would have thought that McClellan's compliments were only too just. Our conversation was in danger. I had witnessed scenes like this already in the baron's company: let one whisper of flattery escape, and he would maneuver for more. The appetite of his vanity seemed beyond satisfaction. Those who obliged it won his complete attention. Perhaps flattery is his only reason now for tolerating conversation with anyone. Thus it was at some risk that I interrupted to ask McClellan to what degree the military principles he had espoused—all in consonance with those of the baron, of course—were in any degree observable during his investigations in the Crimea.

"Alas," McClellan answered, "the principles of war were prominent only by virtue of their absence. Little scientific thought seems to have been given to the grand strategical problem until the neglect of it became so obvious—but by then it was too late. All sides wallowed in mud and ignorance. The movements of all the armies were dilatory in the extreme. Several British and French officers were most critical of the disembarkation at Old Fort. The pace of advance toward Alma was so laggardly that in the face of an expert enemy the Allies surely would have been thrown out of their lodgments. Luckily, the Russians seem to have been utterly insensible of the opportunities their opponents laid before them. Were it not for the suffering of the troops, the whole affair might have been regarded as an elaborate production of the *Comédie Française*."

"At Sebastopol, however, the Russians had constructed their defenses most ingeniously, eschewing masonry for a system of earthworks. Within, the guns had been excellently sited and their fields of fire very finely calculated in harmony with one another. The true author of this system, I discovered, was one Colonel Todleben, a Russian officer of engineers. Happily, I can report that while Sebastopol did finally succumb to General Bosquet's superb main assault on the Malakoff redoubt—an extraordinary feat in its own right—no blame whatever is attached to Colonel Todleben, whose scientific methods excited the professional admiration of friend and foe alike. I may also say I have been told that Todleben's star is yet rising; great service is expected of him in future."

Forgetting any momentary discomfort my interruption may have caused him, Jomini was caught up in the details of McClellan's analysis. "My dear Captain," Jomini said, "we may count ourselves fortunate, Lecomte and I, to have happened upon you as we did. You see, France is happy not to know of her army's doings. France has abandoned her martial dress of old; not even our new Napoleon could reawaken her, even should he choose to do so. He prefers at all hazards a prosperous but quiescent empire and believes he may sustain it by show-playing alone. Public information is closely watched by government officials whose instructions are simple: only triumphs may be reported upon so that public indifference is never disturbed. Details from the war, such as they are, are available to us only through the English press."

Upon hearing Jomini's complaint, which indeed was as accurate then as now, McClellan proposed to prepare a set of sketch maps so that we might have as complete a reconstruction of events as the extent of his knowledge might allow. Might he be permitted to call upon the baron at his convenience in order to rectify this lamentable situation?

Jomini quickly accepted McClellan's generosity and agreed that McClellan should call at his residence in the suburb of Passy, then so close at hand across the river that we could very nearly see it. McClellan thought that he might apply himself to the task straightaway once he retired to his rooms, which he had taken up near the Café de la Paix. He believed he might produce a suitable rendition of the theatre of war by the afternoon of the following day, provided proper pens, inks, paper, and the like could be had.

As it happened, I knew of a shop in Montparnasse that I had used in my own work. I provided McClellan with the address, and without further ado he begged our pardon, saying that if he made haste he might reach the shop before closing time. He strode powerfully in the direction I had indicated, full of purpose and the unreserved good will I have since come to associate with Americans.

During my years of collaboration with the baron it has been my custom to rise early, following each day's course much the same, in a manner best suited to my work. After three hours or so at my desk I repair to my café of habit with merely a coffee and cigar, there to read the newspapers and organize my thoughts for the remainder of the day. I may easily reach the baron's residence at mid-morning in time for breakfast. As it is his own custom to write for a few hours each morning, and without fail, he comes to table rather late, not I think so much for sustenance but to discuss his project of the moment and to make of me some request: to take dictation, to call for true copies of this or that document, to find a particular book, to dispatch a letter, and so forth. Once our morning is concluded, I leave the old man to his reading and pause at some café for refreshment and solitude before attending to the afternoon's duties.

On the day following our meeting with McClellan I saw no need to alter my habits, and so arrived at the baron's residence at my usual time. However, I was not a little surprised to learn from the maid that another visitor had preceded me by several hours. She was in a state of some agitation. A youngish man, quite polite but imposing, had insisted upon seeing the baron at an impossible hour. She had attempted to explain that the baron was in no way to be disturbed, having reserved this time for his serious work. But the young man was a foreigner whose French was execrable, and she had failed to make him understand. At a loss as to what else might be done, she had invaded the baron's study and told him of this strange creature and begged his forgiveness for having violated his strictest instructions.

To her amazement, the old man had promptly abandoned his desk and rushed to greet the foreigner in the friendliest way possible. From that moment, the two had been engaged in the most intimate conversation. Why, she added, they were even now crawling about the floor of the study, which was completely covered with very large papers whose markings were indecipherable to her. The old man had refused breakfast, although he had permitted her to bring coffee and butter and bread and some jams and some fruit. Thus far, however, he had touched none of it. Would monsieur, who is his closest friend, prevail upon the baron to cease his labors long enough to eat? I assured the maid that I would attend to the matter immediately if she would only allow me to pass. She should wait upon my call for breakfast.

The baron's study was as she had described it. The baron is an extremely fastidious man, highly methodical in his attention to his dress as well as to his surroundings. I had not associated with him for long before I understood all too well that one never disturbed any item in his study. Nor had I ever seen him in a state of undress or disarray. When he entered his study each morning to work, he was as correct as if on parade, boots gleaming, coat and trousers well brushed and moustaches neatly trimmed. His shirt cuffs were only occasionally soiled by ink, but when he first sat down at his desk they were spotless.

Now both men had removed their coats and unbuttoned their waistcoats. Their neck scarves were undone. McClellan was actually sitting on the floor with his legs crossed very like some Red Indian. Jomini stood beside him. The air was filled with cigar smoke. McClellan's maps spilled from the desk to the floor. One had been tacked to a bookcase. Scattered about were pens, magnification glasses, calipers, and measuring rods. They had been fairly transported by their amusements. I never saw either man look so happy. And I was happy to be greeted in a jocular and forward manner.

"Ah, my dear Lecomte," Jomini called out, "I have enjoyed the most satisfying morning. The labors of Hercules are a trifle beside what McClellan has done. Look you here: a map of the entire theatre of war upon which is noted all the lines of operation, natural and strategical, drawn with the most exquisite attention to my own principles, correct to the smallest detail. No statesman or general could demand better! And see here, sketches of the Russian works at Sebastopol, together with a depiction of the avenues employed by the grand assault. You know, Lecomte, even from my own vantage point at the elbow of the Tsar himself, I knew far less of the true situation than McClellan has given me here."

"Surely, Baron," McClellan interrupted, "this cannot be true. The Tsar's principal military advisor: you are being too modest by far."

"I am not. I was little more than a prompter at a play, occasionally reminding the actors of their lines. But I was unable to convey understanding to his generals. They sacrificed every advantage they enjoyed. Who else could have tolerated such incompetent campaigns? Their kind know no country. Stupidity, incompetence: these are truly international. I have fought them everywhere."

McClellan said nothing. He smiled as if he had heard only Jomini's praise and none of his complaint.

The maps were as Jomini said. The minutest detail had been attended. I expressed my own amazement and gratitude.

"My task was rather less difficult than I had supposed," McClellan replied. "I found that my notes and field sketches were adequate, so that little was left to the frailties of memory. Furthermore, the doing of these maps has been excellent preparation, for when I return to America I must submit a report of my investigations to Secretary of War Davis. I must confess, too, that a copy of the Baron's *Precis de l'art de la guerre,* which I obtained from a bookseller when I passed through Paris last year, proved a most useful compendium of the Baron's work. I am quite relieved that my depiction has not been found wanting. I felt all last evening as though I was back at the West Point of my youth, preparing for a recitation before the Napoleon Club."

"Indeed not," Jomini said, "no fault at all that I can discern. Would that the marshals of France had been so attentive. I wager my story might have ended differently. I might have commanded, at least."

"You wished to command?" McClellan asked.

"What soldier does not? Once one has seen as much of incompetence in the field as I have, one cannot help but wonder if he could not succeed where others have failed, especially if one has a talent for the business. When one has studied with such discipline and exactitude as I have, one inevitably will look to his superiors for preferment. But my misfortune has been to be subjected to the stupidities of lesser minds that misfortune has made my superiors. Bertier, Chernyshev, others. Dim lights do so often suppress the bright."

Jomini had a familiar dim light in his eyes. Once his memories had been excited, Jomini would become sullen and fix his eyes on some distant point, sitting this way for some long time. I suggested we relieve the servants of their duty to provide us with breakfast. Still somewhat distracted, Jomini nodded agreement, and we repaired to the table.

McClellan and I ate lustily while Jomini as usual ate little at all. He had been trained in the privations of long campaigns. His spare frame, though still then quite strong, required little to sustain his health. McClellan, however, was a man of large appetites; and as I later came to know him, I found these habits extended as well to his moods. He never achieved a happy plane of moderation. He was all enthusiasm or desperation. But my observations on these characteristics were yet years away.

Our conversation drifted pleasantly away from Jomini. I asked McClellan if he found Paris to his liking. He said that of all the cities he had passed through, Paris was the most appealing. He hoped he might return in future for a longer stay to do justice to the museums, the theatre, the opera, the fine restaurants. All were most stimulating to him. He was particularly interested in the vast projects of rejuvenation that were everywhere underfoot, then as now, and that the true engine of such progress was Louis Napoleon himself.

Yes, I agreed, the new Paris is indeed his vision, though much elaborated upon by Baron Haussmann. I explained how the regime's detractors saw these projects merely as an outgrowth of Napoleon's ambition to impose a benign orderliness on the city and indeed on France everywhere. McClellan expressed some surprise when I offered my opinion that Napoleon's new regime was not as benign as it might first appear. The city had then reached a population of one million souls, the greatest number of whom collected in the poorest districts, of which Belleville and Menilmontant were most prominent—as true kasbahs as one might find among the Moslems of Africa. No one might safely traverse such a place. Even police agents, it was said, recoiled at the prospect of entering there.

Were these districts merely breeding grounds of criminality, indeed every sort of vice, that would be one matter. What inspired fear in the new regime, I said, was the propensity for Belleville, in particular, to nurture the most violent political creeds. Socialists, anarchists, the most radical and extreme sorts daily spread their resentments among hopeless people who were happy to hear any complaint to take their minds away from their own destitution. Already, the courts had acquired a certain fondness for political deportation on a scale not matched since the worst days of the restoration. Indeed, after Louis Napoleon's *coup d'état,* more than 25,000 souls had been arrested and transported.

McClellan replied he had seen no hint of unrest in the newspapers, which appeared to him most vigorous indeed. I said no trustworthy intelligence was likely to issue from that arena, as the regime exercised the most stringent control over their contents. At the time, I enjoyed the acquaintance of a police official of a certain station who occasionally allowed me into his confidence. He had told me of several plots, since foiled, against the life of Napoleon himself. He feared that official life in France had entered a new, altogether more dangerous age. Indeed, his fear came true: not one year after my conversation with McClellan, Orsini's dastardly bombs outside the Opera nearly put paid to Napoleon and the empress. Several innocents were killed and wounded.

Should France submit her love of liberty to the necessities of progress, if only for a moment, McClellan wondered aloud, the inequities which so disturbed the unfortunate might ultimately be righted. I asked in whose hands France might entrust so precious a treasure? Why, to men of ability and good will, he replied, else the extremes to which popular government were prone might forestall any intellectual or civic betterment. Such governments were far too fond of mediocrity.

I made so bold as to remind the captain that he himself was a child of a most venturesome republic. Surely he was not repudiating the principles upon which his homeland had been founded? Not for a moment, he assured me, men of talent might always find their way in America, but their way did not often lead to government, where obedience to public passion had become the true civil religion. To his mind, such indulgence would bring his country to no good end. If America would succeed, it must see the necessity of calling upon men of talent. What was wanted was a natural aristocracy of talent such as that established under the first Napoleon. Only later did I understand that, very like Jomini, his judgments were predicated upon how the world treated him. Now I suspect it must be their only true standard.

Jomini startled us both by speaking. I thought he had dozed off, and apparently McClellan thought the same, for we had been talking very quietly. "Lecomte and I have discussed this puzzle," Jomini said. "By themselves, are good ideas enough? Lecomte is a mystic: he believes ideas have a life of their own. I, contrariwise, believe that any idea may be accepted so long as it enjoys a powerful patron. We both believe history favors our own argument and disproves the other's. So you see where we are, McClellan."

"It is as the baron says," I replied. "However, I think I may prove my case by reference to the baron's own history, and with Captain McClellan's kind assistance. Indeed, I may say that Captain McClellan has already made his contribution to our deliberations, as, in fact, have you yourself, my dear Baron."

Both men exclaimed.

"We have by your own testimony, dear Baron, that your career was foiled in several instances by those who were incapable of recognizing the worth of your very original contributions to the science of war. And from your testimony, my dear captain, we have learned that despite the impediments placed in the Baron's way, his ideas traversed the Atlantic, there to take root in the mind of your young army. Have I distorted what you said?"

Both men looked perplexed. "Here, then, we have a perfect illustration of my argument. Ideas may not grow where their authors intend, indeed the life of an idea seems to progress quite independently of those who give them birth. The idea rises above its original time and place and joins the great stream of history, where it may sail on or not."

"How very interesting," McClellan said finally. "And what decides whether it will float?"

"It must survive the test of usefulness. So long as the idea speaks to those who encounter it, the idea will remain vital."

"And what of other ideas, contrary notions, if you will," Jomini asked. "Do these ideas compete with one another?"

"Inevitably they do, and to the degree that they directly oppose one another, my own opinion is that inevitably one idea will die. We may see a shadow of the old idea, but then it is only a matter of interest to intellectual antiquarians. Or we may see yet a third idea which has been given birth by the energy cast off from the struggle between the original two."

"Ah," snorted Jomini, "did you feel it? The Prussians have entered the room."

"Prussians? I don't understand," said McClellan.

"That was Hegel speaking. Lecomte has been poisoning his mind by reading German philosophy. Sometimes he is possessed of the most peculiar ideas. I know they are not his. They were born on the Elbe," Jomini replied.

I tried to defend myself. I said there was much in both Hegel and Kant also for the attentive student. I argued that there was no reason to ignore scholars merely because they were Germans.

Jomini said he had reason to see Germans less favorably than I did. Even their soldiers seemed to believe all wisdom resided in philosophy and that no speculation on war could be worthwhile that did not stem from it. Having fought one or another of their variety for ten years, he said, he was not disposed to accept their pronouncements on war. They certainly had produced no one of merit since before the wars of the revolution. Frederick the Great of course had set the highest possible standards in his own narratives. And yes, Templehoff had written interestingly, if ponderously, of Frederick and had supplied details impossible to learn elsewhere. Von Bulow's strategic appreciations were important, but his work was so burdened with scholarly pretension as to render it impossible except for a determined few.

No, for himself, Jomini said, he owed most to the Englishman Henry Lloyd, whose memoirs of the wars in Germany were so profound and illuminating as to have compelled him to burn his own first manuscript. Only after he had thoroughly imbibed Lloyd and to some extent von Bulow, Jomini said, did he think he was equal to the task he had set himself. And finally, he said, he had completed his task in 1806, when he published his treatise on grand military operations. It was from that work, not some high-flown philosophy, Jomini said, that all his subsequent writing derived, for it was there that he had made known the key to all warfare.

"But now," Jomini said, "the Germans are besotted with philosophy. Truth is an annoyance to them. They confuse order with wisdom. Xilander, Wagner, Theobald, Decker, Hoyer, all their kind. Their infernal systems hang like a black cloud over all experience and common sense. If one protests he is interested in principles, not systems, as I have done, they will say you have a system all the same without knowing so, and attack you with one of theirs. No idea, no matter how soundly formulated, is safe from being assailed in this way," Jomini said.

"The end of the French wars did indeed give way to a very great number of interesting military works, however," McClellan said.

"Indeed, it is true. Some of them were not wholly without merit. General Rogniat, for example, was widely attacked for impugning Napoleon's system, but at least he had the courage to think for himself, without fear that others would disagree or, worse, call him a traitor to the name of the emperor. Vernon, de Presle, Roquancourt,

such works as these merely dilated upon my discovery of the principles of war, without extending true knowledge. During my time in
Russia, I became quite fond of General Okounief's work on the
combinations of the three arms in combat, which I thought was especially pertinent to young, studious officers. However, for the most
part all these works lay in realms subordinate to mine—the techniques and actions of the various arms, incidental tactical forms, and
the like."

"You have no peers, no competitors, it is clear," McClellan said,
rather soothingly, I thought.

"Alas, that has not prevented some from attacking me. My design
for lines of operation seems to have been misunderstood intentionally so as to expose me to criticism. There were complaints that my
lines of operation were indistinguishable from my lines of communication, that my explanation of decisive points of attack was unclear. This has been most vexing to me, and so I set about composing an analytical summary of my conclusions. I had in mind as a
model for this little book the Archduke Charles's excellent compendium of military maxims."

"And you have been satisfied with the result of your labors, no
doubt, Baron," McClellan said. "I have read nothing of late that does
not accord you your proper rank among writers on the art of war."

"I suppose I am satisfied," Jomini replied. "One of my critics, I
am convinced, did not sufficiently understand my work and unfortunately died before I was able to complete and publish my summary.
If only he had the advantage of it, I am sure he would have been able
to do it justice in his own work. I must confess I find it by turns
difficult, impenetrable in places, and certainly pedantic in the extreme. But, all the same, his book was singular."

"And whose book was this?" McClellan asked.

"He was a Prussian. Von Clausewitz. A general. His wife published the manuscript after his death on campaign in Poland in 1830.
It is unfinished. A fragment, really. In a note found among his pa-

pers, he wrote that the manuscript was yet in his judgment a shape-less mass of ideas, a judgment with which I am bound to agree. Still, its publication has led to his celebration. It has been rendered into French since then, but not, I think, English. In any language, it is a difficult text, although I do not find it so difficult as faulty."

"I believe that his achievement is merely a novelty. A common reader can learn nothing from it. Once the novelty has dimmed, the work will be forgotten."

"Did his ideas diverge significantly from your own?" McClellan asked.

"Some say our ideas are contrapuntal, but I am not convinced. Once one discards those homilies masquerading as philosophy, I see nothing that challenges my fundamental principles. His acclaim rests solely on the ornamental features of his work, so to speak, with all its talk of trinities and extremes and magnetism and polarities and such. He uses these illustrations much as I do geometry, which at least has the advantage of precision. There is too much of your much-vaunted German philosophy, Lecomte," Jomini said as his eyes turned piercingly toward me.

He went on, "Von Clausewitz called his work simply *Vom Kriege*, 'On War.' Such pretension! To imagine that the whole drama of war may be so comprehended. He abandons his readers to the complexities he has himself created. So deserted, they are left to wander un-aided through a pedantic labyrinth. It is unnecessary, and it is faulty. What one wants is to find the decisive point of war, the essence where thought and action create the widest and most definitive re-sult. The great geniuses of war have always done this very thing. I have been the only one to say what that thing was. Von Clausewitz seems to glory in his obscurity. One suspects he thought he was some sort of Hegel in military garb. Preposterous," he said.

I attempted to defend the Prussian. I predicted that *Vom Kriege* would be read long after his traducers had been forgotten.

"Does this include me, Lecomte?" Jomini demanded.

I hastened to say that it did not, but that I nevertheless found his criticisms of von Clausewitz too harsh.

"You see?" Jomini asked McClellan, "Lecomte is completely enamored of these Germans. What is to become of him?"

McClellan did not answer directly. "Could one say that this von Clausewitz—what a curious name, full of solemnity—this von Clausewitz was of a particular school of thought? Would he claim an alliance such as you have done with Henry Lloyd?"

"No," I said quickly, "he stands alone."

"So he did," Jomini added, and genuinely, I thought. "He acknowledged no other intellectual authority. But he had the effrontery to imply that Napoleon embodied, personified his system, when I am convinced he knew very well I had made the same claim for my own theories. Indeed, I wrote most precisely, 'Le systèmes de l'Empereur Napoleon présente une application constante de ces principes invariable.' That was in 1809. And that was not the only time this Prussian took from my work. He especially pillaged my work on the campaign of 1799."

"Thus for several reasons I believe we are quite close, von Clausewitz and I. Indeed, I took pains in my own summary of the art of war to demonstrate our essential agreement. I believe this has satisfied those who are interested in this question," Jomini said, evidently satisfied. McClellan seemed likewise.

Looking backward, I am sure now Jomini knowingly deceived McClellan. The thrust of his attack on von Clausewitz seems to have been aimed toward dissuading McClellan from ever reading this work, ever taking it to America, where there was a danger that it might put down roots of some sort. Since the appearance of von Clausewitz's masterwork, Jomini appears to have been filled with dread that someone will see how completely the Prussian's ideas overturned his own. Jomini has spent his long life insisting that of all the parts of war, only strategy was worthy of profound attention. Von Clausewitz explained all that Jomini tried to dismiss.

To satisfy my own curiosity I had spent several months in a close reading of von Clausewitz. It had been rather a trial for me, not because of the density of the text, which was hardly so pedantic as Jomini claimed, but because Jomini and I were collaborating quite closely in preparing his biography. What made this so difficult for me was the necessity of concealing that I was reading von Clausewitz at all. I was concerned that once Jomini learned of my studies, he would withdraw his cooperation instantly. Only gradually was I able to admit any familiarity with his nemesis. Even at that, Jomini would always turn cool at the mention of the name.

Still less could I admit a preference for the Prussian's ideas. I thought then, and think now, that no one had ever written so penetratingly about the fundamental nature of war. Unlike Jomini, who always said to me that his writings were meant to teach, von Clausewitz genuinely wished to understand and explain war in all its great and terrible scope. That was why, I think, von Clausewitz did not appear to be much concerned that he would ever complete his masterpiece. Perhaps he would not have finished even if he had lived as long as Jomini has. I wonder if either of these men would have exchanged their fates with one another? Perhaps Jomini would. But, as for von Clausewitz, I think not.

THE ILLUSTRATED LONDON NEWS, OCTOBER 18, 1862
War News from America
By the arrival of the steamer *Etna* we have received New York
journals to the 4th inst.

Although a small body of Federal cavalry and artillery under General Pleasanton had crossed the Potomac at Shepherdstown, ten miles above Harper's Ferry, the situation of the two large armies on either side of the Potomac remains unchanged. President Lincoln had passed several days in visiting Harper's Ferry and the Antietam battlefield and reviewing the troops. General McClellan officially reports that the total Federal loss in the battles of Antietam creek and South Mountain was 14,700 in killed, wounded, and missing. From the time when the Federals first encountered the enemy in Maryland up to the time when the enemy was driven into Virginia the Federals have captured thirteen guns and thirty-nine colors— they losing neither guns nor colors. The Federals have collected 14,000 small arms on the Antietam battlefield. They have likewise captured 5,000 prisoners, of whom 1,200 were wounded, and have buried 3,000 rebels. General McClellan thinks that these two engagements cost the enemy at least 30,000 of their best troops. *The Richmond Whig* has information that the entire Confederate loss at the battle of Manassas, and in all the engagements in Maryland is about 7,000.

When I reached my customary table at Café Riche this morning and read the latest dispatches from America, memories of this remarkable occasion, now some six years past, returned to me. It marked the beginning of my acquaintance with McClellan, an acquaintance that has endured the most stimulating and dangerous era, one which continues with a full-throated fury even as I write. I refer, of course, to that most dreadful of wars, a civil war, now being fought in McClellan's homeland.

At this distance one finds it difficult to judge the accuracy of press reports of the war. Strict prohibitions against journalists on the American battlefields, when combined with official hostility in France toward the Union and support for the Rebels, prevents one from learning enough of the truth to form any sort of clear understanding. It appears, however, that an important, perhaps even a critical, battle has been fought in the state of Maryland, not too far distant from Washington, along a stream called the Antietam. The number of casualties given in official pronouncements mark this battle as a general engagement of strategic significance. The Rebels seem to be withdrawing to their sanctuaries in Virginia, but the Union forces under McClellan's command do not appear to be pursuing them with any dedication. One can only speculate that both armies were severely damaged and have disengaged to repair themselves.

Neither of us could have foreseen these events that day at Jomini's table. McClellan had not remained long with us. Pleading the press of business, he bade us farewell. He said to Jomini that he regarded this day as the most interesting in his life thus far. I am sure Jomini thought McClellan would never have another to match it. In this, of course, events have proved Jomini quite wrong.

McClellan returned home and spent several months composing the report on the Crimean War the secretary of war had required of him. His duty thus completed, he tendered his resignation from the army and embarked upon a new career in business. With characteristic discipline, charm, and youthful self-confidence, McClellan soon achieved a remarkable success in his new work, becoming a high official in two of the largest railroad companies in America. He had also taken a wife, who was quite his equal in charm and intellect, it was said, and settled in Cincinnati, Ohio, to begin his family.

When the war began last year, McClellan was enjoying the fruits of his talent and labor and could have continued to do so without reproach. But very like most men of his high station and gifts, the great cause of the Union moved him to return to the uniform he had removed in 1857. The first months of the war saw him in command of a small detachment in the westernmost districts of Virginia, beyond the mountains. Chiefly through his own energy and skill, these districts were preserved for the Union, and his success constituted one of the few reverses for the Confederate States in the early months of the war. Because this was such an unhappy time for the Union, any modicum of success brought favorable notice to the commander who had achieved it. In this way, McClellan came to the attention of the superior powers of the Union, and when combined with his excellent soldierly background, marked him as perfectly suited for the responsibilities of a higher commander.

In due course, McClellan was summoned by his president and given command of the body of troops then assembling for the protection of Washington. His appointment gave everyone hope that the war, already so destructive of the fabric of this great republic, could be extinguished promptly by the vast sums then being lavished upon the new army.

When McClellan took his leave of us that day in Paris, I could not have imagined that I would ever see him again. But in October of last year, there appeared in *Moniteur de l'Armée* under the heading *Lettres sur l'Amérique* a series of pieces on the progress of the American war, written by an aide-de-camp to the Prince Napoleon, one Lieutenant Colonel Pisani. The prince had just visited both camps in the first summer of the war. Pisani's letters inspired me to petition my own government for a commission to conduct a tour of observation in America and report on such intelligence as I might manage to acquire.

By the time I formally received my commission from the federal chancellor, McClellan had been appointed commander-in-chief of all the Union forces, as vast a responsibility as any general has ever held in the history of his country. McClellan's elevation as the first military citizen of his land urged me on my way to America, where I arrived a few weeks later. Armed with my commission and letters of introduction, I made my way to Washington, where I was received most courteously by the secretaries of state and war.

After my interviews with leading members of government, I was permitted to join McClellan's headquarters, along with the army proper which was then still in the capital city. Since his arrival, McClellan had been a storm of activity, overseeing the construction of extensive fortifications, attending to a most energetic training program for his troops, seeing to the collection and disbursement of provisions, and formulating plans for a grand offensive against the heart of the rebellion. He was the new darling of society, too, constantly in motion among the gentry of the government by day and in attendance at lavish fêtes by night. Public sentiment had fixed McClellan as the savior of the Union and had awarded him the sobriquet "the Young Napoleon." Everyone seemed to believe he was indeed the very incarnation of his namesake—everyone except the enemy, who stoically held their ground less than fifty miles distant, protecting their new capital at Richmond.

McClellan's army was trembling with anticipation, full of energy for the campaign that lay ahead. Its commander, however, was not, for when I arrived at his headquarters I was startled to learn that he had fallen victim to a severe onset of typhus and was abed in his quarters in the city. Thus it was some time before he was able to resume his duties among his troops, and I delayed requesting an audience with him until I learned he had recovered his health.

McClellan had not changed much, although either the typhus or his constant work had left him in a weakened condition. I thought I discerned in him a nervous frailty that I had not seen in our earlier meeting. For all that, he professed to be pleased to see me again. His manner was all correctness and courtesy, but his conversation flowed along a line that impressed me as much practiced. He inquired after Jomini's health, and when I said the old man was as well as one might hope for one of his age, McClellan quickly turned the conversation to more immediate matters. He did not speak of Jomini again.

He called me to a large table where an array of maps was arranged and explained to me that he meant to move the army very soon and that the object of the coming campaign was nothing more or less than the seizure of Richmond itself, together, secondarily, with the destruction of such enemy forces as might be so foolhardy as to oppose him. He meant to make this movement by sea, embarking his army along the lower Potomac and then sailing to the peninsula that separated the York and James rivers before they joined the sea. It was Richmond, he said, that was the decisive point of the war. Once it was taken, he had every expectation the rebellion would collapse.

He hoped to accomplish this campaign by maneuver so as to reduce the effusion of blood. The wounds suffered by the republic in the war thus far, he said, would be a long while healing. The fewer the better for all, he insisted. The matter was really a very simple one, he said, but he had spent countless hours in contention with the political authorities. The secretary of war was particularly troublesome to him and only seemed happy when opposing him. In an air of confidentiality, McClellan also said President Lincoln was utterly without strategic sense, a crude, untutored soul from the far West who spoke in riddles and was addicted to meaningless stories. He had taken it upon himself to educate the president as far as he was able, but he did not count upon making much progress on this front. All the delays thus far could be laid at the feet of these political gentlemen. The burden of the whole war had fallen upon him. He left me in no doubt that he thought Providence had prudently called him to the task at hand.

Of course I was in no wise inclined to dispute his strategic appreciation, and still less his views of superior authorities, but I wondered at the time what Jomini would have made of it all. Since arriving I had read all the press reports attentively and talked with as many officers as I could. I thought a great deal too much importance had been invested in the respective capitals of the combatants. Richmond was certainly exposed to the seaward approach that McClellan had chosen, but even this presented certain difficulties in my mind, for if it was true that the York and James rivers would protect McClellan's advance, they would also contain it and prevent any important maneuver until the army was very nearly at the gates of the city itself. As for Washington, I had concluded that its importance was only symbolic and that the best place to invest defenses was op-posite a place called Harper's Ferry, some miles up the Potomac from the capital city. Jomini would have said that Washington sat upon an eccentric line, too far removed from what the Confederates would surely see as the most appropriate line of operation, pointing toward Philadelphia and New York.

Even at that, I felt there was no assurance this war would be so easily won as McClellan had predicted. This was no simple war be-tween dynasts. The objectives of the warring parties were in direct counterpoint to one another. Between preservation and destruction of the Union itself, there seemed to me to be no opportunity for the kind of moderation McClellan had hinted at. I thought it was the ar-mies themselves, and certainly not their capital cities, that best em-bodied the causes for which they had taken the field, and that only their physical destruction would bring this vast struggle to a decisive conclusion.

As one who had only recently arrived in this country, however, and bearing no immediate responsibility of my own, I kept my si-lence. McClellan had accepted my commission without reservation and had directed that I be billeted with his headquarters wherever it might be. He promised me an audience whenever I might desire it, but from his manner I concluded this offer was rendered only out of courtesy. As I took my leave of McClellan, I was offered an aide-de-camp to attend to my immediate needs, and this I gratefully ac-cepted in the person of a private soldier named Hans Holder.

Throughout my sojourn, Holder could not have been more atten-tive, nor informative. Indeed, he was my constant tutor, and I have in the days since our first meeting come to think of him as the American of all Americans. One could detect only the slightest sign of Holder's Hessian origins. His family had come to America when he was only a child, after the uproars of 1848. They had helped to colonize a frontier district in Texas after that republic had been ab-sorbed by the United States. His family's fondest dream had come true, and as the great divisions in the land grew to produce the war, they found they were in disagreement with those of their neighbors who advocated secession from the Union in defense of slavery. When the war did break out, Holder was in the port city of Galveston with his father, attending to family business. With his father's blessing, he took passage on a ship bound for New York City and there volunteered for service with the Union army. From the first, it was evident to me that he was not merely a youthful adventurer, and since his enlistment he had made himself into a competent and conscientious soldier, ever ready to lend a hand in any enterprise, sturdy of body and spirit.

The army began its movement to the peninsula while other armies protected approaches to Washington. One, under General McDowell, kept his forces between Richmond and Washington, while another guarded the Shenandoah Valley some distance westward, a valley so formed as to offer a district of operations with but little physical communication with the main theatre of war, save through a few easily observed passes. Harper's Ferry was the northern terminus of the valley, while the village of Staunton was at its opposite end. However, the valley threatened approaches to Washington rather more directly than Richmond; traveling southwestward along the valley, one moved steadily away from the Confederate capital.

Against a Federal host whose numbers could not have been less than 200,000, the Confederates enjoyed by all estimates a similar strength and a superior strategic position. Jomini himself could not have asked for more. While the Federal army was required to dissipate its strength guarding a vast arc from the valley to the sea, the Confederates benefited by the situation: their strategic position was interior to that of the Federals, so that they might move from one point to another, concentrating their forces more rapidly. The Confederates appear to have understood, through a superior appreciation of Jomini's principles, the benefits conferred upon them by this strategic situation. Events were to prove they were equal to their opportunities.

Yet, McClellan had advantages of his own: a new army made to his own design, full of hearty and loyal troops, perfectly equipped and endlessly supplied. In a republic like this one, where the people are the true sovereign, McClellan was favored by a public adoration strong enough to withstand the inevitable reverses of war, at least for a time. All that was wanted from him was an occasional contribution to public enthusiasm. Indeed, the way to victory lay open to him. The Confederates seemed content to wait, but McClellan could not wait. The offensive was his to take, the line of operations his to choose. By the time I saw him, he had already chosen, though I suspect he kept his counsel as long as he could, whether for fear of revealing his plans to the enemy or else running the danger of having his plans interfered with by political authorities.

The grand movement began in the middle of March when McClellan landed troops at the very tip of the peninsula, establishing his base at Fortress Monroe. The arrangements were completed with great celerity and expertness. Within two weeks, upwards of 100,000 troops were thus transported. McClellan himself came forward in early April.

Naturally a movement of this magnitude could not fail to excite the enemy, who for some time had been quiescent. As subsequent events made evident, the leaders of the Confederacy, taking advantage of their interior position, began disposing themselves so as to oppose McClellan's threat. Gradually, their troops were brought from other districts, which nevertheless still demanded guards of their own. Their movements were not conducted instantly, however, so that McClellan had the momentary advantage of a concentration, if he would only seize it.

This, McClellan seemed ill-disposed to do: the great power that had been placed in his hands did not seem enough to him. He framed his immediate plans and disposed his troops in such a manner as to suggest that he believed the enemy's strength equal to his own. Then, word arrived at headquarters on McClellan's very heels that Washington had ordered the cessation of all recruiting in the several states. Having learned that he would have 50,000 fewer troops than he had planned upon, this latest news meant that his government had no way to replace those he might lose in operations that were about to commence. One might therefore forgive McClellan for wondering aloud, as his staff officers said he often did, whose side his superiors favored?

Such were the distractions besetting McClellan from afar, but he had more immediate concerns too. The navy had concluded that the Confederate shore batteries protected the York River so well that no vessel could be risked against them. Thus McClellan would enjoy naval assistance only in the measure to which he could silence these batteries by landward advances.

To all this was added an impediment with which I was directly familiar. No sooner had I debarked at Old Point Comfort than heavy rains began. I have difficulty recalling a single day during my time on the peninsula when rain did not darken our days. When added to the abundant damp already naturally present here, one was required to spend an inordinate time contending with natural conditions which, to my way of thinking, could only benefit those who opposed McClellan.

Faced with so many reasons not to move, McClellan chose the one military course that ensured he would not have to: a siege. His immediate object was Yorktown, which served to anchor a defensive line of earthen fortifications that when connected with the Warwick River spanned the entire width of the peninsula, some fourteen miles in all. Ten miles behind this line another was under way near Williamsburg, and forty miles still further on, merely ten miles from Richmond itself, a third line of defenses had been laid in place.

Fortunately for McClellan's view of the campaign, nature added a powerful argument in the form of more rains. The whole of McClellan's army seemed on the verge of entombment in the mire of the peninsula. My aide, Private Holder, told me, in the most serious voice, of a mule he had seen sink in the mud up to his ears. When I exclaimed, he added that, however, the mule had not been very tall. Holder was always welcome at the headquarters mess, for his mood was in perfect consonance with that of the staff. "How can a man fight when he is sinking?" he asked. "We want to go west, not down!"

Thus, McClellan occupied himself and his army with mighty works. One could see that this mode of war was deeply satisfying to McClellan. Anyone on the peninsula in those days might have thought this great mass of men had been taken over by a frenzy to disturb as much earth as could be done. Roads were laid parallel to the Confederate lines. From these, posts were extended toward the enemy to facilitate the building of the counterworks, gabions joined to zigzags, and fascines by the hundred were assembled by tens of thousands of soldierly hands. Artillery collected everywhere in perfect mechanical grandeur. To add to these, McClellan called for the establishment of fifteen batteries, each composed of ten 13-inch siege mortars. He meant to hold these monsters in check until all were perfectly sited, then discharge them *en masse* to support his assaulting infantry.

Throughout the month, the enemy was little seen or heard from. One would have thought them perfectly entertained by the spectacle but for the prospect looming over them once McClellan decided to act. But beyond our own scene, no discernible movement toward the enemy had actually been taken. All remained, effectively, as it was before: we were still at the very tip of the peninsula, and the enemy attended to their own affairs unmolested by McClellan. Staff officers warned of the most serious danger to McClellan coming from the rear, by which they meant the political authorities in Washington, who, ignorant of the military art, were growing impatient for action.

With these complaints I found myself in some degree of sympathy. McClellan had spoken quite publicly of his government's indifferent support for his campaign; privately, he was even more critical of Mssrs. Lincoln and Stanton. Neither their knowledge nor their constancy was sufficient to win McClellan's approbation: they lived entirely from moment to moment, he was reported as saying, blown this way and that by the multitude of public voices, each one of which offered a view of the way to ultimate victory. However tiresome these might have been, McClellan could only complain if he had himself first accomplished all in his power to effect a decision. If the works at Yorktown were aimed at trapping the enemy, these self-same works trapped him also. They were all trapped alike.

During his sojourn in Paris with us, McClellan had rather coolly savaged the conduct of the generals in the Crimea. Since arriving in America, I had been fortunate to obtain a copy of the report of observation he had submitted to the War Department. His criticisms, now enshrined in print, seem harsher yet: the Russians had failed "to avail themselves of the opportunities offered." As for the Allies, McClellan wrote, "Their measures were halfway measures, slow and blundering; they failed to keep constantly in view the object of their expedition, and to press rapidly toward it." I should think McClellan would not now wish to be reminded of his uncompromising views.

Richmond was still twenty leagues distant from us. My remaining time in America was brief. McClellan had been so long stationary I despaired of ever seeing his army advance. Perhaps he never would have done but for the Confederates. On May the 5th, the very eve of McClellan's grand bombardment, the Confederates evacuated their works, withdrawing slowly and in good order up the peninsula. McClellan's army, likewise in good order, advanced into the enemy's old positions. But they did not then halt their advance. The army pushed on, their forward troops skirmishing with the enemy's rear guard. The campaign assumed a more hopeful character, as indeed did the army itself.

Among the several foreign officers who attached themselves to the headquarters of the Army of the Potomac, one in particular was most engaging and friendly, ever ready to share his own knowledge of the military art. The Prince de Joinville had accompanied two celebrated nephews, the Comte de Paris and the Duc de Chartres, to the seat of war, and hoped to remain as long as permitted. Joinville proposed to write a narrative of the present campaign and perhaps an even more extensive account of the war once it was over. He assiduously sought out everyone who in his estimation might illuminate his own understanding of these great events, together with copies of such written records as he might obtain. To all this, he added a certain talent in conversation that possessed the magical effect of drawing from anyone their most reserved opinions. He was a man easily taken into one's confidence, sympathetic and lighthearted. I was myself impressed by his manner of dealing with the Americans. He did not stand upon his considerable prestige or his familial connections with the House of Orleans; instead, he succeeded in transforming himself into the appearance of the most accommodating and republican of personalities.

Joinville is such an amiable gentleman one does not fear he will be offended by disagreement. Indeed, he always conducts his part of a conversation as if he would be happy to disagree with himself. He had already formed certain views of the campaign that were in direct opposition to my own. For example, he laid the blame for the lack of progress at the feet of the president and his "assistant dilettantes," as he called them, while I believed the success or failure of the enterprise was McClellan's to bear. But for the meddling of Mr. Lincoln and other high officials, McClellan would have had Richmond already, he thought; once the enemy was properly dispersed and its capital taken, the Confederates would sue for peace.

To my way of thinking, the mere taking of Richmond—or Washington either, for that matter—would not decide this war. I said frankly that the decision in this war could not be found in a mere place. I thought no place in America was sufficiently important to the war that its capture would achieve the result Joinville expected.

Joinville asked where the true engine of the war might be found and, so found, be attacked? I replied that it was to be found among the people themselves, and their manifestation in arms, the armies themselves. For that reason, the mere dispersal of the armies, as he maintained, would not in my opinion achieve the aims of the Union. I invited him to look at the soldiers who were all about us. Who were they? I asked. They were citizens of a republic, doing a citizen's work.

Joinville laughed heartily and did admit that understanding the composition of their army had perplexed him. He wondered how a war could be fought with volunteers alone. Save for a small portion of the officers, there were no professional soldiers to be found. Joinville thought the war might be concluded far more quickly, and less expensively, had a professional army even a third of the present size been available. "But of course," he observed, "this solution may be perfectly logical from a military point of view alone, and if one excluded the Americans' peculiar creed. In their way of thinking," Joinville believed, "they are much like the ancient Athenians: Let them once wish for a thing and they behave as though they have it already. Let the Americans wish to be soldiers, and as if by magic it is done. Only a uniform and a weapon need be found, and perhaps not even those: the trick completes itself," he said. "They would rather do war badly than renounce this creed."

"We might not be so quick to denounce them as military primitives," I said. When one considered how these armies looked and conducted themselves only a year ago compared to the vast machines of war that were now entangled with one another from the ocean to the far West, one should be astonished at what they had learned in such a brief time. The generals were learning, too, although I did admit progress was considerably less discernible in this case.

I was preparing to take my leave of this army and this country. My aide-de-camp, Private Holder, expected an order to rejoin his regiment for the general advance on Richmond. When I expressed my fervent wish for his good fortune, he said he did not expect God would favor him much longer. He thought much hard fighting lay ahead. "We have not seen the worst of this war," he predicted. I did not say that I feared he was right. "But we are on the side with the best cause," he added. "Justice must win in the end, even if I am not here to see it."

Holder's grandfather had been severely wounded fighting with the Prussians at the great battle of Auerstadt and afterward had become a schoolmaster, bringing up a family surrounded by books and genteel learning. Hans had inherited his grandfather's taste for reading, and when duties permitted could always be seen with a book or a newspaper that he had foraged. In this he was not unlike a great number of his comrades, who exhibited a lively interest in affairs beyond their immediate camp and carried knapsacks full of reading and writing materials. When not reading, Hans found time to write letters to his family, hoping that somehow they might find their way home through the naval blockades.

When Hans offered his dire prediction, I understood instantly that he was not giving way to needless apprehensions. He had turned his excellent mind toward the most immediate part of his war, that of its fighting methods and weapons. "These guns are too good for our tactics," he said to me with an air of finality. "The guns aim and fire just as you want, and the boys just stand there, all together, waiting for them to do their worst. The officers do their best to find good ground, but they can only do so much. The generals haven't put on their thinking caps, so the old boys find what cover they can. I don't think I would have lived for a minute if I hadn't. The new boys always start by crowing at us when we get behind a tree to shoot, but after the first exchange of fire, they know better, those that are still alive," he said calmly. Hans said he hadn't minded the siege at all.

One could arrange a few comforts, trade for tobacco or sweets, attend to one's kit and weapon. "All that is about to change," he said.

Knowing that I must pay my respects to the general-in-chief before departing, I offered to ask if Hans could be found duty in headquarters, but he would have none of it. "I came here to fight," he said simply, "not lark around the tents with the grandees, excepting yourself, of course, Major Lecomte," he added quickly. So I left Holder to his duty after pressing into his hands such money as I could spare. He protested, but I would not be denied. Without his knowledge, I asked Joinville to watch over Holder as well as he could.

My call upon General McClellan was all formality and courtesy. He had surrounded himself with staff officers of every description who were copies of himself—young, avid, confident, and proud, convinced they knew the truth of any matter before them. I counted myself fortunate to have been permitted to see him at all: only a few days before, President Lincoln himself had visited, and McClellan had sent word that he was too busy at the front to attend to his commander-in-chief. I gathered it was not the first time McClellan had behaved this way toward his president. This was a McClellan I did not know, nor wish to know.

My interview with him confirmed that the McClellan I had met in Paris had all but disappeared under the weight of enormous responsibility. Not having recovered completely from his earlier illness, now he was showing early signs of recurring malaria. a disease he had contracted as a young man during the war with Mexico.

"I promised to show you Richmond, Lecomte," he said, "and if you were to remain with us a while longer, so I should."

I replied I had no doubt Richmond would eventually be in Union hands.

"I should have had it already," he said, "but for the gorilla in Washington." I took him to mean Lincoln, toward whom he had conceived a most considerable and public dislike. "He and that fool

Stanton have thwarted me at every turn, promising all with one breath and denying it with another. No general ever suffered such impediments."

But, he said, now that the Confederates had broken, he would pursue and defeat them. He had hopes of reinforcements that had been withheld. Having said this, he stared distractedly at the maps laid out on his camp table. "It all seems so straightforward, Lecomte. But it is difficult in the doing."

I spent only a quarter of an hour with McClellan, fearing to ask for more. I had many questions to pose for him, but this was not the time. The war had a complete hold on him; he was in a contest with the war itself, and it seemed to me that it was slipping beyond his control. I left him to his struggles.

Once leaving the peninsula, I quickly made my way to New York City to spend a few days at ease before taking ship. I had no wish to idle in Washington, which now struck me at once as an official village and a tropical desert. But while I hoped never to see Washington again, I found New York entertaining, so full of life one would scarcely know that a war was in progress.

The weather on my return passage was most agreeable, permitting me to take the air on deck whenever I pleased or to remain in my cabin arranging notes for my report to the federal chancellor. Because my commission was in no way confidential, my arrival in Lausanne brought forth a number of invitations to dine with various officials, all of whom wished to hear my observations on the war. My obligations were satisfied by the end of August, and not soon after I traveled to Paris.

All these activities served as useful preliminaries for the book I intend to write. I have determined to spend the remainder of the year here, conducting such research as proves necessary and remaining abreast of the most recent developments in America. Of course, I could not fail to call upon Jomini, for I could hardly have avoided him and in any wise did not wish to do so.

Very soon, my old habits of living resumed, and if my work prevented me from making a daily visit to Passy to sit with him, I found time to see him at least once a week to converse on military affairs near and far. He had likewise kept to his routines. Most mornings found him in his study as usual, attending to his correspondence, and abed in the afternoons.

During my visits I attempted to encourage in Jomini a true appreciation for the unique features of the American war. Often I would bring such news as had reached the continent; and with the aid of maps I had obtained in Washington, we would trace the grand movements of the armies as they became known. On these occasions, Jomini showed the most intense and intelligent attention to detail and posed questions that I often did not have sufficient information upon which to form an answer. Most of Jomini's questions pertained to the details of this or that operation. He evinced no interest whatever in the political aspects of strategy, regarding the Americans' supreme political authorities as mere rustics, nor was he very curious about what he called minor tactics, or the actual clash of soldiers in battle. To him, such affairs were no more significant than railroads.

When I called upon Jomini today he was still at table, ignoring his breakfast under the gaze of a disapproving servant, as usual. As I took my place, Jomini looked at me and without a word passed a London newspaper to me that I had not yet seen. A dispatch, dated from the 8th instant, announced the relief from command of General McClellan.

Jomini watched patiently as I read. They had finally done it. McClellan had been given every opportunity to learn, and he had not learned. The campaign that showed promise after Yorktown had gone to ground again only a few miles from Richmond, and then the Confederates had harried him from their peninsula during a fighting retreat in which he had shown no little defensive skill. The political authorities had ordered him to withdraw altogether, and I had thought then McClellan's days as a field commander were over. But when the secessionist army, under General Lee now, had taken the offensive across the Potomac into the state of Maryland, Mr. Lincoln had called McClellan back to command. McClellan, I had no doubt, would have taken his reappointment as a vindication, not as the act of near desperation that it was. The casualties at Antietam exceeded even those at Malvern Hill, the costliest of all McClellan's peninsula battles. And now this. Although General Lee had taken his army back to Virginia, McClellan had not pursued him. McClellan's promises of action apparently no longer impressed Mr. Lincoln, and so the general had been set aside, once and for all. No successor was named in the dispatches.

Jomini wanted to know by what right Mr. Lincoln presumed to interfere so in this war. He said it was inexcusable. Once declared, war ought to be left to the soldiers. The Aulic Council of Austria had never done so much to wreck a strategy, he thought. I replied that Mr. Lincoln acted by the right of his Constitution, but Jomini would not be satisfied with this answer. A Constitution could not make a strategist, he said. No more than a book can make a strategist, I thought to myself. I said to Jomini that to my way of thinking Mr. Lincoln had shown himself far better suited to the demands of the war than his generals, and that many people had been misled by his rusticity to think him simple. I said Mr. Lincoln was far from simple.

McClellan should be president himself, Jomini said; he should take steps to secure the office. I said that no small number of people felt the same, but that they were of a party too closely associated with the secessionists. The northern people would never surrender their ideals to the secessionist creed. Jomini dismissed my observations as mere romanticism. The time had come, he said, to place the war upon a truly scientific basis. One need only observe a few simple principles, by which he meant his own principles, and the war would be quickly concluded. Politics need not be involved at all. Once the war was won, politics could resume their normal operation. In such a temper, Jomini was not to be persuaded of a different view, and I did not wish to be unkind. Our conversation turned toward less contentious themes, and I soon left him to the care of his servant.

This latest war news has left me strangely unsettled. The war in America seems to have escaped those who would direct it. What was that wonderful phrase von Clausewitz had written? "As if chained to a stag in the forest." America is now so chained. No war was ever so simple as Jomini imagined. He has seen the worst that war can do, yet he has closed his mind to what war had to tell him. He made war into an elaborate game with edges as clear and hard as a chessboard, a game of the purest kind, unencumbered by reference to life beyond the board, war and strategy as one and the same. The war in America is not Jomini's kind of war. McClellan thought strategy was the war, and the war engulfed him, sickened him. The war is von Clausewitz's kind of war, one whose shapes and purposes lie far beyond the chessboard. Jomini and McClellan do not understand this war. Nor do I. The difference between us is that I do not pretend that I do.

I think Mr. Lincoln cares not at all for strategy except as it permits him to preserve the Union. He will use strategy or not, as circumstances dictate. No, he is not the strategist Jomini and McClellan would have him be, but the antistrategist. Perhaps the day will come when he finds others who understand the war as he does, but I do not think it will be soon. In the meantime, we are all in winter quarters, living day by day until the spring.

8

THE VERY LAST
CIVIL WAR HISTORIAN

Death stalks one victim among thousands in the hospital tents at Gettysburg, as modern industrial warfare makes its grisly debut.

JULY 5, 1863, 8:30 A.M.
Hdqs., Army of the Potomac

Maj. General H. W. Halleck:

The enemy retired, under cover of night and heavy rain, in the direction of Fairfield and Cashtown. All my available cavalry are in pursuit, on the enemy's left and rear. My movement will be made at once upon his flank, via Middletown and South Mountain pass. I cannot delay to pick up the debris of the battlefield, and request that all those arrangements may be made by the departments. My wounded, with those of the enemy in our hands, will be left at Gettysburg. After burying our own, I am compelled to employ citizens to bury the enemy dead. Every available reinforcement is required, and should be sent to Frederick without delay.

Geo. G. Meade, Maj. General

July 7, 1863
Nr. Gettysburg, Penn.

My dear Wife,

I shall remain at this place a while. Gen. Meade and the army
have moved south after Lee—not with so much avidity as to over-
take him, mind you, for no one could wish to bring on another general engagement just yet. This affair has been so disastrous, I wonder if we might have finally spent our enthusiasm for fighting. The
lustre of martial glory must be dimming considerably these days,
tho' what I know of history gives me little hope.

I am prevented from moving about very much on account of my
wound, but I hasten to say that it is more inconvenient than serious,
so you must not seize upon this news as an opportunity to worry on
my account. Something—one knows not what—struck my right leg
just above the ankle. I count myself rather fortunate, too. The blow
knocked me senseless, and when I awoke I was well to the rear of
the fighting. A very great many of our wounded have not been so
promptly collected owing to their great numbers and a deficit of ambulances, and so the past several days have been hard on them as it
rained prodigiously after the battle and is only now giving way to a
clear and hot day. If the damp did not take these unfortunates, the
heat that now falls upon us surely will. At least I am away from the
damp and the sun besides.

One hears all manner of stories after a fight, and this must be especially so in a hospital such as the one I am in at present. A Ver-
monter told me of several of his wounded comrades being swept
away by a sudden freshet. They had been deposited along a little
creek that looked inconsiderable until the rains came. He said he
only escaped by dragging himself to higher ground. Someone else
said there were more than 20,000 of us left here, and this would be
scarcely creditable were it not for what I had seen with my own
eyes.

Whoever brought me here took care to see that my kit came with me. My old journal and all my writing implements are unspoiled, and so the happiest part of my predicament is that I am allowed to make use of them. The kindest of young ladies, a Miss Hancock of Philadelphia, has been quite attentive to my comforts by arranging my blankets and finding a small board so that I may prop myself up and write, which I do happily in spite of frowns from the stewards.

A wound is not the worst part of being in a hospital and if it were within my power I would quit this place. The surgeons are badly outnumbered and have labored without pause since the fighting began. The boys complain of the doctors being too quick with their knives to take off injured limbs that might be saved with a little care, but I suspect their misery causes them to be too sharp with their opinions. My own wound has been deemed of insufficient severity to warrant a visit to the surgeon, and so I am making do with most impressive bandages. It all looks a good deal worse than it is, and the stewards see that I am supplied with opium. After all our hard marching I am happy to light upon this place and really feel like a daisy, so you should have no fear for me.

I shall write again soon, dearest. Kiss the little ones for me.

> Your husband,
> John

> July 7, 1863
> Nr. Gettysburg, Penn.

Dear Father,

I have only just written to Sarah, telling her of my present situation, or so much of it as can be told without disturbing her overmuch. I expect she has told you what she knows now. I do not want to add to her worries, nor those of the children.

I have landed in the field hospital of our corps, which is a sight better than roasting in the sun. At this juncture I cannot foresee when I might be invalided home, but I am fairly certain I shall not be returned to my regiment. My leg is utterly wrecked just above the ankle, but I still have it, wrecked or not, and only today have I had much pain, which the opium holds mostly at bay. I take these as good signs, but as a physician you know the signs better than I do. The wound is very tightly bound and from time to time an attendant will come by to drip water on it and sniff at it. He says the water will keep the wound *sweet,* by which he means that so long as his nose is not insulted, I am free and clear of infections. Is your nose trained so well too, father?

One cannot imagine what our generals must have been thinking to take away with them all our ambulances when they decamped. But as I wrote to Sarah, I am one of the fortunates. Here we are four days after the fight, and some of the boys still lie where they fell. They will lie there for eternity if someone does not fetch them soon. The heat is downright infernal.

The boys who are brought in are not so well off either. We have so few surgeons we are using the ones the Rebels left behind. For all the hospitals, I am told, there could not be more than thirty. Even three times that many would not be sufficient. So the boys most in need await their turn wherever they are put, and they are put everywhere. The whole district must be covered with them.

The surgeons have had much practice at separating those who have a hope of living from those who do not, a division which is not always apparent to my eye but which I am sure would be no mystery to you. I do not mean to paint a false picture of good order, however. This place is a perfect bedlam, and its inmates have been forced to rely upon the good will of the local citizenry, which one must admit is well intentioned if not expert. From what I have observed anyway, the distance between those who may be deemed expert in this particular business and those who may not is far from great. Judging from the numbers who have passed on since arriving here, one cannot be too favorably impressed. Perhaps I am being unfair, as I am only seeing the business from an invalid's cot.

I would tell you all of what happened if I could, but a soldier is the last one to tell anything about a battle. The newspapers will have revealed much that I never would have known, and even if I was in the middle of it all, the mind saves its power of remembering anyway for more immediate uses. For the larger part of the fighting we were little worried, having been placed by Gen. Hancock in the very strongest part of our lines along a little rise people hereabouts call Cemetery Ridge. Out in front of us was a sloping field more than a mile across to the enemy's lines. We could not have wanted a more nearly ideal place, and all the boys were saying the Rebels were not so mad as to have a go at us here, and at first they seemed right. Well off to both flanks, some distance away, hard fighting could be heard but little seen on account of the clouds of smoke. Behind us, mostly away from the reach of the enemy's guns, all manner of activity around the various headquarters caused a hubbub. But all this was merely annoying. We were snug as bugs.

We were about to think we could have our battle without fighting, which notion seemed mighty appealing to the few veterans among us. They were not at all anxious to start anything with the Rebels and were not as skittish as the green boys. That was why I often used them as skirmishers. One of these cool heads wandered in Friday morning with news that the Rebels were moving as if to assemble in the woods across the way. Several of the strategists among the boys thought all the commotion meant the Rebs had seen how unassailable we were and were making ready to leave. But one of the other boys was so outspoken and firm in his disagreement that Major Holder began calling him Private Jomini, and although the rest of us did not know who this Jomini was, after Holder explained we all took up the sobriquet. Private Jomini was in no wise dissuaded from making his pronouncements, and Holder said this was in the way of Private Jomini's namesake as well. Private Jomini insisted Lee no longer enjoyed the interior lines he had used against us so famously in Virginia, lines he must now retrieve if he was not to be cut off from his bases back home. Disaster loomed if he did not, Jomini declared loudly. One of the boys asked him if interior lines were how come our sinks were always laid within our camps! Though sometimes offending the politer delicacies, our boys' humor is always good natured before one takes himself too seriously, as Private Jomini certainly does. The boys may complain about him, but no one will say he is not a pistol when it comes to fighting. So when he continued to declaim his strategical estimations, someone called him an old windbag and soon fisticuffs were being threatened. As I was nearby, the prospective combatants looked to my direction to see if I would permit a go-round, but I shook my head no, and that concluded the matter.

Just then one of the other skirmishers came back in to say he thought he heard caissons moving just to our front, and I passed his report to the rear. Down the line someone shouted, "What do you think of that, Jomini? The damned Rebs heard your advice, and ain't you happy now?" But we were all pretty sure that Gen. Lee meant to stay put. And if Gen. Lee had decided not to go, we could not let him stay. So that was that.

About noon the Rebels opened the most furious cannonade, but as they were aiming at our artillery we were mostly untouched by the fracas. We bade the boys lie down, where they were protected by a low stone wall. I myself sat down against the wall, facing the rear so as to watch the thunderous spectacle. Though there was the most infernal banging, still I do not think our batteries much suffered.

All the same, it was a fine demonstration but for the certainty that the Rebels would not spend so much artillery on us if they did not mean to follow with their infantry in the usual way. As the boys always did when vexed by imagining what was to come, they began to fuss with their caps and belts and cartridge boxes, even though all were well and correct. Those who had not affixed their bayonets now did so, without anyone's command. I don't suppose any of them meant to stab Rebels, for never in any fight did I see anyone use these things. The boys acted like they felt better for it when they had these articles on the end of their rifles, however. One of the boys, having just fitted his bayonet on the rifle for the second or third time, seemed well satisfied with the result. He looked directly at me and smiled and shook his weapon. He struck me then as quite the perfect savage, one who could have found company among pagan warriors of old. What a state our race has come to after such a long history! I might rather wish history itself had come to an end than continue in this way.

Off to the left our guns opened a cannonade of their own and I took this signal to stand up. The enemy's colors, perhaps a division's worth, were advancing toward us. From such a distance their lines appeared solid but pliable as a set of reins; every now and then the Rebels would fetch a swale and disappear momentarily, only to reappear closer yet. The whole mass advanced steadily and with determination. I thought them a dignified picture, painted with dangerous hues. Holder was close by me, as usual. I heard him say, in a low voice as if for me alone, "There'll be no running today."

All time and sound and movement went strangely dull and dreamlike. I thought the whole scene must be populated with apparitions. As I looked down the line, I realized all the boys were looking to me for a sign that they might open fire, but I motioned for them to stand fast, judging the enemy to be yet too far away to do much good. Our batteries continued their murderous work with an almost languid heartlessness. Whole men or pieces of them exploded into the air. The boys shifted themselves. Every now and then one of them would stand up and wave his cap as if transported with mad delight.

How I do wish, father, that my powers were adequate to convey a soldier's feelings in the moment when he sees he will and must fight for his life. In that instant a most perfect electrification takes over his mind and body. All the senses are excited to a wholly unaccustomed degree of clarity. Did not events require one to act, the experience could be likened to a trance. To an outsider we might have been like so many pointers, poised so sharply that we were fairly shivering, anxious for the game. And then the cry, "Here they come!" though everyone could see so perfectly well. I think soldiers in battle for all time must have heard such a cry.

Thus ended my dream, and the speed of emergency overtook me. I sent the drummer boy to the rear and nodded toward the color-bearer to take his place beside me.

Our cannon fire was wrecking the Rebel formations most terribly, but what remained of them came on even faster than before. When I judged the distance between us to be correct, I ordered firing to commence. It was like the opening of a floodgate. All the boys' impatience and fear now fairly poured from the end of their weapons. On either side of us, I saw other regiments advance beyond our line and wheel to stand in perpendicular to the enemy's flanks, so that now they suffered from shot and shell on three sides. Far from abating, our fire increased as the Rebs drew closer, so that with every step they were made to redouble their exertions. The peculiar slap of bullets could be heard, but the noise seemed not at all threatening to me. Several of our boys fell immediately after the Rebels returned our fire, but fell so matter-of-factly and with so little drama they could have as well been swooning.

I may wonder for the rest of my life how I spent the next minutes, for I cannot begin to recall them to my mind in an orderly way. When the Rebels closed with us, it was as if a thunderstorm had burst over us, so drenched were we with the violence of it all. I do hope and pray never again to see my fellow man reduced to such a state. We had all descended to an animal ferocity. It makes me fear for the future of our kind.

The heaviest part of what remained of the Rebels fell over a little battery to my right, and for some reason I know not I began to make my way in that direction. I had not gone far when I was hit. I only remember being surprised and thinking I had only stumbled, but when I tried to regain my footing I fell again. After this, my memory fails me altogether.

From what I have learned since, the Rebels had spent too much of themselves crossing the field, so that when they came to us they had not sufficient strength to contend for long. I am in wonder that they made such headway against the fire we brought upon them. I reckon the Rebels must have been under our fire for half an hour before reaching us. They must have lived several eternities in that time.

Their reckless bravery was not without cost to us. I should guess that more of our regiment is dead than alive, or will be before too long on account of the wounds suffered. I saw the redoubtable Private Jomini leap beyond the protection of the wall, disappearing headlong into a mass of Rebels. After our firing commenced, I lost sight of Major Holder. I imagine they, and many others, are on the field to this day. I am thankful for the opium, which helps keep my dreams of these sights from my mind.

I know, father, that my lack of religion has ever been to your regret and disappointment. I can imagine you now, hoping I will allow your God into my heart in the extremity of my present situation. But I have seen no God on this field of battle. Such a congregation he could have won here on that day, and the days since, when so many pitiful voices have cried out his name. I think this suffering must have dissolved all religion for me. And should the steadfast claim we are paying for our sins, I should reply our debt had been paid most completely, so that we are as innocent now as any babe.

I am bidden to give myself a rest for the present, father. I hope to write again very soon. I know you will look to Sarah and the little ones as you have ever done.

    Yr. son,

    John

July 10, 1863
Nr. Gettysburg

My dear Wife,

I am in high spirits today. Our situation here is much improved. Where before there was only chaos, now some purpose can be detected. The army has rediscovered us at last and so also have any number of citizens who have come from well beyond the immediate district. Depots are taking shape in the vicinity, and we are fairly cosseted. I am given brandy whenever I may ask for it, and my bandages are seen to with efficient regularity.

Miss Hancock, the young Quaker miss I told of in my last, is still with us. These past days I have been struck with admiration at how she passes among the boys—some of whom do present the most alarming aspect—with perfect calm, pausing here to fix a bandage, there to offer a drink, yet elsewhere to assist another to eat, or to write a letter for those who have not the wherewithal to do for themselves. How one so innocent could have persisted so helpfully in such a place is beyond knowing. Perhaps she would say her faith has been her mainstay, which answer no doubt would please you and father, but in truth she says little of it. Leaving aside whatever sentiment moves her, she does move, to everyone's benefit and to her credit. If she were a man, I would say she is quite the little soldier and would ask for a regiment's worth of her.

Of course it is in the usual nature of things that along with the good one finds the bad. Our provost has been beset by scofflaws of every description, who detect advantage in the suffering of others. One such was a man who was said to have gone about the field on the day after the battle asking the wounded for one hundred dollars to carry them to safety. And there is plenty of scavenging as well, from those who merely wish a relic of the great fight to possess, to several men who were arrested while trying to carry off a cannon. Our troops have even chased away children from rummaging about the wreckage. By fair means or foul before long, nothing will be left but bones, and even these could be made into a monument to this history. I pray no such will ever be erected. It is to our shame that events here suggest it, and the sooner we purge them from our minds the better.

For all that, I am most heartened by the reappearance of Major Holder, whose loss I had most sincerely dreaded. I should have had more confidence, for I have never known a man more quietly possessed of talent for survival, not in an arrogant way, surely, but in a manner that gives all about him hope in whatever may come. He has certainly made a friend of good fortune. I had completely lost sight of him during the fighting and did not lay eyes upon him until this day. He did not go entirely untouched, however, being wounded in the head, and he now goes about his business topped off with an impressive turban that gives him the appearance of an Araby sheik. As soon as his wound satisfied the surgeons in the field hospital where he landed, he was permitted to set off in search of me.

He had made a tour of the entire district in his quest and has just spent the entire morning relating the sights along his journey. Up along the Chambersburg Pike west of town there stands a seminary where not only the boys from I Corps were collected but large numbers of enemy wounded too. Here, Holder chanced upon a Rebel officer, one Colonel Powell, with whom he had been acquainted in Texas before the war. The colonel had been hit during the earlier fighting for a small hill that guarded the southern part of the battlefield, and the seriousness of his condition prevented him from joining Lee's retreat. Despite his painful wound, he had greeted Holder as a fond old friend and did not seem at all insulted by the color of his fellow Texan's uniform. Once his captors learned that the colonel had commanded the Texas Infantry, he told Holder, they seemed to be ever watchful of him, as if he were on the verge of doing something Texan-like, such as killing a man before breakfast. In truth, Holder says, he is not quite the bloodthirsty savage his captors imagine, and is quite a civilized man.

The two of them were allowed nearly an hour together before the colonel was ordered to rejoin his compatriots, Rebels of the higher ranks who also had been made prisoner by their wounds. One of these was the infamous Baltimore incendiary Trimble, who had been unhorsed by a shot during the assault on our positions and had since had his leg removed. Holder thought him a strong old man to have gone through so much, but he wished Trimble had been dismasted, to use his word, rather than only shot in the leg. I hastened to agree, for this Trimble is the very worst example of a traitor, heartless in every season, beyond any means of persuasion other than brute force. Men like him are the true engines of this despicable rebellion. Trimble's gaolers let on that the old man was a constant trouble, letting no opportunity for protest get by him. I think no one will allow him a parole and should expect he will end up in the Dry Tortugas, where there is nothing to fire and too much water anyway.

We hear talk of a more permanent hospital in the making hereabouts so that the medical department may be able to combine their efforts and strike down all the temporary miniatures thrown up during the emergency. This may suit the doctors, but as for myself I am persuaded that any kind of hospital is genuinely unhealthy and dread going together into any such collection. If I must continue in this way, I had rather continue here.

I cannot say that I am quite ready to dance, nor even move about, but I am encouraged by each day that passes, being determined to outrun my discomforts in the end. When we are moved I shall write to you again, dearest. Hug and kiss the little ones for their loving father.

     Yr. loving husband,
     John

July 11
Nr. Gettysburg

Dear Father,

Either I am on the mend or I have grown strangely accustomed to my present state. I have had several days of turpentine application on my wound, which continues its aggravations, quite swollen round the edges and very red and draining prodigiously. My attendants insist the debut of this noxious material, which they call by the rather infelicitous name of laudable pus, bodes well for my recovery. No one is venturing to predict how I might actually walk on what remains. They will say only they look forward to when the wound begins to slough away its scabrous excesses. Should my corpuscles not meet expectations, the doctors mean to draw larger calibers from their armory and apply some form of acid so as to expunge the evil humors once and for all. This has already been done to some of my fellow inmates, who allow that the unpleasantries are softened by a mask of chloroform. I hope one day you explain to me how one steels himself to a life regulated by the laudability of pus or the value of slough. Once, I suppose, such events would have struck me as grotesque, but I confess to taking a rather greater interest in them these days.

It has been over a week now since, like Gulliver, I awoke at this place. About half of the wounded have gone elsewhere. Our keepers reckon we number 10,000 or so at present. We have established our own town, a most singular metropolis composed chiefly of recumbent citizens. It is in no wise a republic. We are governed by a standing elite. We vote with our wounds. Let sufficient improvement be seen, and we may be allowed to stand also. Any detection of poor performance, and we forfeit any hope of independence. Indeed, we lose our voices entirely. Our attendants speak of us in our presence as if we are not here, or rather as if our wound is a thing apart from the rest of our body. It is the wound that has all their attention, and the rest of us is expected to follow along obediently. Suggestions of any kind are not wanted from the body connected to the damage.

Our town has its own clock. It is the pain that provides the springs and counterweights. The hours strike with each attendant's visit to perform, often in silence, this or that piece of work demanded by the gods of our time, the doctors. Our emergencies prefer the deepest night for their time to call. Perhaps the hubbub of day keeps them away, or at least less worthy of attention, but in darkness one is awakened by the shuffling of feet or tiny sounds—a tin cup against a basin, a low breathless moan. More feet. A gasp of exertion as the attendants lift the dead weight off the cot. And come the dawn, a newly vacant spot. Or was it a dream? One cannot tell. No one speaks of the night's transactions. The day's commerce goes on in this city of pain, with currency made of bandages and concoctions and cots still full of hope.

Until yesterday a feeling of complete abandonment had taken me over. Perhaps Sarah will have told you of Major Holder's miraculous return. I had felt certain none of my officers had survived, so that on top of my discomforts was laden the heaviest grief, and it was for Holder I felt the greatest remorse of all. To have died so far from home, after so many travails as he has had, I thought the cruelest injustice. But suddenly here he was beside my cot with his wry grin and an enormous wrapping about his head. When I inquired as to the nature of his wound—an impolite question in any other place, as you will readily agree—he said he'd seen a cannon ball coming and thought it best to stop it with the least useful part of his body!

His memory of the affair is no clearer than mine, although I gather he was left standing longer. He remembered the crisis of the grand assault, and he remembered being in front of the wall with Private Jomini, but he did not see the boy disappear as I did, even though they were closer to one another. I think he was fonder of that boy than I was. He said, in a sad way, that Jomini reminded him of himself when he was first with Gen. McClellan down on the peninsula, full of the cause and ever watchful of the war's mechanics. He had loaned Jomini several books which a kind Swiss officer had given him in those days, and the boy would take them away only to return a few days later with all manner of questions. Toward the end, Holder said, the boy professed to understand all that came before him, and took to sketching maps on the writing paper he carried in his knapsack. These he would deploy for Holder upon the slightest encouragement, and they would sit into the wee hours by the fire, discussing the finer details of the struggle. As I know myself, these meetings did not go unremarked by the other boys, who accused Jomini of going for a brevet. For his part, Holder did not cavil at the idea of raising Jomini to a commission, and while I did not oppose the proposition—if only because Holder was well disposed toward it—I suggested we might wait to see how the boy did in the next fight.

I should have permitted the boy to go up. Then, at least, we should have had at least two who understood this wretched war, for I certainly do not and see little sense above me. Holder has been saying since I first met him that our tactics were so hopelessly out-moded that our methods of attack amounted to little more than orga-nized murder, that no one stood much of a chance except in a well-protected defense, and I could not disagree except to say that we were seldom allowed a choice, especially when our brief was to at-tain some degree of progress against the Rebels. But even at that, Holder averred, our formations, so tightly packed, presented the best of all targets for even the worst marksmen. Our only recourse, he said, was to disorganize ourselves as we attacked, for all of us to take up the habits of the skirmisher. Greek-like struggles, wherein great phalanxes crashed into one another with sword and shield, are no more. We should not mind the loss of power our bodies once pro-vided in battle, for the dreadful machines in our hands express this power a hundred-fold. Yet we do persist. We neither of us see the slightest hope this hard-won knowledge will ever be admitted by the grand conductors of the war. Our latest fight seems but a harbinger. We shall fight on 'til exhaustion, and then that will be the end of it. Holder has conceived a theorem, one that he says embodies all that this war has taught him: when our guns are better than our tactics, our men must be better than our guns.

July 12

Dear Father,

As it is still not possible for me to write very much at one go, I thought it best to leave off and continue when I felt a bit fresher. My mornings go well enough, but my afternoons are marked by a bit of sinking. My nights are best not spoken of.

Major Holder returned this morning with the news that I am being favorably considered for a promotion to brigadier, and that he is to have a brevet along with temporary command of the regiment. But, he says, our colors are so faded there are few men left to do much with. He commanded almost as many when he first took a company. As for my ascendancy, the army must be at the bottom of the barrel. We must have lost a good many officers if we are looking to invalids to fill the empty places. I do not flatter myself that any other reason recommends me. In truth, very little skill was wanted from me, and I should think even less is required from a brigadier. Such creatures are never free but are fenced in on every side by orders and obligations. There is no soul more a prisoner of circumstance than a brigadier. And anyway, once the grand high powers understand the extent of my wound, I am sure the nomination will be withdrawn. In my present state I could not even be roped to a saddle, though I've heard such has been done. I believe my war-like days are over. My only wish now is to return home to my family.

For the present I am spending such time and energy as allowed in attempting to write down as much as I have learned in this war. My conversations with Holder are of considerable assistance, for at this moment it is hard for me to discern what I remember and what I imagine. You know better than anyone, father, how I have ever had this passion to record everything. Holder has often remarked upon my habits as well. The other day he laughingly hoped that I should run out of war to record and so become the very last historian of the war. I believe what he meant was that the war had finally overflowed its banks of reason and was now being fought simply because it could—reason having deserted us, no reason could be summoned to explain it. Although his remarks were cloaked in good humor, I wonder if he is not right.

I shall close this poor effort, father, with my usual injunction to see to Sarah and the children, and to yourself as well. I shall write again very soon.

> Yr. son,
> John

July 14, 1863
Nr. Gettysburg

My dear Wife,

Dearest, you will not recognize this hand. It belongs to our Miss Hancock, who has graciously consented to assist me as she has so many others these past days.

Late yesterday, the surgeons, having delayed as long as they dared, were required to remove my foot, from just above the ankle. The condition of the wound permitted no other course. It had taken on a dangerous appearance, and rather than attempt to ward off any further decline, they thought the removal best calculated to arrest it once and for all.

Would that I was not forced to write to you so, for I know how you will worry, and my most fervent wish is to convince you there is no cause to do so. I am fairly comfortable and in surprisingly little pain after what most would consider such an extravagant operation.

Also, I am fairly surrounded here by many who have been saved from their tortures in just this fashion, and since being here I have seen a number of them enjoy a marked improvement toward their healing.

I am told it is possible these days to fix upon the leg a device that will enable one to move about with very little impediment and that once my surgery has sufficiently healed I will be given one of these machines. So when you next see me I shall appear as a whole man with perhaps only a bit of a list to one side, like a bay fisherman in the lightest of breezes.

There can be no question now of my coming home at the first possible opportunity. Our arrangements here are daily becoming more efficient, and it is reckoned that there are not more than 3,000 of us remaining. The new hospital camp on the outskirts of town is in its final stage of readiness, and we have been told that we are to be moved there before long. The new camp is said to be commodious, airy, and clean as a new whistle, with plenty of stewards and matrons to go round. A change for the better, or indeed any change at all, will be very welcome here. I do not blame the army so much for the time it has taken to set aright its original deficiencies in seeing to our needs. No one could have foreseen what this battle would leave behind it. And anyway, as Miss Hancock is fond of saying, Uncle Sam is very rich, but also very slow!

Looking forward to brighter days, I send you love, dearest, and to the little ones. Please say to father that I shall write before too long.

> Yr. husband,
> John

July 18, 1863
Nr. Gettysburg

Dear Father,

We are being moved, very gradually, to a new establishment east of town. I find the hubbub irritating; before, I couldn't have been bothered. I feel as though I am slowly being abandoned. I shall probably be among the last to be moved, owing to my condition. The easier ones, it is said, are to go first.

The amputation was not so horrible as one would fear. I certainly did fear it and at first refused to countenance any suggestion the surgeons made in that direction. In the end, the surgeons enlisted Holder to their side, and I could no longer withstand the weight of their combined arguments—that, and what I saw with my own eyes. The wound had grown so red as to appear dark, and my fevers were visiting more often. No amount of opium seemed equal to the pain at the end. Once I saw no other avenue of relief, I gave my assent.

The whole business was over in a trice, and anyway I knew nothing of it, for the surgeons dosed me with chloroform. By then I was actually grateful to be going ahead, tho' I awoke with a ringing headache that did not subside for some time. Since then I have been liberally supplied with brandy and other spirits for the shock, and these in combination with the opium have kept me rather befogged until today.

What remains of my leg is tightly and cleanly wrapped, but I have the strangest feeling my foot is still attached, whereas before the operation I could not feel the foot at all. The surgeons say this often happens, and may happen well into the future if I let it. I am told to put the notion of ever having had a foot there right out of my mind, which I think is very good advice if one has both feet while offering it. Only the pain running up my leg told me it was there at all before, but that has now been replaced with merely the pain created by the surgeon's instruments. If we are not friends, my pain and I are now old acquaintances.

Holder has been most loyal and attentive to me. He takes my merest whim as his command, disappears and returns with the most impossible articles. He even brought me an orange and bade me eat the skin and all, extolling its salutary benefits, which had been taught him by sailors on his childhood voyage to America. His own great turban has been replaced by a lighter and certainly less fashionable dressing, which he says he will substitute for a zouave's fez when he can, so as to keep up his imposture of an eastern potentate, even if it is of a slightly lesser rank. He admits to continued headaches and poor sleep and is indifferent to food, but he turns away my concerns, as usual, with a joke, saying the headaches would not last much longer anyway because his brains had spilled out of the turban when they took it off.

I suppose the sum of these signs bodes well for him, but not for me, for I dread being deprived of his company when he rejoins the regiment. He will be as fine a commander as anyone and certainly better than I was. Were it possible, I would leave now and serve under his command. But his war has been longer than mine if you count his troubles in Texas, where he was made to fight a duel before leaving. Of course, father, I know you disapprove of such proceedings, but you must not hold them against Holder, who by his account had no choice but to meet his assailant on equal ground. I never saw anyone whose temperament was further from being a real duelist than Holder. The boys saw his true nature in a wink, for they have become expert in gauging the real worth of those who are privileged to lead them. Who knows, now, how many of the old originals are left, so he will be a stranger to the larger part of them. But they will see as quickly as the old ones what they have got for a colonel, and the old ones will help them understand their good fortune. I hope one day you will have the pleasure of meeting him.

I do so look forward to leaving this awful place, in whatever condition. There is so much wreckage about—tents deranged, piles of cots, old dressings floating about on the wind, and a large inferno that has been kept going since we first arrived. Materials have been burned on that pile that I dare not speculate on. It is not even a fit place for the dead. Perhaps it is only my long confinement here, but I have had difficulty resting even at night, so that when morning comes I feel as though I have been hauling and pulling all during the wee hours. I expect the new place to drive away my discontents, however.

JULY 20, 1863
II Corps Field Hospital
Nr. Gettysburg

My dear Sir,

Your son has bidden me to write thee, telling of his recent reverses in health. On the day before yesterday the colonel's wound worsened, to the alarm of his doctors. They determined that another amputation was necessary to prevent further decline. The operation subsequently performed removed that part of the leg below a point equidistant between thigh and hip. The doctors believe and trust that his travails are over at present.

Your own reputation as a physician is well known here. I know your son's doctors would ask me to have you believe they are doing everything within their power to see that your son will receive proper and attentive care, to which I presume to add my own pledge. Your son is very highly regarded here for his courage under the most trying of circumstances, for he never fails to have a friendly word for all who meet him. I have myself been the beneficiary of his kind temperament, when it is I who should have lent him comfort. I am told the regard in which he is held here extends to the Army of the Potomac at large, not only because of his gallantry in the recent battle but because of his service before as well.

Although suffering somewhat from delirium, your son is resting as comfortably as it is within our power to effect. I know he will write to you when he is able, or if he so desires I will happily serve as his agent to ensure that you and his family remain abreast of the course of his recovery.

> I remain, Sir, your humble servant
> Cornelia Hancock

July 24, 1863
Gettysburg

My dear Sir,

With the heaviest of hearts, I must inform you that your son passed away last evening at 11 o'clock. I as well as several others were by his side. Toward the end he was without much pain and able to speak clearly of his abiding love for his wife and children and for you. He hoped earnestly that his love might remain forever in your hearts. This thought seemed to comfort him most profoundly. Then he passed into a deep and peaceful sleep from which he did not return.

Sir, I would wish history at an end sooner than the colonel. He was my best and truest friend, and I do not expect or wish he shall ever have a competitor. Never was there a finer man or a braver one. On the day of our fight no one was more conspicuous. While he was most solicitous of our safety from the enemy's shot and shell, he would seek no protection for himself, knowing that the men would take heart from seeing him and hearing his calm voice explaining what they must do. When the battle was joined he did not shrink from the death that enclosed us on every side. I myself saw him engaged in the fiercest duel with several of the enemy while attempting to protect one of our batteries. All about him the fire was white hot. When finally he was struck down, several of our men left their place of comparative safety to join in guarding him until he could be removed from the field, which was done over his protests.

At first the doctors thought they could save his leg, but as events proved his infections got the best of them and left no recourse but to remove the injured limb. For some time after the fight our medical services were sorely tested for want of proper supplies and surgeons, necessitating the crudest measures to save those who were most dangerously wounded. We were short of everything. To your son's everlasting credit, he would not countenance any treatment until he was satisfied that the medical officers had regained their balance and, as you will understand, thereby placed himself in even greater jeopardy.

When finally the surgeons were able to persuade him to allow the first amputation, our meager supplies of chloroform had entirely given out, so that the colonel bore the pains of his operation without any kind of sedative. He only asked that I hold his hand, which it was my honor to do. It was a mark of his *sangfroid* that after his surgery he amused us all by observing that I seemed to have suffered the ordeal more, knowing well as he did how the very sight of blood sickens me. Throughout he was the most uncomplaining of all the wounded and was ever watchful against receiving extraordinary favor on account of his rank. When Miss Hancock, one of our nurses, chided him for endangering himself with his own unreasonableness, he replied that in an army of free citizens rank should only confer responsibility. He only grew irritable when he suspected his wishes were not obeyed.

I was able to find him a few days after the battle and since have been given as much time with him as his condition allowed. We had our peace for a while and indulged ourselves as we had often done, with the best of conversations. He held that I was the scholar of this war, but to my mind he possessed the completest understanding of anyone. He had come to think that this beast of war had escaped its cage of reason, and I could not disagree. But he had no thought of retiring from the fight and saw no other course but to bring the beast to heel. To do otherwise, he thought, would be to abandon duty and honor.

What he did not say to me he wrote in his journal, which was his constant companion. He meant to record all the sights and sounds that impressed him and to arrange all he had learned as intelligently as he was able. The men often joked about their colonel's mania for writing, which he would do whenever the mood took him. He was famous for writing when under cannon fire, and indeed his habit was so well known that whenever he drew his journal from his pocket, the men would look at one another and say, "Duck." Certainly, no disrespect was ever intended; on the contrary, their jokes about his little peculiarity were signs of their real affection for him. Between us privately, and only half jokingly, we came to call his journal his private history of the new 30 yrs. war. I pray now that soon we will have no need for any more historians of this bitter struggle.

I have collected all the items in the colonel's kit together with his sword and pistol. Among these are letters to you and to his wife which appear to have been most recently written but never sent. These I have had wrapped in oilskin so as to preserve them for your safekeeping. All this I send to you now by this trusted courier, a young private who so distinguished himself in the fight that he will soon be raised to a commission, and of whom your son was very fond. He has been ordered to report to me when all has been safely delivered into your hands.

I am ordered back to the regiment without delay but I have taken steps to ensure the proper return of the colonel's body to you. The stationmaster here assures me that you may meet next Monday's 3 o'clock train at your place. I have attended to the expenses of the colonel's return so that no burden of cost falls upon you. The colo-

nel will be escorted by a guard of our regiment by order of General
Meade. If fortune favors me, I hope one day to call upon you and the
colonel's wife to pay my respects properly.

I would have given up my life not to have written this letter. I remain, Sir,

Yr obt svt.

H. Holder

Bvt colo

9

HUMAN RAIN

A war between ancient empires in the Manchurian wastes unveils the face of industrial combat at the dawn of the twentieth century. Now soldiers must fight not only against each other: their common enemy is now the war itself. Is modern war too terrible for human beings to fight? Will war annihilate itself with its own efficiency?

CHIN-CHOU, FEBRUARY, 9, 1904, 0200 HOURS
Headquarters, 5th East Siberian Rifle Regiment

His hand would not have trembled so had he been fixing the bayonet to his Mosin. That was not so different from his old axe, or hay rake. But he rarely handled paper. Its properties were foreign to him. So fragile, so easily soiled. And by the Holy Father, the wrinkles appeared as if ordained.

He had never before served as a runner, nor had he seen his regiment's headquarters. He was not even certain he knew what a headquarters was, except that important persons and orders issued from it. Now he had in truth seen headquarters. It was a wondrous thing indeed. Paper abounded there: strewn about on the long tables, or stacked in bales and tied with colored ribbons, even disrespectfully cast onto the earthen floor. Important matters were committed to paper, he suspected; could it be that these last contained that which

227

was no longer of importance? Here and there were wondrous machines as well, one of which gave its tongue of paper to an officer, who remorselessly ripped it from its place and rapidly pasted it to another, larger piece of paper. The soldier rolled his own tongue around the roof of his mouth, in silent sympathy.

The officer had beckoned, "Here soldier, deliver this telegram to the colonel. You will find him on the heights, at the old bombproof. You know the way?" "Yes, your honor," the soldier said. "Quickly then," the officer grunted, and turned back to his papers.

The soldier did know the way in daylight. This night was moonless, starless. He stumbled out of the building toward his pony, an ugly, runty, ill-tempered Manchurian. In his younger days on the estate, he and his family would have made him into sausages. Mounting, coaxing, he rode his little sausage down the quiet streets of Chin-chou and past the sentries at the town's south gate. Drowsing, they hardly acknowledged his passing.

Then, he was along the rough road, which in truth was more a path. This was the path that would take him up onto the hills to the south. The climb was not difficult if one stayed on the path, which the pony would do without further interference from his rider. He merely waited in the saddle a bit, thinking of little, perhaps an hour, and then he was challenged by another sleepy sentry, who pointed him on his way a little higher. Not once did he turn in his saddle to see the town below. Nothing in this country was so interesting as to warrant an expenditure of energy.

These hills were not interesting to him either. They were like all the others. Perhaps higher, but none were very high at all. Perhaps two hundred meters. One could shoot from the top and easily hit his target at the bottom. Nothing grew in the way. Here and there a scrawny bush. Ravines everywhere, cut by the snows when they melted in May. At the top of this one in daylight, though, he could see the bays on either side, each giving into the larger sea. If he looked southeastward, he could see the railway going on to Darien and Port Arthur.

The cold winds picked up as he reached the summit. Not his coat, not his boots, not even the pony's own warmth interrupted their effect. The ground was always frozen in this accursed place, it seemed, the air was frozen, now he was frozen too. He thought he smelled snow. He hoped there might be something warm to drink at the top.

The pony must have been asleep. He nearly took them headlong into the deep trench, but recovered himself at the last moment.

When another sentry challenged him in the usual way, he remembered his mission, the most important of his brief career as a soldier of the Tsar. "A message for the colonel, from headquarters," the soldier replied loudly.

This caused immediate motion. His horse was taken from him. He was led down the gallery of the huge trench toward the bombproof and bade to enter.

After the gloom of the night, the electric lights of the dugout blinded and confused him. He looked this way and that. None of the several other soldiers and officers there paid him any attention. Finally, he saw the august personage to whom he was to report. As he brought himself to attention, he withdrew the paper from his tunic and held it before him. My Holy Father, he thought, what a mess it looks. How did it become so in such a short interval? And so his hand trembled. "A message, your honor," he announced, forgetting for a moment that he was no longer the peasant boy addressing the lord of the manor.

The colonel's aide-de-camp administered a glance, eyebrows arched, as he whipped the paper from the soldier's hand. Had the colonel not been present, he would have cuffed the young idiot for his offense against form. The colonel looked up from the makeshift desk and bestowed a smile on the soldier. The soldier stiffened himself in acknowledgment.

The colonel read the note so quickly, the soldier saw. He only had to glance at it to know its meaning. An educated officer, the soldier thought. Refined, by the look of him, and kind as well. The colonel handed the message back to his aide. "Well," the colonel said finally, "we are at war with Japan."

To no one in particular, the aide read the telegram aloud: "The Japanese fleet is 50 miles from the coast and making for Port Arthur. Signed, General Glinski."

Japan? the soldier thought. But we are in Manchuria!

THE TIMES, FEBRUARY 9, 1904
Latest Intelligence: War Begun
Russian Warships Torpedoed; Night Attack on Port Arthur
From our correspondent in Odessa

The following is a close translation of a telegram which has just been published, addressed by Admiral Alexeieff to the Tsar:

"I most devotedly inform Your Majesty that about midnight between the 26th and 27th of January (February 8 and 9), Japanese torpedo-boats delivered a sudden mine attack on the squadron lying in the Chinese roads at Port Arthur, the battleships *Retvisan* and *Tsarevitch* and the cruiser *Pallada* being holed. The degree of seriousness of the holes has to be ascertained. Particulars will be forwarded to Your Imperial Majesty."

This news has created the profoundest impression amongst naval and military circles here. Its suddenness has stunned them. The population remains calm, but great anxiety prevails.

THE TIMES, FEBRUARY 10, 1904
The War in the Far East
From our correspondent in Tokio

The Japanese navy has opened the war by an act of daring which is destined to take a place of honour in naval annals. On Monday night a number of Japanese torpedo-boats surprised the Russian squadron in the outer road stead at Port Arthur and delivered their

attack with such good effect that two of the best battleships of the
Russian squadron and a cruiser were disabled. The Japanese boats
appear to have made good their escape without injury. It will be observed that the careful translation of Admiral Alexeieff's telegram
to the Tsar, sent by the *Times* correspondent, shows that the three
ships were fairly hit and "holed," and the interesting account of the
fight brought by the steamship *Columbia* to Chi-ful discloses that all
three Russian ships were beached to save them from sinking.

From the memoirs of Akashi Motojiro
Lieutenant, Imperial Japanese Army

In the fourth month of the thirty-seventh year of Meiji, my division was mobilized and ordered to the front. Only two months before, after years of resentment and mutual suspicion, relations between Japan and Russia escaped from the polite salons of
diplomacy and plunged into the abyss of all-out war.

Of course there were reasons behind this new state of affairs—
there are always reasons. But the real one is that people on both
sides wanted to test themselves against each other and against the
trials of mortal combat. Youthful enthusiasm and bravado seemed to
infect everyone in my prefecture. As news of our relations with Russia worsened, the air thickened with the emotion of a religious festival. Any sort of occasion was used to whip up enthusiasm for war.
Reservists like myself conspicuously visited the shrines to offer
"mobilization prayers" and "orders prayers." Young regulars, allowed a final home leave, strutted through village streets in uniform,
collecting admirers as they went. The most outrageous proclama-
tions were made. "I will fight them all myself at Liaotung," one
youth cried to an admiring crowd. Fathers gathered their families
about them, as indeed did my own, and with great solemnity offered
up precious ancestral swords to their sons, praying that honor would
be done in their use in the days ahead. The tide of joy was relentless,

irresistible. It was our duty to be joyful. His August Majesty had proclaimed it so, and if one were so daring for a moment as to consider disobeying his will, our fellow subjects would have torn him to pieces and left him and the reputation of his family in the dirt of our streets, and our march toward war would have continued without pause.

So I went along. I left my school and my students behind. My wife and children were just as happy as my students over my mobilization. They were glad to think that I might die a righteous death in battle and thus contribute to our family's fine history. I offered my own "mobilization prayers" insincerely, for the sake of my family's reputation, even as my throat was swelling with feelings of dread too strong to be spoken.

How obliging were the gods! Even after detecting my insincerity, my prayers were answered all the same. The gods took my private joke away from me.

My wife took great pains to prepare my kit, polishing my boots to a great shine, brushing my uniform to perfection, laying out my other necessities with parade-ground precision. At the foot of this array lay my family's sword, held expectantly in its sheath, its goldwork gleaming with pride. On the appointed day, I slowly removed my ordinary attire and stepped into my uniform. "All correct," my father grunted approvingly.

And, indeed, he knew what was correct, for he had himself fought in Liaotung nearly ten years before. With General Nogi, he and his comrades had stormed the defenses of Port Arthur, crushed all resistance, and, some said in hushed tones of voice, exacted a terrible vengeance upon their Chinese adversaries. Now, my father said, once again our sword must taste an enemy's blood.

At the announced time, I and all the reservists of the prefecture and their families gathered at the railway station to depart from Osaka. Hundreds gathered on the station platform, beset with emotions poorly concealed. Of course my attire distinguished me as an officer, and as I moved toward the train with as much dignity as I could summon, ordinary soldiers and their families retreated to allow my passage, bowing in respect before an officer now on the active service of the emperor himself. Their respect was not for me. To all of them, even my family, I was merely the physical representation of an idea, the embodiment of our emperor's will.

I no longer felt in command of myself.

THE TIMES, MARCH 13, 1904
Latest Intelligence: General Kuropatkin Leaves for the Front
From our correspondent in Paris

General Kuropatkin left for the front today. The correspondent of the *Echo de Paris* at St. Petersburg has had an interview with an aide-de-camp of General Kuropatkin. He affirms that the commander-in-chief, who "expects to have done with the Japanese at the end of July," has made the following declaration: "I know the impetuous temperament of Linievitch, but my good comrade will have to wait. I do not intend to sacrifice needlessly a single man. We shall operate in great masses. To give the Japanese a lesson we shall make a little promenade in their island after having crushed them in Korea and Manchuria. If I have anything to say in the matter, we shall sign the treaty of peace at Tokio and nowhere else."

CHIN-CHOU, LIAOTUNG, APRIL 2, 1904
From the private day-book of Colonel Nikolai Alexandrovitch
Tretyakov
Officer Commanding, 5th East Siberian Rifles

The 3rd Battalion arrived today. They are a fine lot of men, having gained much experience hunting the Hunhutzes. As they have been in the field much of the time since the declaration of war, I have quartered them here in the town and moved the old companies to the villages just in front of the Nan Shan positions.

The weather is turning fine. The ground is still frozen hard enough to break our pickaxes, but I can see the beginnings of the kaoliang sprouting along the hillsides. In the ravines, the water is still frozen, however.

Our progress in fortifying the Nan Shan heights has been slow, all of the positions having fallen into ruin since they were first constructed during the last China campaign. The whole scheme of our defenses here must be repaired and extended without delay. Fortunately, Major Schwartz, of the engineers, has arrived from Port Arthur with sufficient monies to hire Chinese workmen for the repairs, thus lessening the burden on the regiment and allowing for more time in their own training and preparations.

Every day for several weeks I have had 200 mounted scouts in the field, sending detachments by company along the railway toward Mukden, toward the northeast and Mount Sampson, and along the coast as far south as Dalny. What remains of the regiment, regulars and reservists, is here kept at drills, marksmanship, and maneuvering in front of and within our positions on the heights.

I take it as settled that very soon the Japanese will attempt to force a passage across the Yalu. The enemy's actions thus far admit no other possible course. Yet I do not believe the danger to us will come from that quarter. The enemy must have Mukden and Port Arthur together. Singly, they are of no use to them. Each, if remaining in our hands, would threaten the other. Each is the terminus of our lines of communication, the one by land, the other by sea. Therefore I believe so much of their army which is now before the Yalu has Mukden as its goal, whereas the army meant for the investment of Port Arthur has yet to materialize. The Japanese may not plunge into Manchuria unless their own rear lines are secure. Korea must be indisputably theirs before they will venture more. Now that the weather is daily improving I do not think we must wait long before the enemy's plans manifest themselves in action.

I admit this only to myself: I am not sanguine. To an undiscerning eye, these heights promise excellent opportunities for defense. Situated as they are, on the very narrowest neck of the peninsula, they seem to bar the way to Port Arthur. Indeed, that is the very purpose they served during the last China campaign. And, indeed, in the 60 versts between this place and that, few other obstacles of useful terrain intervene, whereas here the long slopes of these moderate rises, laid perpendicularly to the line of operations, present the best observation and fields of fire in this vicinity for musketry and artillery alike.

But this topography, which outwardly frowns so sternly upon all below it, possesses weaknesses that give me concern. Without complete command of the sea, a command now contested by a most enterprising and dangerous enemy fleet, both of my watery flanks are open to naval gunfire. Too, without the reliable protection of our own fleet, the enemy may descend at any one of several points from Takushan or Pi-tsze-wu southward even to Talienwan Bay without fear of much resistance from any force but those of weather or tide. Naturally the enemy will be interested in seizing control of the railway at some point; only one point, strongly held, will suffice for the effect he desires—the severing of all connections by land between our main army under General Kuropatkin at Mukden and the garrison now standing to Port Arthur's defense. And we are in the middle.

Our work at Nan Shan has come to a point at which we must begin to reckon more precisely the force we will commit for its defenses. Every request for more men and heavier guns, however, has been turned aside. From the outset of the war, or even before it began, we have dismissed the thought that the Japanese were in any way equal to ourselves.

Still, when word came to us that Japan might indeed resort to war, I thought that although they might be so bold as to attack Korea, to which they had long laid claim, they would certainly avoid any direct conflict with us, not least because of the presence of our fleet. When our fleet was torpedoed, no one was more surprised than I myself.

But my superiors do not share these opinions. They seem to think a certain public bravado sufficient to intimidate the Japanese. Almost immediately as the war began, General Stoessel, who commands Port Arthur's defenses, announced he would never surrender and issued a declaration to all those in his command, ordering preparations to fight to the last man. My own divisional commander, General Fock, who advanced to his present rank through the police rather than the army, appears to have taken on General Stoessel's attitudes. At our last divisional parade, he addressed the regiments, assuring the men that the Japanese were fools because they advocated a wide dispersal of troops while assaulting a position. This done, he called out to the front rank, asking them why they thought the Japanese were fools, to which they dutifully replied, "Because they advance dispersed very widely." One of my fellow officers, whom I should not name even now, said to me under his moustache, "It appears the general is something of an expert on fools."

The front of my position, from bay to bay, measures 4,000 yards if one does not add the very wide coastal flats that reveal themselves at lowest tide. And although these flats would work to our advantage by keeping the enemy's gunboats farther from our positions, neither can they be effectively defended except from the heights themselves. An enemy as enterprising as this one has shown himself capable of mastering any feature of terrain. Our positions are marked throughout by intrusions of deep ravines that point themselves as if by design toward the summits of our main positions. If we fight here, these will be of inestimable value, protecting the enemy's infantry advance within as few as thirty meters from our positions in some places. We must cover these positions, which can only be done by means of firing blindly at targets calculated beforehand.

All this and more I explained to General Fock, who answered my request by ordering me to defend this place to the last drop of blood. I said that, unless we were reinforced at least to the strength of a division with additional support of heavy batteries, that was precisely how the fight would end.

I cannot imagine what reasons lie behind such orders and so must trust that they are sufficient for the task that lies before us. Thus, our preparations continue with even greater urgency than ever.

THE TIMES, APRIL 4, 1904
Latest Intelligence: The War
The Naval and Military Situation: The Japanese Advance in Korea
From our correspondent by DeForest's wireless telegraphy
Aboard the *Times* special steamer *Haimun*, Wei-hei-wei

I returned from a four-day cruise today, having visited one Japanese base, and yesterday passed within view of Port Arthur. The last wireless message which you received from me, giving details of the attack on Port Arthur, was sent from the coast of Korea, a distance of over 100 miles.

The situation at present would appear to be as follows: As regards the land forces, General Kuroki's army is now in a position to attempt to force the Ya-lu whenever and wherever the general may select to strike, but it would seem that, having secured the necessary strategic position, he is waiting for the development of the second Japanese mobilization before making a decisive move. This development is already under way, but it is not possible for me to say where until the blow has actually fallen.

The Times, April 15, 1904
Latest Intelligence: The War
Attack on Port Arthur: Further Russian Losses
London: The following telegram from Tokio has been received at the Japanese legation

Admiral Uriu, commanding cruiser squadron, reports as follows: According to the report of the Third Destroyer Flotilla, our fleet attacked Port Arthur on the 13th and sank one battleship of Petropavlovsk type; also destroyed one destroyer. Our fleet is quite safe. No official report has yet been received from Admiral Togo.

The Times, April 16, 1904
The Russian Government and Wireless Telegraphy
War Correspondents Threatened
From our correspondent in New York

A Washington Associated Press dispatch says that the Russian government has given notice that newspaper correspondents using wireless telegraphy will be treated as spies and shot.

The Times, April 21, 1904
Japanese Military Dispositions
From our correspondent in Tokio

On the 18th and 19th inst., the citizens of Tokio gave a send-off to the First Division, which entrained on those days for Hiroshima, there to be combined with two other divisions into the 2nd Army Corps. Tokio's normal garrison consists of the Guards and the First Division, the former of which left the city some weeks ago to join the First Army. All the men of these divisions belong to the city and its suburbs, and thus the farewell to them had something of sadness to leaven its enthusiasm. The crowds lining the streets were not numerous, but at the railway a great concourse assembled, and most hearty were the cries of "Banzai!" that rent the air.

This Second Army will be commanded by General Baron Oku, an officer of much distinction. His first brilliant service was performed 27 years ago, when, as a major, he commanded the battalion that raised the siege of Kumamoto during the Satsuma rebellion. In the China–Japan war of 1894–95 he had command of the First Division. The men of the Second Army believe that they are going to Liaotung.

THE TIMES, **APRIL 21, 1904**
Japanese Patriotism
From our correspondent in Tokio, April 21

The War Office here has been flooded with thousands of requests from men of every age and condition of life for permission to go to the front. Many, following the Samurai custom, sign their applications with their own blood, several requests being wholly written in blood.

From the memoirs of Akashi Motojiro
Lieutenant, Imperial Japanese Army

Colonel Aoki seemed the happiest of men to me. When I observed so to one of my fellow officers, he asked why the colonel should not be? Of all the men in the regiment, he is the only one to have experienced combat, when as a young man he fought in Liaotung against the Chinese. "Only he knows how one may soar to the heavens in the crucible of battle," said my comrade. "We should soon feel the same," he said.

The colonel was not alone, by any means, in his excitement. During these days of hard training and preparation for departure to the theater of war, I was accosted everywhere by the most enthusiastic moods among the officers and men alike. All professed an impatience to come to grips with the Russians. Even my sergeants, who attempted to stand aside from all this, so as to present a solid appearance of calmness, were affected. My own servant could not suppress a constant smile.

My fellow officers attended to their duties with purpose and dedication, but as they filled out their kits they were issued new revolving pistols, which, now encased in their holsters, hung from every belt on the offhand side. Their swords remained placed where they were. The pistols were mere ornaments to them, and several officers disdained to practice firing them at all. "It improves the balance of one's belt," one of them said to me, "but I shan't use it. It is the sword for me, all the way to the bitter end." He said this in a way that suggested he would greet his "bitter end" with pleasure.

Every day, after our men had finished their rifle practice, I tried out my pistol, firing as many times as I could at a target only a few feet away. Once, a sergeant lingered after his men had departed. He was from my own town. In fact, I had taught one of his sons. As we had a local connection, he was slightly less formal than he would have been. Ordinarily, the other ranks, even sergeants, did not approach an officer on any account other than regimental business. When I had fired my pistol a few times, he grunted in approval, nodding his head. Until then, I had not seen that he was nearby. I nodded to him in recognition.

"May I speak, sir?" he asked, saluting.

"Of course, sergeant."

"I have seen you working hard with your revolver for several days now. The other officers seem to ignore theirs," he said, "May I ask why you are taking such pains with yours, while the others exercise with the swords?"

"I exercise with my sword as well, sergeant," I answered, "The colonel demands it."

He was silent for a moment, nodding his head. "Yes, sir. I have seen you. You are as good as any of them, while not quite the master. But I think you favor the pistol over the sword."

This was presumptuous indeed. No soldier could speak to an officer with such familiarity. But I saw from his face he meant no reproach. Nor was he indulging in the casual curiosity one sees in so many of our more rustic men.

"Sergeant, what is the role of the officer when engaged with the enemy?" I asked.

"Why, to lead, sir," he replied quickly.

"And how does he lead, sergeant?"

"Why, sir, he places himself at the forefront of action, so that his men can follow his example."

"Yes, very good, sergeant," I said. "And while his men follow his example, what do you suppose is on the officer's mind?"

"Sir? Why, to conduct himself with honor."

"Yes, of course, sergeant, otherwise the officer would not be an officer. But in addition to that, which we all must assume will govern every one of our actions, the officer must see to it that he and his men meet the enemy at the time and place dictated by orders from our superiors. Is that not so, as well?" I asked.

"Indeed, sir, but even if we do not find the right place, we must always conduct ourselves in the best way," he answered.

"Of course, sergeant. As I said, we must all assume so. And what of the enemy? Has he honor?"

"Sir, I must think he has honor as well. We all join in the honor of combat," the sergeant said.

"In the old days, the days of our grandfathers, and their grandfathers before them, sergeant, with what implements did they fight?"

"Why, sir, with the sword, the lance, the arrow, face to face."

"And, face to face, honor was done."

"Honor was done, sir," he said. He bowed slightly. Across his face, a whisper of a grin appeared.

"And in these days and times, sergeant," I asked, "how do you suppose our battles will progress?"

He thought for a moment, considering my question this way and that. Finally he said, "Sir, I believe we must suffer much before we are allowed to approach the well of honor."

"Yes, sergeant. And when we drink from this well, do you suppose we shall set aside our modern weapons and resort to the weapons of old?" I asked.

"Sir, our officers and our men pray daily that they may be allowed to drink from the old wells," he said, "and so we see our officers exercising daily with their swords."

"The Russian officers, sergeant: they wear swords as well. Do you suppose they mean to use them?"

"Well, sir, they are not like us, I think. They will use their guns."

"I think so too, sergeant. And your gun, sergeant, your rifle. How far will your rifle reach?"

"As far as I can see, sir, and farther still," he answered with some pride.

"And seeing so far, sergeant, can you discern whether your target is officer or soldier?"

"No, sir, I can only see a target at the longest distance."

"And you will fire at the target, officer or soldier. It is all the same to you, is it not?" I asked.

"A target is only that, sir. Bullets have no sense of honor," he said.

"So we can see that many swords, theirs and ours alike, will never leave their sheaths. Our killing distances have grown very greatly in recent times. Your honor will be walled off by the fire of weapons."

"I believe you are correct, sir," he replied. Hesitating for a moment, he continued, "But will there not be occasions in which we are face to face with our enemy?"

"Yes, I believe so as well, sergeant. And on those occasions, one must assume the rifles and pistols will not be discarded. To do so would surrender advantage."

"One surrenders honor as well, so?" he asked.

"If one fights as well as he is able, even on such occasions, the weapon he uses is of little importance. We must remember that now we fight, not merely for our own honor and that of our family, but for the honor of our whole nation, the honor of His Imperial Majesty."

At the mention of the emperor, the sergeant bowed deeply, as I knew he would. The emperor's name was always the best way to seal an argument, or to fix a point squarely in a student's mind. In life as in war, reason is never enough.

"And so, you see, sergeant, I have not forsaken the old ways and tools of honor but, for the sake of our emperor, I have added new tools so that I might serve him better. Who knows? I may even ask you to teach me how to use your rifle?"

At this, the sergeant came to attention, bowed, and saluted. "I am your servant, sir," he said warmly, and respectfully took his leave of me.

A few days after this encounter, the regimental adjutant called me to his side. "Do you know the sergeant, Sakurai, in Company B?" he asked. I replied that I did, that he was from my own town. "He has requested formally a transfer to your company. Would you accept him?" I asked if the sergeant had given a reason for his request. "He merely said that his honor demanded that he serve under your guidance. Do you know what he could have meant?" I replied, as casually as I could, that we must let honor have its way, and so the sergeant's transfer was approved.

MAY 2, 1904

From the private day-book of Colonel Tretyakov

The Japanese, under Kodama, have forced a passage over the Yalu near the town of Wiju. General Zasulich is said to have suffered heavy casualties—more than 2,000, if rumors are to be credited. All agree, however, that the Japanese have come across into Manchuria and are now advancing along the old Mandarin Road toward the city of Liao-yang, 180 versts away. Along the Japanese line of march lies a paradise of defensive positions waiting to be employed. Hills and mountains guard the old road, which itself is little more than a track in places, certainly not one that will stand up easily to the demands of moving a large army. The most difficult place awaiting the Japanese must be Motien or "Heaven-Reaching" pass through the mountains. A mere company could hold up a division there, so narrow is the defile.

As yet, General Kuropatkin has not come out from Mukden with the main body of our army, and my informants are not able to say when and where he intends to make his stand. It is said there is bad blood between Kuropatkin and the viceroy, Admiral Alexeiev, the former insisting on taking the offensive, the latter insisting upon a defensive campaign. By all accounts, Kuropatkin believes that beating the Japanese army is much more important than protecting Port Arthur.

We are but a morning's journey by train from Port Arthur, so I am not wanting for news here, even if most of it is unreliable. Nor am I neglected by my superiors, who day by day appear with inspiration and advice with which I am meant to agree. Naturally, these are accompanied by experts from the staff, who bring their own advice as well as firmly held predictions of our future. Many of these remain the entire day and help themselves in the evening to the generosity of the officers' mess that we have established in the safety and comfort of Chin-chou. Sated with our food and drink, and uplifted by their trip to the field, they find a place on the last evening train to Port Arthur, where their opinions may be taken as having been anointed by their dangerous visit to the front. Nan Shan has thus become a favorite day-trip for those fatigued by the comforts of Port Arthur.

Major Schwartz's supply of rubles is almost extinguished. Schwartz himself is not. He is tireless. Lieutenant Colonel Eremeiev, my old friend from Plevna days, and before that the academy, arrived recently, having volunteered to come out to us. Although I was delighted to have his services, I scolded him for leaving the comforts of Port Arthur. To this he replied, "I would have joined a regiment in Hell before spending one more day in that place. Up here, at least, people seem to know what they are doing," and with that he stomped off in search of what he said was "honest labor." In Schwartz and Eremeiev I have the advantage of two of our army's finest engineers. Between the three of us, we had no difficulty finding employment for 5,000 Chinese, preparing more bombproofs and gunpits, repairing and covering trenches, laying down fougasses, and chevaux-de-frise. Toward the rear of our positions we have established field bakeries, wells, and ambulances.

These last improvements in particular have excited no little criticism from my superiors, especially General Fock, who insists that Nan Shan heights should have no rear area, that it must be contained entirely without reference to other positions, troops, guns, and so on. Following the suggestion made by General Kondratenko after a visit here, Fock wants us to spend all our energies on the construction of a huge redoubt in the central part of our position. That, he says, is where we should plan to die. I am puzzled by his orders and cannot dislodge this passion for glorious martial suicide in favor of a precise calculation of the best tactics we can employ here. Surely, the longer we can hold our positions here, the better. Surely, the defense of Port Arthur would benefit more by our survival than our prompt death.

If we are to put up a serious, effective defense, ought we not improve all our positions as best we can? On the other hand, if we are meant merely to delay the enemy's advance, we must at least think of the most unpleasant contingencies. We cannot allow ourselves to be thrown off these heights, if thrown off we must be, in disorder and confusion. If we forfeit the protection of our positions, we expose ourselves more completely to enemy fire from the heights they will have just taken. We are much more in danger in retreat than while resisting in our positions. Professional soldiers have known this elementary fact for a good long while. Indeed, I hear a French officer has just written a book, which says exactly that.

None of these arguments make the slightest impression on Fock. His obstinance enrages Eremeiev, who has the habit now of referring to General Fock as "the idiot" or "that crude policeman." When I admonish Eremeiev not to speak so, especially in front of the men, he says "That man, not the Japanese, will kill us all."

But I cannot change my generals, and so I will not allow myself to dwell upon these disappointments. Not knowing from my superiors whether to delay or to hold, I plan for both courses of action. Our position grows stronger with every passing day, the men more confident. I have had experiments conducted with our rifles at various ranges, so as to measure the effects of small arms fire on our protected trenches. Loopholes protect our soldiers from aimed fire until the range closes to 200 yards, after which targets that appear in the loopholes offer themselves more clearly to the marksmen. If our fortifications, artillery, and machine guns can hold the enemy at the base of the hills, we may well succeed where all seem to expect us to fail.

I hear we are to have a Schneider-Canet gun delivered before long and have issued instructions to prepare for its emplacement in the central redoubt where it can cover the bays on both our flanks. This, along with our 56mm guns, will add immeasurably to our advantages. I am told the Japanese field guns are quite light, compared to ours, and that they do not possess quick-firing improvements as ours do. Still, as Plevna showed us all, any position, regardless of how stoutly it is defended by fire, can be taken, provided the attacker is not disheartened by high casualties.

THE TIMES, MAY 4, 1904
Latest Intelligence: Savage Naval Actions, Shocking Acts
From our correspondent by DeForest's Wireless Telegraphy
Aboard the Times special steamer Haikum, Wei-hei-wei

Last night the Japanese fleet attempted, with evident success, to put the final seal upon its blockade of the harbor at Port Arthur by boldly sending upwards of a dozen decrepit vessels loaded with explosives into the teeth of the Russian defenses.

Immediately beyond the harbor entrance the weather was filthy, with high seas running under a steady gale. More inauspicious conditions in which to launch such an attack can scarcely be imagined.

The Japanese raiders were taken under fire immediately as they came into view. Several seemed to veer off course, but one by one stupendous explosions were observed across the harbor entrance opposite Golden Hill. Whether these explosions were the result of Russian gunnery or explosives carried on board is impossible to say at this juncture, but in any case the raiders' purpose seems to have been accomplished. One ship came aground at the port itself and promptly exploded.

The fate of the Japanese sailors who carried out this daring attack can only be guessed. With commendable promptness, Russian vessels crisscrossed the harbor in search of survivors. Only a few, burnt and injured by their ordeal, were taken from the water. There was debris everywhere on the water: swords, cups, binoculars, bits of uniform.

One report heard early this morning is most disturbing: a lone Japanese lifeboat is said to have come ashore some distance away.

As a Russian torpedo boat made to rescue the survivors, sailors were horrified to see the Japanese on shore calmly beheading one another. By the time the Russians were able to land a party, every one of the Japanese was dead, the last of whom dispatched himself by a pistol shot with the cry of "Banzai!" still on his lips. In all, seventeen Japanese officers and men are said to have put an end to their existence in this fashion.

This is the first instance in this war in which we have seen the Japanese resort to their ancient custom of ritual suicide, or *seppuku,* the ultimate act of atonement, a redress of dishonor. While in the West suicide is looked upon as a shameful act, the Japanese regard it as an honorable means of extirpating shame itself. This episode contributes, quite forcefully, more evidence of the vast differences animating the two nations fighting this war.

From the memoirs of Akashi Motojiro
Lieutenant, Imperial Japanese Army

Only a few days after my meeting with Sergeant Saito, our division was commanded to move to Sasebo, where we were put onto a collection of ancient steamers for our journey to the seat of war. One of my fellow officers, who was always quick to measure all that can be measured, counted 3,500 passengers on our vessel only—if passenger is the correct word for those who can hardly stand upright or even sleep without jostling a neighbor. There being insufficient space below decks for all to sleep at once, mats were used in four-hour turns. Some of our soldiers were too excited to sleep, while others, made sick by the motions of the ship, could not in any case stand the thought of descending into the stale airs below and so milled about on the main deck. When too many seemed to gather on deck, we officers would attempt to shoo them below, but we knew that some were so miserable they would do anything to evade our orders.

Naturally, accommodations for the officers were better. Cooking was impossible for the men throughout the first part of our voyage because as we made our way into the Yellow Sea the weather assaulted us with a fury. For a time, even we were made to subsist on iron rations. We were six or eight to a cabin and had permission to move about as we wished and when our duties permitted. I could hardly bear to remain in my cabin and sustained myself mostly on brandy, which, if it did not assist in warding off my seasickness, at least helped me to care less about it. I spent as much time as I could on the main deck in all weathers. Because of these conditions, then, we had no shortage of lookouts, night or day, but no lookouts were ever more wretched than we.

Lookouts were indeed necessary, for although the weather had turned quite foul the ice had by then relaxed its grip on the Russian squadron at Vladivostok, and it was from that quarter that the greatest threat to us now came. Already we had heard news over our ship's wireless of a disastrous encounter between one of our transports, the *Kinshu Maru,* carrying our 37th Infantry Regiment, and a Russian cruiser from this squadron. Having intercepted *Kinshu Maru,* the Russian cruiser demanded surrender. This the captain and crew seemed willing to do, but their passengers refused utterly. As the crew of the transport took to lifeboats, the soldiers began firing their rifles at the cruiser. After several warnings, the cruiser torpedoed *Kinshu Maru.* While she sank, the soldiers turned their rifles and bayonets on each other, and the officers committed seppuku in their quarters. Such, at least, was the story from the crew members who were able to elude their attackers and were later saved by another of our ships. Not one soldier seems to have survived.

Without exception my fellow officers pronounced themselves completely in accord with the conduct of our comrades in the 37th. Not a few were heard to hope that they might themselves be favored with such an opportunity to sacrifice themselves so nobly for His Majesty. I suspect now that our censors allowed the incident to be known precisely to inspire us to greater effort when our time came. But with or without the example of *Kinshu Maru* before us, the flame of war burned with the brightest purity in our hearts. We were frantic to be discharged from our confinement and set loose upon our enemy, who, we were certain, had no means of opposing the violence with which we would meet them on the field of battle. And so for the remainder of our journey, in our most disconsolate moments, when the gales of the Yellow Sea were at their harshest, we invoked the noble spirits of those who went down with *Kinshu Maru*. "What about that 37th?" someone would say, shaking his head in wonder and admiration. Or more simply, as we passed one another on the companionways, "The 37th."

Lashed by the storm-crossed seas as I held to lifelines on deck, or listening to feverish talk in the officers' mess, I had no trouble keeping my opinions to myself. By then I had acquired a reputation not only for efficiency but also taciturnity, which my fellow officers preferred to regard as evidence of approval for even their most extravagant declamations. I was able to conceal my true feelings. My fear of what lay ahead had nearly rendered me mute as I struggled from moment to moment with the thought of destruction. I found I could only banish these fears by plunging into work, and quickly accomplishing my own, I cast about for the work of others as well. My aim was to rid my mind of any serious reflection at all. I meant to become a blank.

But this was not so easy for me. Most of my fellow officers were younger than me. Some had been to military school, as I had not. Since our military schools had expunged French influences and taken up German principles of war, our army had progressed enthusiastically. Now the most advanced of our higher officers had studied abroad in order to master Western methods, and it was even possible to say that the time had come to cast off our own warlike traditions if Japan was to survive in this modern world. Of course there were those who would never agree, and like Saigo the Great, go down fighting to preserve the old ways.

Between these two views lay the greater number who believed it possible to combine the best of the old and the new, and indeed this middle way was the one that seemed to have been chosen by the Genro. Steady hands had guided the army's way since Saigo. Our strategies toward the foreign world, the human material from which our army is drawn, our military methods and equipment, all these are now for the most part indistinguishable from the army of any major power. Yet our spirit, it was said, is drawn from the unique history of our own people, the spirit of *Yamato* that infuses any modern implement with the special power of our traditions.

Our little fleet made the safety of the harbor at Chenampo on the Pyongyang inlet by the first day of May. Officers were allowed time ashore to take their ease at houses requisitioned for this purpose. At home, officers were expected to conduct themselves simply, modestly, as befitted one who acted directly in the service of the emperor. Indeed, during my own training as a cadet, *Guntai Naimusho* had been a required text, one we virtually memorized.

At Chenampo, however, no such strictures as laid down by *Guntai Naimusho* were observed; on the contrary, every sort of impropriety was permitted. It was as if, having entered this foreign world, crudities that would have offended politeness at home were here acceptable. Korean temperaments simply were not thought sufficiently refined to be insulted by personal excesses. The time we spent at Chenampo was too brief for us to become accustomed to profligacy, thankfully. I have heard since we departed that our officers had acted outrageously against Chenampo's inhabitants, and that these acts were never given more than a dismissive shrug by local authorities. One tale of debauchery was so offensive to me I protested that such conduct was the same as an insult to His Majesty. "Relax," my major consoled me, "Korea is our colony now, to do with as we will, and when we have finished, Manchuria will be ours as well. We must learn to command inferior peoples, as the Europeans have done."

Perhaps I was only envious. Perhaps it was not my virtue but my wretchedness that kept me from going ashore with the rest and behaving as they did. Everyone was wild to set their feet on the soil of Korea, as if they might win a small share of our victory. Unable to abide the thought of going anywhere in a tossing boat even smaller than the one I was now on, I volunteered for extra watches and other incidental duties. Thus it was that Colonel Aoki and I were the only officers left aboard during our interlude at Chenampo.

Such was the colonel's dignity and bearing that no junior officer like myself would dare approach him in any way. Since returning to active service, I had seen him from afar on several occasions, but unlike others of his kind he never presided over our mess or felt it necessary to offer heroic pronouncements when the regiment was drawn up on parade days. So far as I knew, he had never raised either his voice or his fist. On the other hand, he looked as though a terrible and violent animal had coiled itself up within him. The picture of inner power he presented was unmistakable; it said, "Do not test me, for I will pass your test."

Naturally, he had distinguished himself in battle. From his first combat at Castle Hill, to Formosa, to the capture of Port Arthur ten years earlier with General Nogi, our colonel's superiors had no cause to complain of his conduct. He was always in the vanguard of battle, the most dangerous spots of all, yet behaving as if he were strolling in his gardens. Like his samurai ancestors, however, he alone was the final judge of his honor. Had he found himself wanting, no one doubted that he would avail himself of seppuku. In this respect, he was much like his mentor, General Nogi, who was at once the most traditional and most modern of soldiers.

During these discussions I was always silent. Beyond my own observations of the colonel I could contribute little. The only revelation I could offer was that I had actually seen an example of his writing, which I thought quite beautiful and refined. Someone else said the colonel spent much of his time composing poetry. But I had seen only an old poem he had copied over and over on the paper, as if doing school exercises.

On our second day in port the winds gave way to clear cold air that hardly stirred. The bay was as still as my garden pond. Somewhere, off to the north, beyond the Yalu, our soldiers were fighting Russians. After seeing to the needs of my charges, I permitted myself a cigarette on the fantail. Looking landward at the bare winter hills, I was overcome by how greatly I missed the beauty of my own home, set with other neat houses along forest-covered slopes and happy streams fed by the melting snow. Until this moment I had not allowed such thoughts. I had made work for myself and sought the work of others when my own was done. As I gazed over the gray winter sea, I was too sad to be angry.

At my elbow came a stirring. Turning about, I was startled to see Colonel Aoki. In my haste to collect myself I completely forgot to salute and bowed deeply instead. This, he courteously returned, then moved to my side and leaned upon the ship's railing. Searching his pockets, he finally retrieved an exquisite case from which he drew a cigarette. While I wondered helplessly if I might properly offer him a light, he quickly found his own matches and was soon puffing contentedly. I kept as silent and still as the bay, not knowing if I should speak or even further acknowledge his presence.

After a few moments he spoke, "Even at rest many duties require us, is it not so?"

I agreed that it was so.

"You have taken much upon yourself," he said after thinking for a bit.

I wanted to reply but could not imagine what he wanted me to say.

"Your diligence is to be commended. You appear to have an aptitude for this work."

Finding my voice, I said I was glad to be of some small service to the regiment.

"Your service is not small," he said. "The men want to see their officers are concerned for their well-being, as a father is for his sons."

"We were so trained in cadet school," I replied.

"But you are the only one here," he said abruptly, glancing at me. "You are possessed of a habit of mind that will be of great value to you in more difficult times. In these new days, few have this discipline."

I took out another cigarette. While lighting it, I saw my hands shaking. Why should I behave like an idiot? I was disappointing myself. I yearned to discuss all manner of things with my colonel, but I could not make my tongue work, nor the mind behind it.

"You were a teacher, were you not?" he asked. I was able to nod yes.

"And you taught what?"

"Literature, and history, sir," I answered firmly.

"Then you are well-equipped to understand what is happening here, and what will happen in the coming days. Our nation has taken a new path, as I am sure you appreciate. We have no choice but to take this path, but the way is barred by adversaries of great power. They make wars as a . . . as a machine would turn a gun barrel."

"A lathe?" I offered.

"Yes. Of course you would know this. You are a modern man. It is true: as their armies employ machines their armies try more and more to make themselves into machines. So then," he sighed, "the person is less than the war he makes. That is the spirit of modern war, and we must submit to it if we are to take our place in the new world."

Then he looked me straight in the face. "You will see how it all works in a few days," he said. "I have enjoyed talking with you." Without further pause he cast his cigarette over the railing and withdrew toward his cabin.

A few hours later my major issued orders for all parties ashore to return to the ship. All the junior officers were directed to prepare their men for another sea voyage and to begin drawing ammunition stores for distribution. At dawn the next day, our transport joined with nearly forty others and steamed westward, guarded by our faithful destroyers.

CHIN-CHOU, MAY 5, 9 A.M.
From the private day-book of Colonel Tretyakov

By telegraphic report from Lt. Golenko, commanding 3d Scout detachment, via Sanshilipo station, the Japanese are landing in force south of Pitzuwo at Yentai Bay. Golenko reports 39 transports and 3 warships. Enemy naval detachment began landing at 5 a.m. Hostile fire has been received and returned. I have ordered Golenko to keep the enemy under close observation and to avoid direct engagement. All outposts have been ordered to the alert. I have reinforced the 10th company at this place to 400 men and am sending a cavalry column up the railway line toward Sanshilipo, Pulantien, and Wafangtien. Two dispatch riders bearing copies of Lt. Golenko's message have been sent by different routes to apprise General Fock of the present situation. It seems to me that this is the appropriate time to move the 13th and 14th regiments forward. I am confident these landings are not merely a false demonstration or reconnaissance.

MAY 5, 2 P.M.

By telegraphic report from Lt. Golenko via Sanshilipo station: the enemy's main body is debarking and sending out strong patrols in the direction of Sanshilipo. Two other strong columns have been observed moving in the direction of Pulantien station. For the present, the enemy appears content to establish themselves ashore preparatory to general movements. Expect outpost action and probing movements as soon as the enemy reaches sufficient strength. I shall make an inspection of our positions and outposts today and tomorrow.

MAY 8, 12 NOON

A sharp action between our cavalry and enemy raiding parties at Pulantien has been reported. At approx. 6 this morning a strong enemy detachment entered Pulantien station and severed the telegraph lines. Skirmishing in and around the station. At 8 a.m. the Port Arthur–Mukden express received enemy fire n. of Pulantien and was halted. Someone on the train hung out a Red Cross flag, whereupon the enemy withdrew and permitted the train to proceed unmolested. Subsequently, the tracks were torn up for some distance. I have received unconfirmed reports that Wafangtien, some 6 versts distant up the railway line, has also come under attack with similar results. As a consequence, the telegraphic communications between Port Arthur and Mukden as well as our line of general communications with General Kuropatkin must be deemed insecure. General Fock, who was here this morning, stated his belief that these events mark the onset of the enemy's campaign against Port Arthur. If it is obvious to General Fock, we must expect the high command to commence offensive operations very soon. Even the viceroy should by now see the urgent necessity to arrest the enemy's progress in this quarter. Thus far it has been unimpeded. It is clear, too, that we cannot rely upon our navy to save Port Arthur, especially since the death of Admiral Makaroff last month. General Stoessel, who was only recently appointed commander in chief of the garrison, shows no signs of willingness to sortie from his well-defended fortress.

Yesterday's tour of inspection revealed a weak point on our left, covering approaches to our position from Chin-chou Bay. Having insufficient men to cover every yard of our front, I have arranged for four machine gun emplacements here. The belt of wire entanglements at the base of the heights is defended by three trench lines, and these are supported in turn by five battery positions higher up. We have about eighty 56mm and 6″ short guns in all. Our two heavy gun positions watch over the whole from north to east, and our searchlights are in good working order, as is their power station. Telephone lines to the rear are in good order after some trouble with frozen diaphragms on our phones earlier this spring.

The troops are kept busy with such improvements as can be made, although I am concerned by the lack of communicating trenches between the main lines of defense. General Fock has said that such trenches would offer too appealing opportunities of retreat for the men. We must think of these trenches, General Fock says, as useful for containing our own men as for opposing the enemy. They should be made to stay where they are placed, with no provision for withdrawal—this, in keeping with his defend-to-the-last-man philosophy. Nevertheless, I have taken the officers who are to command these various positions on inspections of the rearward terrain, so as to fix in their minds the best avenues of withdrawal should events require. I recognize that by so doing I have violated the spirit of General Fock's orders, but I cannot see how arranging for the death or wounding of my soldiers will advance our tactical situation. It is not by dying, but by fighting, that our soldiers will win this war. With this, no doubt, General Fock would disagree.

MAY 12, 4 P.M.

An earlier unconfirmed report that the telegraphic lines at Wafangtien had been cut proved false. Wafangtien fell this morning to an enemy party of undetermined strength. Now nearly 30 English miles of railroad and telegraphic line to our north are either threatened by the enemy or are already in his hands. No part of our lines of communication beyond Sanshilipo may be considered secure. For several days we have had no word from the station at Pitzuwo, to our n.e., and must assume this also has been lost to the enemy. Our mounted scout detachments from the railway line, eastward to the coast, have found it increasingly difficult to patrol without encountering strong bodies of enemy infantry. The enemy's cavalry is not yet in evidence, but this is not unexpected as we have been told that cavalry is the weakest of their various arms.

I have assigned my old comrade, Lt. Colonel Eremeiev, as commander of Chin-chou garrison. Major Goosov has command of the 10th company, which makes up the bulk of our strength here. The 3d Scouts are commanded by Captain Koudriavtsev, but I have given young Golenko 60 men as an independent detachment. Golenko has proven to be an able and enterprising young officer, one of the new sort who does not abuse his men. The regular companies have occupied several outlying villages for the time being, to serve as an outpost line across the isthmus. When I review these dispositions, I am reminded how thinly held are our defenses.

Late on the 8th, all these dispositions were disturbed. General Fock had determined upon a strong reconnaissance toward the enemy's landing sites, maneuvering to the southeast of Shisanlitai station and past the foot of Mount Sampson. It had been Fock's intention to march throughout the night with all the regiments, including my two battalions, in hopes of discovering the dispositions of the enemy. However, our maps were woefully inadequate: the place names were unreadable and the elevations of the various hills were nowhere given. Local guides could not be induced to help us by any amount of threats or money. When I appealed to the division staff about midnight that going farther in the dead of night would be folly, these orders were amended, postponing our advance until first light at 3 A.M. About an hour before, I arose from an unsuccessful sleep and saw to rationing the men. No fires being permitted; the men would march without their tea, and so there was much grumbling.

Owing to the state of our maps, it had been decided that the chief of staff would lead our column, but for some reason he did not appear until two hours later, and at 5 A.M. we resumed our march, stiff from waiting in the cold. However, he neglected to leave guides at the various crossroads, and we were left to guessing at each junction. Meanwhile, without my knowledge, General Fock was directing my flying battery to take a line of march to our left that separated it from the main body, and in fact placed it some distance ahead, beyond my protection, perfectly outlined on the crest of a small ridge line. When I discovered this, I rode in the direction of the battery, only to encounter General Fock riding quite alone, cursing the battery for going so far ahead. He claimed the company commander had allowed the battery to wander off in this way, but as the battery itself was commanded by Lt. Colonel Romanovski, I think this unlikely. He is the best of my gunners and knows his tactics. He would not have taken such a dangerous line as this without being so ordered. Still, Fock swore to no one in particular, "Such officers are a curse to us." When I attempted to defend Romanovski, Fock waved me away impatiently.

After a time our buglers sounded assembly, and the whole expedition retraced its march back to Chin-chou. The men sang loudly and happily. I myself was happy enough that we had not encountered the enemy on open ground. Watching our troops deploy into skirmish line earlier, I saw they did not advance with any determination and seemed confused as to how to avail themselves of the natural cover offered by the ground. Unless their officers were very near, the men acted very much as if they were on a stroll. These habits are permitted by the indifferent training of our infantry, who are good enough at obeying but not at thinking. Yet, in modern war, as General Dragomirov has said many times, we must have "thinking bayonets." It is just as well we are on the defensive, where our talents, such as they are, will be put to best use.

MAY 16, 4 P.M.

This morning General Fock led another reconnaissance in force, this time in the vicinity of Mount Sampson. This is to the good, for we are utterly ignorant of the strength and dispositions of the enemy. Eremeiev argues that I worry over nothing. They will be here soon enough, he says. We needn't look for them. Then we will fight: strength, dispositions, none of that will make the slightest difference, he says. We will fight the Japanese, and we will prevail because we are Russians, children of the Tsar, soldiers of the Tsar.

I remained behind to observe from Battery No. 13, where I had a fine view for some distance across my front and all the way to Mount Sampson, six or seven versts away. Our troops marched out in column, completely exposed. As they came up to Mount Sampson our bullock batteries unlimbered and began firing at targets I could not see. Soon, the enemy replied, and smoke enveloped our regiments. After an hour or so, during which the artillery fire never subsided, our regiments reappeared from out of the smoke and retraced their line of march. When the wind turned, I could hear bits of singing from our columns. So far as I could see, neither rear guard nor flank guards were ever thrown out. General Fock and the Japanese appear to have agreed that this is not the proper time to bring on a general action.

MAY 19, 5 P.M.

Small arms fire has commenced all along our outpost lines. Company commanders report enemy probing attacks at all points. All the outlying villages are either contested or already overrun. The station Shisanlitai, 1.5 English miles n.e. of Chin-chou, has been taken. Guards along our own walls here are receiving sporadic small arms fire. Carts bearing our dead and wounded, perhaps a hundred so far, arrive as in a procession now. Of course, those unwounded soldiers pushing the carts make no attempt to return to their places of duty, so the town is filling up with able-bodied men as well as casualties. I will direct the sergeants to collect all those who are milling about and apportion them to various posts here. Soon, anyway, no one will think of Chin-chou as a place of safety. As I was passing from the officer's mess to my command post earlier, bullets were already singing down the streets. The sound these bullets make when they strike our mud walls is the same as when they strike a body. Thus I was somewhat distracted. Every time a bullet found a spot, I feared one of my staff had been hit. So does the mind play tricks in its agitations.

The cooking fires have been lit all around the village. The odors of tea and bread are coming through my windows. And there is the singing, as usual. I will retire to sleep as long and as well as I can. After tonight, I expect, we will not be allowed such freedoms.

MAY 21, 11 P.M.

The Japanese have not commenced their general attack, though for the past several days one has been expected at any moment. Chin-chou is still ours. Our outposts at the smaller villages to the east and west are still with us, but the skirmishing gives them no rest. Observation at every sunrise reveals some new enemy emplacement or trench line, each a bit closer but never quite within reach of our guns. That the enemy is composed of more than one division is now undeniable. I make their strength at three or four divisions. There could be more.

The Japanese must be impressed by our defenses. Their hesitation must mean they believe the problem before them is worthy of close study. All is conjecture, naturally. The Japanese commanders are only doing what I would do. They must know any attempt they make upon us, from any direction, will cost them dearly. Calculations now will save them troops when the time comes.

But the waiting is annoying, and it tells when we bicker among ourselves because we cannot fight them. Today, General Stoessel visited our positions and surprised General Fock by demanding to know why Major Gomsiakov, the commander of our 3d company, had been left wounded during a sharp engagement n. of this place. When Fock asked General Nadyein why he had retired and permitted this to happen, Nadyein produced an order signed by Fock himself. Fock had no explanation, so he relieved several officers of their commands. This does no one any good. It is too bad about Gomsiakov, an able and gallant officer, but poor Gomsiakov is rather beside the point. The simple fact is that General Fock's experience has not prepared him for the responsibilities he faces now, and his high rank is no protection from his deficiencies. Nan Shan will be his classroom, and the Japanese will be his teachers. My regiment, however, may not survive the lesson. Three days ago I asked General Fock for reinforcements from the 13th and 14th Regiments. He replied, "So you want to command a division now, do you?" Today, two scout detachments of about 60 men each arrived, bearing instructions that these were to be held in strictest reserve. But I need them on the lines, where my losses have been greatest. Seven hundred yards of trench lines near Lt. Colonel Beilozor's position on the right are undefended. Not even our machine guns can compensate for this weakness.

MAY 23, 8 P.M.

We have been given a 6″ Schneider-Canet, which I have ordered emplaced in the central redoubt. From there it will command both bays, but laying in a gun of this size requires enormous and exacting labor. Because I must oversee the matter myself, I have moved my own command post to this position for the time being. The telephone lines virtually fix me to this spot anyway. Of course, the machine is constantly ringing, calling me to answer this question or that. Now I have left the thing to my adjutant so that I might attend to more pressing business.

It is becoming more difficult to move about, even in the trenches, or should I say, because of the trenches. I try to avoid them while going from place to place, but enemy fire often drives me into their protection. These transactions always cost me time, of which I seem to have less and less. I have not rested for more than half an hour nor washed nor had my boots off for five days. My adjutant, the same. My new orderly—the old one having been killed by shrapnel three days ago—seems to have a talent for finding a corner of our bombproof where he can roll himself into a ball under his blanket. The shelling does not seem to interrupt his sleep.

NAN SHAN, 1230 A.M.
Battery No. 13
True copy, msg. by hand fm. Tretyakov to General Fock

Sir—We are receiving the heaviest artillery fire to date. The thunderstorm we are now experiencing has not interrupted it. No word of enemy infantry movement as yet. I believe the enemy is firing a program preparatory to a general assault which will commence as soon as the storm has abated. All troops have been ordered to stand to their guns. My messenger will remain with you so as to return with any orders you may desire to compose.

From the Memoirs of Akashi Motojiro
Lieutenant, Imperial Japanese Army

The smoke from the funeral pyre rises through the still, damp air. How can the smell be sweet and rotten too? Silence envelops us like a thick fog. Only the muted sounds of the working parties can be heard. We who miraculously are still alive stumble from corpse to corpse. We are sorting the dead.

Our regulations tell us how. The particulars of our task have been carefully specified. We need not think if we so wish. Solemnity and stupor appear the same to those who observe our work. We are solving human puzzles. We must divide the Russians from our own kind. The sons of Russia and the sons of Yamato will take different paths to heaven. Whole bodies are collected, one for the Tsar, one for the emperor. The emperor's collection grows larger by the hour. We must search for pieces too. These we place to one side, so that we might rejoin them with their hosts. Often, we are confounded: if the piece is naked and the flesh greatly disturbed, how does one decide if it is Russian or Japanese?

We have dug separate trenches for the Russian officers and their soldiers. Kaiolang stalks are placed in the bottom, then the bodies, shoulder to shoulder. The Russians were fond of their crosses, amulets, and other trinkets which they wore about their necks. Some were found with their talisman clutched in a terrified grip. The night air has made them stiff. If possible, their hands are placed upon their breasts. Photographs, pay books, watches, and other personal objects will be given to the Red Cross so that they might eventually find their way home. The once-white coats of the officers are laid over them. The soldiers greet the lime and ashes and red earth with naked faces.

Our regulations insist these graves must be to the depth of one meter. The staff officer who composed these regulations could not have known of the great Manchurian dogs who roam the battlefield even now, carrying away what we have not found, or digging furiously for what we have. In a fortnight, the dogs will have full bellies, and Nan Shan will be strewn with Russian bones. We have found 700 Russians so far, and 4,000 of our own.

Our own dead require different care. Small boxes have been constructed so that locks of hair and bits of bone may be returned to Japan. They will rest in military cemeteries if they are not retrieved by their families. From our soldiers' pay books, often torn, covered in grime and blood, we compile a list of names, ranks, companies, divisions, and other information of value to those in headquarters who will study the battle. What remains here will lie in graves, separated by rank: officers, NCO's, privates. If the pieces cannot be identified, they will be committed to the fires, while the division priest prays over them. Each grave will be marked with a tomb-post made to face southward, toward Port Arthur, so that it might lend its spiritual power to ours during the battles that lie ahead. Thousands of posts, marking the places our soldiers spent their last breath, make a crude sketch of the course of our battle: there, a forlorn hope detachment was caught in the wire by Russian searchlights and machine-gunned to the last man; over here, a battalion gradually bled to death as it advanced up the slopes; farther up, tomb-posts at the counterscarp of a Russian trench grin like so many white teeth.

I awoke this morning in one of the enemy's gun-pits. Someone had covered me with a blanket during my dreamless sleep. I had no sense of place or time. The emplacement was a macabre trash heap where bodies had been thrown about by some vicious being and come to rest in ridiculous poses. I dared not move, lest one of them spring back to life to fight me again. Frozen by my terror, a stirring across the way startled me to move. My old friend Saito's face peered at me from the gloom, grinning foolishly. "I knew you were alive," he said.

Standing up, I looked about for my old pistol and my sword, only to discover them still in my hands. When I made to return them to their places, I found mere vestiges. My holster was gone but for its flap, my scabbard torn to shreds by some maelstrom. I dropped the weapons to the ground and stood stupidly, not knowing what to do next. Saito came over to me. "Permit me, Lieutenant," he said gently as his hands began to brush the filth from my uniform. "Your kit is much abused, Lieutenant," he said. "We will do a proper job of this when we go back down the hill."

Now a horrific thirst came over me. I meant to ask Saito for water, but only a croak came from my mouth. Understanding, he handed me his canteen. The tepid water coursed down my throat. I felt life returning to me. As I drank, Saito fashioned a scabbard from a gun sling he found in the debris. He slipped my Mauser under my belt and fixed my sword, its filthy blade exposed.

"Are you hurt, Lieutenant?" he asked, taking me by the shoulders and turning me front and rear. I did not think so. I did not seem to be damaged in any way.

In that instant, however, I was overtaken by a black wave of sadness impossible to resist. I felt I might lose control of my limbs under such an onslaught of feeling and be hurled to the ground by its weight. I began to cry helplessly. I gazed about as if blind. How long this outburst lasted I do not know. Gradually, my feelings retreated before the profoundest exhaustion I have ever experienced. I had run a thousand miles. I felt older than my father's father.

All this time, Saito remained beside me. When I had emptied my well of tears, he bowed silently. Then he took me by the arm and led me out of the gun-pit. The early sun was joyless. Smoke streaked across its face.

We were very high on the hill. The summit was only a few meters away. Everywhere below, across the slopes, in ditches and ravines, along the counterscarps, in the pits and huge redoubts, were corpses beyond counting, an army of the dead. Among them, living men were stumbling about like children learning their first steps. Others stirred with purpose. Little cooking fires were winking in the dawn light. Their smoke mingled with plumes rising from the enemy's positions. Here and there the ground itself smoked.

"Our men, Saito, where are they all?" I called.

"As you see, Sire," he answered quietly. His voice had changed. He had addressed me as one might a noble lord.

Saito spoke with his head bowed. "All were left behind, Sire. The samurai legends came to life in you. You fought as if you were already dead. There was no stopping you. At the last redoubt, down there," he pointed, "we fought the enemy face to face. Your sword sang through the air, first against one, then another and another. From every quarter the Russians came with bayonet and sword, teeth bared like tigers, screaming in their strange tongues. You were screaming, and laughing too."

"There were so many. I could not protect you. I fought to save my own life. But I was thrown to the ground by an attacker. Before he could bayonet me, you killed him with a great sweep of your sword. And then we stood alone. You raced madly about the redoubt and fell upon the machine gun with your sword, striking the instrument, again and again. When it would not return your blows, you leapt out of the redoubt and thrust your sword to the heavens. 'We shall fight our way into the clouds,' you screamed, and then you ran upward through the explosions, far ahead. I could barely keep you in sight. Finally we came to this place. It was already filled with the dead. As I came into the pit, you were hacking the dead to pieces. Then you collapsed and fell asleep. I was afraid you were dead too, afraid I had seen a dead man fighting his way toward the afterlife. The bottom of my soul turned so cold."

He looked up at me then. I searched his face for the truth. His eyes were wide, unblinking, shivering like a rabbit at my stare. Could all this be true? I tried to remember, but only a haze came forth, hanging like a gauze before my eyes. Shame began to creep into my heart. Shame has a memory all its own. I could not speak to my faithful companion.

Gradually, carefully, I began climbing down the hill, Saito following along. We picked our way past shell craters, mangled turns of wire, guns pointing queerly at the sky. Bundles of flesh often barred our way. Once I lost my footing and stepped on one of these, my foot pressing into the soft mess. Sickness rose in my throat.

Little knots of soldiers paused as we passed by. "What company are you?" Saito would ask, "How many are you?"

"We are 7th Company, sir. We are no more than this," came a reply.

"We are twenty, sir," said another.

From yet another, we heard, "I do not know where the 12th Company is, sir. I fought here." Saito bade him to follow us.

Saito asked after the wounded. Had they any? No. All had been sent to the rear. Those too serious to move had died already. All who remained were fit.

"Tell the others to report down the hill when they are ready," Saito ordered. Some gathered themselves up and joined our procession.

And so eventually we came upon a demolished house where our regiment had established its forward post. Officers and men were striding about importantly. Our adjutant, Major Sugimura, was speaking to a cavalryman astride his horse, evidently passing along orders. Saito quietly bowed and left my side, taking our refugees with him. Finally, Sugimura looked toward me.

"Motojiro!" he exclaimed. "We reported you missing, believed dead. Where did you come from?"

I pointed to where Saito and I had slept. Sugimura inspected me closely. He pointed to the hill. "Look," he said. "No. To the right. Do you not see our flag? Did you not bear the colors yourself? You went several hundred meters more?" I could think of nothing to say. Without warning, I began to cry.

"Never mind," he said. "We shall amend our report directly, so as to spare your family further concern." A question intruded upon my mind: would father be pleased or disappointed by this news?

Sugimura led me to a pavilion that had been erected alongside the house and pressed a bowl of soup into my hands. I sat down against the wall. Then, under the shade, I fell asleep with the bowl of soup in my lap. I slept an hour, two? three? Saito sat on the ground next to me.

"Sire," he said simply.

"I am only your lieutenant, Saito," I said, "Pray address me so."

"Sire," he said obstinately, "the colonel desires you join him after you have bathed and changed."

"But my duties, Saito."

"Those will be attended to by others, sire. The colonel's order was plain," he said.

I obeyed. Someone had fetched my spare kit from the regimental trains. All had been cleaned to perfection.

"All correct?" I asked Saito when we had finished with me.

"All correct, sire," he saluted smartly. I bowed in reply.

Colonel Aoki sat upon a camp stool in the sun, gazing toward the heights of Nan Shan. I came to a halt and bowed deeply.

"Lieutenant Motojiro, you really must learn to salute. It is the modern way," he said, but not unkindly. All the same, his fatherly rebuke embarrassed me. I could feel other eyes upon us. I came to attention and saluted.

"Forgive me, colonel, I meant no . . . "

"Yes, yes, Akashi," he interrupted me, surprising me so, using my familiar name. Since our few moments on the ship at Chemulpo, I had hardly seen him.

He bade me sit beside him. Looking past my face, he raised his eyebrows, perhaps to signal his aide, for a moment later a service of tea appeared along with a small table. He waited patiently for the aide to withdraw before speaking.

"Your father's?" he asked, looking at my sword.

"Yes, sir, and his before him, and so for many generations," I answered.

"No more, Akashi. The battle has made it yours. No one in this generation, nor your fathers, nor theirs for a thousand years, has ever seen this kind of war. Our old ways seem like play-acting."

To this I had no adequate reply. Of course he spoke the truth. The tables of history had turned. Once war was an instrument in the hands of men. Now, we are merely the servants of war.

I looked at my sword instead. "I'm afraid it is much deranged," I said stupidly. Of course, anyone could see its disgraceful condition. A great wedge had been knocked out of the filthy blade.

"You used it. You used your pistol too?" he asked.

I could not remember, I said, although at that very moment I recalled having no cartridges left in it. They must have been fired sometime.

"I observed your attack, Akashi. Medatashi," he said, "glorious."

"My attack, sir?" What could he mean, my attack?

Colonel Aoki fell into a silence I dared not interrupt. He stared at a faraway place. With great deliberation, he withdrew his cigarette case from his tunic, removed a cigarette and absently tapped its end, never lifting his mind from wherever it had traveled. Then, ceremoniously, he held out the case to me. I accepted his generosity with gratitude.

My colonel smoked in great contentment, happy in his faraway place. He appeared untouched by sadness. In this man, who once seemed so formidable to us juniors, I thought I saw now the simplest of characters, hardly so complicated as we had imagined.

All about us, the headquarters was decamping. The colonel saw me looking around.

"Yes. We will move forward soon," he said. "The enemy is in retreat. Our patrols will skirmish with his rear guard, merely to worry him along. Eventually, he will regain his balance, he will go to ground again, and there will be more battles like this one . . . no," he corrected himself, "they will be more difficult. We are all learning as we go."

How could anything be learned from all this? I wondered silently.

But as if he read my thoughts, the colonel answered, "We had no idea of the punishment this modern kind of war could exact, nor how much we could suffer and still succeed. Our preparations, though excellent, were quite inadequate."

"Perhaps you will not know," he continued, "that as a young man I studied military science in Germany just after the war with France. The Germans, and especially their paramount kingdom Prussia, had prepared meticulously. But even they were caught off guard by the casualties. In the end only their hard fighting won their battles, but not victory. France did not surrender. Defeat in battle no longer meant what it had. So an unsatisfactory peace was negotiated. Afterward, some wondered if the costs of war were beyond the power of human beings to pay. All seemed to depend upon the power of machines, if anything. Only the great war in America foretold of such things, but the Europeans disdained of learning from any but themselves. And now we know these costs can be met, but only if we are true to ourselves. Yamato damashii will prevail. Because our duty is clear, our hearts are strong. The Russians are decadent. They believe in nothing, not even in each other, and nothingness shrinks the heart. Our hearts are full. Therefore, victory will be ours. You, Akashi, of all people, should know this by now."

He saw the indifference on my face. He looked at me questioningly.

"I was thinking of the red surf, sir."

"No. Having seen battle, you could have no interest in the higher questions you contemplated as a teacher. Such matters of theory no longer hold their appeal. You want to know why our regiments were kept on the fore shore so long," he nodded. "It was because so little was expected of you."

"So . . . little . . . was . . . expected?" Anger rose in my throat.

"The honor of breaching the enemy's defenses was meant for the center of our line—Prince Fushimi's 1st Division, with the 3d to his left in close support. That was the Baron Oku's intention. Our division, our regiments, were to wait until the enemy had cracked."

"And we did wait," I cried, "We did. Faithfully. But from the moment we took our places we came under enemy fire. The regiment nearly bled to death in the surf. Shell bursts, machine gun fire. Bodies everywhere."

"Yes," Aoki said, "and the other divisions, Prince Fushimi's 1st especially, struggled all day toward the enemy's trenches, to little avail. I begged that we be allowed to go forward too. 'But what can Osaka men do that our best men cannot?' was the reply. We had done so poorly against Chin-chou the night before, you see. Prince Fushimi had grown impatient over our lack of progress and had sent his own men to storm the gates. Of course we couldn't take the town, Fushimi insisted. After all, our soldiers were all city boys. What could be expected of such men? We must first pay our debt to honor, as Fushimi's men had done."

Pay our debt of honor. Aoki's phrase exploded in my head. Again I felt the flagstaff in my hands, jerking and twisting violently as bursting shells whipped the wind like a typhoon. The water was lapping at my boot tops, and higher it came with each passing minute. Ahead, our 19th Brigade stretched along the shoreline in perfect formation, columns of company. The fire from the heights crashed into them. Whole ranks were swept away. Shell bursts tore men from their places, hurling them upward in high arcs. Bloody projectiles, bits of uniform, caps, and kit flew through the air. An arm ripped from its moorings splashed into the water next to me. The sky was raining pieces of human beings. Human rain. The 19th was disappearing before my eyes. The waves were a bloody froth. Behind me, someone cried out, "Are we all to die in this filthy Chinese water?"

Now the water was at my belt. The sand below clutched at my

boots. We lived instant to instant. I felt every pulse. All eyes froze on the heights. If only we could go on, dash to the top. But no. The sun began to fall toward dusk. Was this to be our day in hell?

Our company commander, Matsumaru, posed with his arms crossed, impervious to the slaughter, like Fudo. Several men cringed when a shell burst dangerously close. He turned on them with a ferocious scowl, "Shame!" he yelled, "Who is it that salutes the enemy's shot? Stand fast!"

Whistles and bugles suddenly called out to us. At last we were to be freed from our watery prison. At last we were to be freed from life. Joyous feelings of gratitude swept over me. I raised our Sun Flag as high as I could reach, then higher still. To the front I saw the 19th's flag, dashing ahead furiously, then turning out of the surf toward the heights. Rapid volleys of fire erupted from their piteously meager ranks. The enemy's machine guns replied. Invisible fingers of death filled the air. Captain Matsumaru drew his long sword and made the signal to fix bayonets. So, it was to be as Saito had hinted so long ago at camp: the enemy's fire could be extinguished only by an offering of blood. As the soldiers rammed their bayonets home, a low animal sound issued from a thousand bellies. Matsumaru raised his sword. "Tokkan!" he screamed. "Tokkan!" answered the men. Across the flats we raced. My fatigue vanished. I felt an ecstasy. Dreamily, I floated toward the heights, carried on waves of air toward the enemy's fire. We plunged headlong, screaming, into the smoke. After that, nothing. I had outrun my memory.

The colonel's voice brought me back from the surf. "Now, no one will ever doubt the men of Osaka. No one will be so ungenerous again," he said. "I watched you advance with the flag. Then the smoke obscured the field, and I was sure you had been killed. Just before sundown, I saw the flag go up on the heights. The Baron Oku saw it too. That is when he ordered the general assault. The rest you know."

But I did not know. My memory was dark. The battle had consumed my mind. None was left for any thought at all. When one is certain to die, what is the good of a memory?

So now I am to be promoted, the colonel says. All the other officers of my company are killed or wounded. I shall have command of 12th Company. My first duty is to oversee our burial parties. Colonel Aoki says this is the most sacred of duties, a great honor. Honor: how easily the word passes from his lips. How is it, I wonder, that honor could live in such a barbarous place? I think it must have been killed with me.

Major Sugimura has told me that Army Headquarters would be pleased if I would accept a fortnight's leave home. My refusal has been seen as a commendable devotion to duty, loyalty to my soldiers, reverence for comrades who have fallen. The truth is that my thoughts for home are dead, as I am already dead. I am a war ghost.

I have constructed a tiny funeral box for myself. It waits, suspended in a cartouche from my belt, bouncing against my hip as I march on. Soon the storms of battle will form again. Soon my earthly reflection will be obliterated. Soon the smoke will rise from my funeral pyre. I shall join as one with the clouds.

THE TIMES, LONDON, SEPTEMBER 1, 1904
A Fallen Hero

By latest dispatch from the Ministry of War in Tokio, it is announced that one of Japan's first heroes of the war, Major Akashi Motojiro, was killed leading his battalion against Russian positions at the so-called 174-meter hill, one of the strong points guarding Port Arthur.

Readers of *The Times* will recall that it was Major Motojiro who, while still a lieutenant, planted the flag of The Rising Sun atop the Nan Shan heights during the desperate fighting in that vicinity last May. His exploits in battle came to the attention of the emperor himself and became the subject of many patriotic verses and articles in the newspapers of Japan.

Major Motojiro's remains have not been recovered, the hill still being in Russian hands and under constant fire. Military authorities in Tokio have announced that when it is possible to do so, a proper ceremony of burial will be conducted at the Yasukuni Shrine to Japan's war dead.

In one of the many coincidences of the war, it is known from other quarters that the Russian commander in charge of the defenses at this place is none other than Colonel A. N. Tretyakov of the 5th East Siberian Rifle Regiment, the officer who put up such a spirited defense of the same Nan Shan heights where Lieutenant Motojiro won his laurels.

Lt. Gen. Sir Ian Hamilton, K.C.B., D.S.O., who is detached on observer service with the Japanese First Army in Manchuria, has commented: "Major Motojiro's valiant death in combat underscores my contention that in modern war, morale must be the deciding factor. Modern armaments are such that only the strongest will can oppose them. We must take our lessons from the Imperial Japanese Army in this regard. Superior discipline, when combined with a relentless and aggressive spirit, are the keys to future victories," General Hamilton said.

10

RAIN STOPS PLAY

Within the wars of nations, another war is being fought between tradition and science for the soul of the soldier. Romance or knowledge: which best sustains a nation in the violent extremes of modern war? In the aftermath of the Great War, a professional soldier fights a personal war he does not understand.

Hmmm. God! Not another one of these bloody interviews for Southborough's lot. What a waste of time, and with this headache returning it will be agony. Must take some more powders before this chap arrives.

There. Thus fortified—well, a brandy would be better, but as it is still early in the day, mustn't set the others talking.

Right. Where's that dossier? Somewhere in this mess. Ah, there. Might as well have this fellow brought in. Get it over with. How many of these talks have I had? A dozen, two dozen? Every one of them dead certain he's right, and every bloody one of them contradicting the other. It's enough to drive one . . . Miss Banks, has Mr. Rivers arrived?

Ah, splendid, splendid, here you are already! Do please come in. Please be seated. Yes, just there. Splendid.

Well, sir, my name's Fortnum. How do you do, Mr. Rivers. Oh, I do beg your pardon. Dr. Rivers, yes indeed, Dr. Rivers. How foolish of me, of course it is; I see it just here. Ha ha. Well, not a very good start, is it? Early innings though. Shall I have Miss Banks bring in some tea—I would like some myself. Late night last evening, you know, and our days around here start earlier all the time, what with the reductions. *Àpres la guerre finis,* perils of peace and all that, you know, economies. Miss Banks, tea please.

Well, now, sir, I suppose our telegram was not very revealing, so I should just begin by saying how very grateful I am, indeed, how grateful we all are that you have merely taken us at that brief word to interrupt your work and come down to W. O. for this meeting. Yes, grateful.

I beg your pardon? Ah, no, nothing really wrong, merely a bit of a headache. Sure it will pass in due course. Let's see, where was I?

Ah yes, well, *de quoi s'agit-il,* eh? Perhaps you will have heard that questions have been raised in Parliament regarding the matter of what has been called, for want of a better name, shell shock. Yes, of course you have. It was in all the papers. Deuced complicated, if you ask me, don't pretend to understand half of it, the medical parts anyway. As for rest of it, the politics, you know, the Lords have registered concern over whether shell shock is to be regarded as, well, a legitimate, shall we say, authentic, war wound, although I must say that I myself can't see how one could come round to such a curious notion. As I say, it's all well beyond me. I wouldn't claim any sort of knowledge about the thing. No.

My role in all this? Yes, an excellent question. Yes, you should not regard me as anything but a minor clerk, you see. My only task is to vet, as it were to examine in advance, those who've been recommended by various authorities as persons who might contribute to the enquiry now in session. Lord Southborough, who I believe initiated the debate in the Lords, has the chair. Viscount Peel accepted Lord Southborough's motion on behalf of government, and the whole was given over to the War Office. That's where I come in, you see, yes. Think of me as a kind of Cerberus, ha ha.

Ah. Miss Banks, you and the tea are just in time. Rather warm in here, don't you think, Doctor? The tea should help. Yes, Miss Banks, just leave it. We'll attend to it ourselves, thank you. Now: thus fortified . . .

Yes, well: I would calculate we've had more than thirty witnesses before the committee thus far, all sorts, and I must say—for myself only, you understand—it has all been deuced interesting. General Lord Horne, of course, Lieutenant General Sir John Goodwin of the medical service, and many others have given most generously of their time and very extensive knowledge of the war. Rather like a history lesson to me, I can tell you. I didn't know the half of it, the parts I could fathom. Quite a lot of doctors, too, yes indeed, and, well, I must tell you I have been completely at sea, listening to them go on. Fearfully bright, every man of them. Not the sort of thing a soldier would hear in the mess, I can tell you, no. Still, a chap can learn a great deal, just by listening. It gives one a great deal to think about, it does.

Do listen to me go on. Quite absorbing all this is, to me at least, although I imagine you experts take it all on board without any bother at all. Yes. Well. Let me see, I suppose I should add to what I have said already that certain members of the enquiry have voiced a particular concern over the matter of pensions, you see, especially in our present circumstances. The general view seems to be that the cost of these will only rise with the passage of time. That is, veterans who 'til now have not come forward with applications for assistance with their medical problems will inevitably do so.

So we can only look forward to using more public monies, even as the government are trying to recover the costs of the war to the country. There are always the reparations from Germany, of course, but then one can hardly be sure of those, especially as she is in quite dire straits at the moment. None of it looks very good, you see, from any point of view. So I think it was in the way of looking ahead to these problems that Lord Southborough brought the motion in the first place. I've heard it argued in committee already that if shell shock be accepted as a legitimate result of war service we stand a good chance of being bankrupted by that malady alone, quite apart from the pensions we shall have to pay out for ordinary wounds, amputations, the blind, those who were badly gassed, and such. Well, I mean to say, we already have returns of more than a hundred thousand men claiming medical attention on account of, what's it called, neurasthenia. Deuced if I know what that is.

Well, anyway, I know this must sound quite ungenerous, Doctor, but among the members there is serious doubt that we can afford to recognize this particular disorder by itself as being worthy of a pension.

As against all this, there stands the question of the public's opinion. A goodly number of our fellow citizens, and most especially those on the Labour side of things, have been excited by the whole affair. Indeed, shell shock seems to engender very strong feelings all round. Private clinics and charities popping up everywhere to attend to these chaps. Very odd to me, I can tell you, that a chap who's lost a leg don't signify alongside one who's shell shocked. Can't account for it myself, most odd indeed.

Too, I would venture to say that the chances of public amity are not at all helped by the rather extravagant arguments advanced by some public figures, the general thrust of which is that the government are taking the side of ingratitude for the sacrifices made during the war, whereas the government were grateful enough when our victory hung in the balance. Throwing up to us that "home fit for heroes" business that came out during the war—promises casually made by members when we were in the thick of it, to boost morale and such. I should say, as well, that quite a number of former serving officers have not been helpful to the government side of the question. They seem not at all sympathetic to government's natural desire not to spend a farthing more than necessary. But if we save what we can, it all redounds to the public good in the long run, don't it? You will recognize, of course, how several quite complicated problems meet one another on this ground.

At all events, then, the government must protect against charges of ingratitude, of insensitivity to truly needy veterans, those actually wounded I mean, as well as against the view that the government are simply niggardly or perhaps incompetent to face up to these challenges, and I should think . . .

What, I beg your pardon?

Well, now that you mention it, I do believe this heat is coming up on me rather. The tea doesn't seem to have helped. I say, I wonder if you would mind awfully if I took a dram or so of brandy? Yes, that should do nicely, if you really don't mind. Would you have one as well? No? Well, so long as you are not put off.

No, actually, as you mention it, I do seem to be having these little spells. Spent some time in the Middle East, you see, before I went out to France. I may have picked up some bit of unpleasantness along the way; can't quite shake it. Yes, you are quite right, you and my friends agree: I should see a doctor, but, ha, ha, isn't that rich? Here I am, sitting right across from one! No, I'm sure this will pass. I shall be quite all right. Don't trouble yourself for a moment. But if you don't mind I believe I shall relieve myself of this tunic, yes, I think I will. Beastly hot in here, don't you think? There. Thus fortified.

That ribband at the top? Oh, well, the MC. A fellow's been around as long as I have is bound to come in the way of something like that, don't you know? Especially if one traveled about France in those days, you know?

Yes. Out in '15, after a year in Palestine and a bit in Cairo. Deuced hot there, I can tell you! Never let up, the heat. Most unpleasant. Mind you, some of the fellows liked it there, couldn't get enough of it. Blazing bloody thermometers as far as I'm concerned, though. Couldn't wait to get to France anyway, felt left out, don't you know? My own regiment went in fairly early on, so my posting out to the fringes of empire, as it were—well, I was left out of the big show, wasn't I? Doesn't do much good, being a soldier, if you aren't permitted to actually do any soldiering. The old ME was just about sweating in headquarters. No life for a solder. Good for the other johnnies, though. Happy to get back, myself. Happy as anything to see the old chums out in France. Good days for me, all in all, though, mind you, we had a few rough patches. Well, you know all about that, I suppose.

Well, what am I saying? I suppose I don't know very much at all about you, and that was to be the purpose of our meeting in the first place. Do forgive me, won't you? All that carrying on about the ME and France and whatnot.

There I go again, you see. Must be age: can't quite keep my mind on a thing very long, ha, ha. Well, Sir Frederick Mott put you up for our list of expert witnesses, Dr. Rivers. Quite complimentary, if I may say so. Said you had to be the one to talk to if we called no one else. I wonder if I might inquire, did you actually see service yourself?

No, I'm afraid I don't know Craiglockhart. Sounds a bit out of battery, ha ha. Where was it, Scotland? Yes? My lord! Farther out than France. And before that? Let me see, somewhere in all this paper, I seem to recall . . . yes, here we are: took degree at St. Bartholomew's, M.D. in '89, FRCP in '99, by then university lecturer in psychology, elected Fellow at St. John's in '02. Most impressive, I must say. But, look here, there's a note about some sort of expedition, Good Lord, to the Torres Straits, of all places. Good Lord. And then a book on it all, too. I shouldn't imagine I should understand a word of it: *The History of Melanesian Society.* Perhaps one day you could tell me of your adventures out there. My, my. And so on the basis of your professional standing, as it were, commissioned captain, RMC, in '14, with the following four years, ah yes, here it is right before me, in this Craiglockhart place. Tell me, was it a sort of asylum?

A shell shock hospital? An old hydro? My, my. Didn't know such a thing actually existed. Well, I knew some of the chaps were sent down, as it were, but I never dreamed . . . Most interesting, indeed.

But the front was a deuced big place, don't you know? All sorts of things happening I didn't know about, and happy for it. The regiment held just the tiniest of places; it was our own little world, don't you know? Yes. The world was literally whizzing by, and we saw little of it except the few thousand yards of front and our rear areas. I didn't even get back home after '15. I knew some chaps who took off for old Blighty whenever they could, but I never did. One has to hit a kind of rhythm out there, you see. I think going back home would've spoilt the rhythm, just when one had got used to it all, don't you know? Yes, two years before I was wounded and sent back. Yes. Close on to three, it was. Started as a lieutenant, came out a major, as you see. Family hardly recognized me. Well, there you are—as it is.

Now, if you would, Dr. Rivers, I don't suppose you could tell me a bit about this, this Craiglockhart place. What was it all about? What kind of work did you carry on? I must say, an entire hospital, just for shell shock? What sort of men came to you?

Mostly officers? Really. Well, I say. Wouldn't have thought that at all. I don't recall any of our witnesses thus far having made distinctions of rank. Indeed, my impression was those funking it came from the other ranks, don't you know? Well, my, my. What, er, could you, did you make of that? The mostly officers bit, that is . . .

Well now that you ask, I should have thought just the reverse would have been true. I mean, the officer chaps came from good stock, good families, well educated, public school and all. I grant you, of course, the best ones went first—Mons, Ypres, you know. Later on, as the casualties mounted, of course, it was true enough some pretty rum fellows came in behind. Not quite up to the mark, some of them. Funked it pretty badly, they did. But what could we do? No one else available, you see? I can see what you're getting at:

after the Regulars were used up and the Kitcheners and Lord Derby's men started coming in, I can imagine your trade improved, as it were, ha ha. Yes.

No? You saw cases like these straightaway as the war began? Among the old sweats? Well, I swear. Never heard of such a thing. Of course, being out in the ME then I wouldn't have known, would I? But look here: those young chaps were top drawer, real gamesmen, you know. Knew some of them before they went over. I mean, it wasn't as though they were the weak sisters. I could understand some in the other ranks, giving way like that, but the early officers . . .

I must say, Dr. Rivers, I wonder if you've got it right? Surely, a man's character stands for something? I mean to say, one could understand a young town fellow, no education to speak of and all, no family—well, none of any distinction that is—well, they wouldn't really have anything to fall back on, would they? What I mean is, well, you and I know very well there isn't much self-control in such people. Surrender to any notion that comes into their head unless they're watched over properly, what? Well, I must imagine more than half my time in France was spent trying to keep them out of trouble, just watching over them, seeing they did the right thing, you know?

Oh, well, now that you ask, I didn't pay much attention. I mean, I was hardly the one to mind about that sort of thing anyway, what with the tactical side of the game always in play. I don't know that we had very many shirkers in the R.W.F. Oh, excuse me, Royal Welsh Fusiliers. It was quite a special mob, you know. May've been a few, of course, always in the other ranks naturally. Didn't see any among fellow officers that I recall. No. Had a few cases of misbehavior and like that, usual run of things, a few lads not wanting to go out again, going absent after time in the rear areas, that sort. But even those you'd think doubtful at first stood up all right. One fel-

low, most extraordinary, couldn't bear his manner in the mess—
why, do you know he once claimed Homer was actually a woman?
Something of a bore. But a good officer, all the same, did his bit,
just like everyone else. No, the ones we sent back mostly were all
knocked about by shells and the like.

If I had to describe the lads I was with, I'd say they were, well,
stoic. Didn't seem to get the wind up, if you know what I mean.
Other ranks never blamed of that anyway. Well, if one doesn't have
the breeding, er, the background I mean, well, one hasn't the imagination to be afraid. Take things as they come, what?

Well, yes, naturally, there were those who came loose a bit after
being shelled and the like, you know, had their voices or hearing or
whatnot just blown out of them. One can't imagine the power of
those explosions 'til one's been through it. Never felt anything like
it. Fairly take your breath away, even if you're not very close. Feel it
all through your body, you do. No, a chap don't forget something
like that very soon. But with a little rest, one's right as rain, you see.
A little brandy or a tot of rum will always help too.

Well, it goes without saying some chaps couldn't repair on their
own, and that's where the old MO comes in. Ours were always first-
rate chaps. Right flash, some of them, just out from Harley Street.
Didn't go around mashing up the technical words, though. Straightforward. Yes, our lads thought the MOs were worth their weight in
gold. Chap's got a problem, off to MO, who likely as not was close
at hand, right with us in the trenches or not far back. Dash off to the
old doc, you know, get some powders, right back, that's what the
officers did. Then we made sure the other ranks got to see the doc at
regular intervals. In between, if one ran into trouble on patrol or
caught one in the trenches, the old docs were right there, yes, right
there. Can't say enough about their service.

Helped me a good deal, I can tell you, yes indeed. Just in the
summer of '16, it was, right before the Somme mess began in ear-

nest. The old ME unpleasantness came up on me again, caught a fever or something, couldn't stop shaking, sleep impossible, no appetite, sick to my stomach, that sort of thing. Well, old doc had me up again in no time. Kept me back for a while, let me sleep it out. Brandy without end. Best medicine in the world, brandy and a little sleep. Well, the headaches kept on, but what could anyone do about that, don't you know?

And I would have to say my experience was more or less typical in the battalion. Everyone, man and boy, got the wind up every now and then, you see. Just had to press on, no help for it. Keep yourself under control.

Afraid? No, not after the first bit, is one? What I mean to say is, it's only natural, that first time out and all, that one is bound to get the wind up. But after the first show why then one settles down, gets the rhythm of it. After that, should be all right. That's what I told the lads, I said, "Now lads, it's all right to get the wind up first action, perfectly natural, but then you'll see you can take it, and there'll be nothing to it. Act like you've been doing this all your life, you will," that's what I said to them. Well, I mean, there must be some little germ of fear here and there, don't you know, but then a man controls it, you see? Rather like riding a horse or driving a motor car. One grows accustomed, as it were.

I think our training had a good bit to do with it, too. What I mean to say is, a chap's new to the army doesn't know what to do, so we show him, show him what he must do in a certain situation, say, how to cover oneself during a barrage and the like, little things, how to use his rifle, the bayonet, and so on. Well, after all that, he knows what job he has to do, and what job the officers do, and this helps enormously, you see. Steels one for eventualities as it were.

Mind you, there were some of the lads who never should've been recruited in the first instance. Not at all up to the mark, and well, one way or another the front would show them up, so we'd send them away as quickly as we could. A goodly number of those were killed straightaway, however. Just not up to the mark. War has its way, you know, of seeking out those who aren't quite up to the mark. If the shells don't actually get 'em, the concussions will, don't you know?

Of course, that meant the show'd be carried by those who persevered, but isn't that always the way? No small number of the lads picked up the game, time and again, when the weak sisters funked it. Yes, those who stayed out the longest carried the heaviest loads.

Too heavy? I don't quite see what you're driving at. Well, now that you mention it, a chap could see rather more than his share of it. I suppose one could say there comes a point . . . well, I mean, how much can a man take of that sort of thing? One has to admit there is a limit somewhere.

Look here, this war . . . well, one couldn't say there'd ever been another like it, what with the constant shelling and patrolling and sniping and whatnot. And then the bloody MGs, the machine guns, you know, my word, the Boche were awfully good with them! Knock over a whole line while a Lark whistled his tune. Bloody dangerous, all in all. Smashed 'em down as best we could, but they always popped up again, you know, just like one of those children's toys. Didn't really have to kill a fellow to do the greatest damage, either. Wounding was just as good, from Fritz's point of view. Always had to tell several lads to drag the wounded back, then Fritz'd take on the stretcher bearers.

Well, I could go on, but you get the idea. That's the sort of thing that'll build up. Some of the lads just hit their limit, that's all. That holds good for the war as well. What I mean to say, no one would have thought it'd have gone on so bloody long. Of course, our side won the game, but, you know, I wonder now if anyone really won. One wonders if the war didn't just stop, you know, rather like a game when the weather's heavy. What's that the papers always say?

Rain stops play? Weather got too heavy, 's all. No blame there. Have to be sensible about it, you know.

Mind you, some weren't. Brigadier, fellow I knew from before the war, fairly got steamed up about the shell shock thing in '17. Said he wouldn't permit it in his brigade, said anyone claiming it'd be brought up on charges, court-martialed. Just wouldn't have it. Said a man had to control himself, that's all. Saw him at an *estaminet* somewhere round then. Said he'd turned over several to the provost already. Hope'd they'd be shot, he said. When I said "Steady on," he fairly flew at me in a rage. No good talking to him at all. Well, if you ask me, he seemed a bit out of it himself, poor fellow. Caught one in '18, when Fritz made his big push. 5.9 landed right on top of him, they said. Can't imagine what a shell will do to a man 'til one's actually seen it. Most fearsome. Looks like one's been ripped to shreds by some monster, if you can find the shreds, that is.

It was all so fickle, you know. Same thing could happen to anyone, any time. One just couldn't dwell on that sort of thing, just had to get on, you see, do one's duty. Anyway, that's all by way of saying there were some officers, mostly old seniors like this chap, never would give an inch. But for most of us, those on the line, you know, well, one couldn't be so sure . . .

Duty to what? I say, what a funny thing to ask. Well, to stick it, I suppose. That, and one's chums. Yes, that was the thing. One didn't want to let the side down, you see. Had to play up. Ah, no. I see what you mean. No. No. Didn't take long to know where one's real chums were. They were there, right alongside. Not in Blighty, for heaven's sake. Not with the strikers in the munitions palaces, to be sure. That's one of the reasons I didn't go home, you see. I saw too many of the lads come back, spirits all down because no one back there seemed to have any idea of what we were going through out here. Some of them came back hating their families on account of it.

Didn't want any part of that. Wanted to keep the war where it belonged, myself. Rather like bad wine, the war—didn't travel well.
Best left in the past, you see.

And now you have these shell shock johnnies, all's they want to
do is talk, it seems. Don't know why they don't just . . . well, stop
complaining. Goodness knows, there's enough to keep one occupied. Well, I mean there was the flu last year, bloody awful, all those
people taken down. Lost my daughter. That sort of thing'll bring
you up smart, what? So who are these fellows to complain about
their nervousness?

Anyway, the stronger one's character . . . Beg your pardon? Character's obsolete? Well, I swear. Then, if you're right, what's to replace it? What I mean to say, without character, man's not got a leg
to stand on. I mean . . . I mean, look here, you don't really fall in
with all that German psychological mumbo-jumbo? What do they
call themselves? Freudians, is it? Like this Meyers fellow, is that his
name? Deuced uncooperative, he was. Refused to attend the enquiry
at all. Said the establishment wasn't mature enough to hear what he
had to say. No. Rum fellow. Heard he resigned his post out in
France in '17. Fit of pique, just because no one'd listen to him. And
who's this other chappie? Yes, here it is, a Dr. Elder. Bit of a controversy out on Malta. I don't suppose you know either of these fellows? Do you then? Meyers was with you at Cambridge? Well,
then, what's his story anyway?

Shell shock is Meyer's invention? My Lord. But I have it on good
authority he's dead set against the whole notion. Changed his mind?
So the concussions haven't anything to do with it? But look here,
Dr. Mott thinks the matter of the brain is deranged by explosion
somehow. And didn't Meyers believe the same?

Well, sounds as though he came round to a more sensible notion.
Don't quite hold with all that, well, you know, all that rot about hating your mother and such. Wouldn't you know the Boche'd come up

with it. Far's I can see, well, they might well've hated their mothers, but no well-bred lad . . . So this Freud fellow's Austrian. Well, much the same, if you ask me.

So I say, what's the game now, as you see it, I mean? You know these chappies, what they think, and you've got your own experience with the shell shock business. What's your best guess? I mean, is it real?

I say, steady on. You won't get very far with the committee there. Courage is obsolete, or dead already? What do you mean, doesn't work? Well, if it's born into a chap . . . No? Breeding isn't important? Well, yes, I do remember your saying officers dropped out faster at first. All right, I follow, but still, family notwithstanding, a man's in charge of his own behavior, right? Well then, who is?

Sub . . . subconscious? Yes, I've heard some of the witnesses talking about that, though I can't say I quite get the thing straight. You mean, a chap's mind works on a kind of automatic? Yes, I see. I suppose I should make a note or two here. The committee chaps will be, well, intrigued by all this. Mind you, some of them are dead set against . . .

Repression, now what's that? A process and a mental state? Hmmm. Yes. And this comes about because of a conflict. Well, do you mean the fighting? No? A struggle between one's fear and one's sense of duty. Well, I say, this is most original. And what about old Freud's mother? Unnecessary. Well, I'm with you there, Dr. Rivers. Yes, indeed. Don't hold with all that mumbo-jumbo, as I said.

Look here: let's say this struggle, as you call it, goes on. Where does it lead? Wait a moment, must write this down: memories, even of recent events, pushed out of the conscious mind into the subconscious mind. Well then, what happens? A kind of rot sets in? Struggle to get out? Nightmares? Paralysis? My goodness, you mean a chappie could lose the use of an arm or leg just because of repression? His eyesight or hearing too? What about the shakes? I mean, could a fellow just not be steady? Suffer headaches and the like?

If I have you right, Dr. Rivers, I must say, your view differs substantially from that of some of our other witnesses. I mean to say, we've had Sir Robert Armstrong Jones in; he says all a chap needs is a bit of electricity and a doctor exercising firm authority to put him right. Says plenty of the lads have responded to his treatments. But it sounds as though, regarding this repression business, he demands that a chap simply put the bad memories out of his mind. I gather you and he are on opposite sides, as it were. Is that about it?

Yes, I can see how you would be. In your scheme, a cure comes about when a chap talks it all out, as it were, whereas Jones and others—there's this Yealland chap, for instance—they say just the reverse. Deuced complicated, if you ask me. What's a fellow to decide?

Yes, I agree with that, certainly. See what actually works. Well, did you have a measure of success at your hospital? Could you give me an example?

Sassoon? Why, yes indeed, I did know him. First class young officer. MC. Quite aggressive. Knocked about quite a lot, he was. Mad Jack, the men called him. Bit on the funny side, liked to go out by himself, hunting the Huns. Ran into a patch of trouble the year before the war was over. Something about denouncing the war and all. Well, I can't say I had any problem with that. Bloody f'ing mess by then, and everyone knew it. He didn't say anything the rest of us hadn't said. Well, he came back anyway. Stayed 'til he was hit again, just before the war was over, as I recall. Yes. Quite a remarkable fellow . . . You mean, he was one of yours? Well. I say. What's he at now? I mean, did he recover?

A poet? Yes, now that you mention it, I did hear something about all that, or, yes, I actually saw a volume in some bookstore or another. There was his name right on the front. I remember thinking, well, what about that. Old Mad Jack. Yes, I do remember. Well, good for him. Good for anyone who got out of the mess, more or less whole. Good for us all. Out into the new world, we are, though things don't look quite as bright as they did, mind you.

No. Thank you for asking, my headache is quite gone now. Knew the brandy would do it, after all. Best medicine there is. Good for the heat too.

Well, I think that will be all, Dr. Rivers. I believe on the basis of what I've heard here today that your testimony before the committee would be quite valuable indeed if you would consent to appear. I'm sure the committee will be quite grateful to hear what you have to say, yes, I'm sure of it.

And, with that, if you'll just allow me to shake your hand, Dr. Rivers. Yes. Thank you very much for coming down to talk. It's helped me a good deal, too, I must say, what I've understood of it all. Ordinary chaps such as myself can't hope to get it all on one go-round, ha ha, but I think I've got the run of it. Once again, thanks very much. Perhaps we'll see one another again when the committee reconvenes.

Good day, Dr. Rivers.

JUNE 3, 1922

The patient is a 30-year-old serving officer who joined a distinguished regiment in 1912 after Sandhurst. At the outbreak of the war he was on detached service with the Foreign Office in Cairo and spent much of his time in Palestine. While in the Middle East he married the daughter of a Foreign Office official and had one child, a daughter. He had also spent several months in hospital for recurrent episodes of severe fever of unknown origin but thought to be malaria and was so treated. When his regiment was sent to France he immediately petitioned for return to battalion duty, and this was granted in due course. He rejoined the regiment on the front in December 1915 and, notwithstanding repeated urgings from his superiors, remained continuously with his battalion until he was severely wounded in March 1918 and returned to England for a period of hospitalization. He was passed by the Medical Board as fit for light duty in August 1919 and was seconded to the War Office. Eventually, he was appointed principal army secretary to the War Office Committee Enquiry on Shell-Shock, in which capacity he was serving during our initial meeting.

On that occasion the patient appeared a fit, mature man of average height and weight. From his manner and mode of speech I reckoned him to be the product of a good country upbringing, perhaps of the middling class or slightly higher, which he later confirmed as being brought up, as he himself said, during an ordinary, untroubled childhood on a small estate in Devon. His family consisted of both parents, two boys of whom he was the eldest, and two younger girls. As he did quite well in school, it was thought he might make a scholar, but he had in mind from his earliest memories to become a professional soldier, a decision of which his parents did not approve but tolerated.

However, when we first met his complexion was somewhat florid, and he sweated profusely and complained in a rather casual way of sleeplessness and headaches. The absence of his right arm seemed to pose no obstacle to his movement or agility. Indeed, he did not once refer to the loss of his arm during the course of a conversation lasting the better part of an hour. He spoke with the rather rapid jollity common to serving officers of his type. Whenever he made reference to his own travails during the war his manner was rather dismissive, as if these were of no account. He spoke in a normal voice, neither raising nor lowering it unnecessarily, and to all appearances was perfectly at ease with his present situation. His only mention of any difficulty was in the form of an offhand admission that he was treating himself with "powders" and brandy, of which he drank several glasses during our interview. He seemed willing enough, perhaps mildly grateful, to discuss the war with me, even though he may have thought it slightly off-colour to do so, as among fellow officers talking about the war is even now considered bad form.

Two weeks after our first encounter the patient called upon me at surgery. He had been present in chambers during my testimony before the committee and appeared to be listening intently, alternatively frowning and smiling as I spoke. Afterward, he came up to me and thanked me more than profusely for agreeing to appear, saying he was sure the many misconceptions held by the several members would be put right because of what I had said. At the time he offered no hint that he was himself suffering any difficulty or that he would come to see me.

In our subsequent meeting he was as ever polite, calm, and well-spoken. By way of explanation for his unexpected appearance he said that his headaches had steadily intensified, that he had difficulty sleeping all night, and that his appetite was "not what it used to be." Upon further discussion, he admitted occasional sensations on his right side, as though his arm were still present. These sensations took the form of tingling, as when one took a hard knock on one's elbow. At times, he said, these sensations were of such intensity as to prevent his sleeping altogether, whereupon he would rise and take several brandies and eventually doze off just as dawn was breaking. After a short nap he would gratefully dress and go to his offices at the WO, where he would plunge into his work without pause until midafternoon, when he would go to his club and remain until dinnertime.

When asked what he thought was troubling his sleep, he answered that his domestic life had taken a turn for the worse after the death of his daughter during the flu epidemic just after the war. His wife had been inconsolable at the time, and as he was himself still in hospital he felt he had badly let her down just when she most needed him. He had convinced himself that he was in some way to blame for the loss of his child, thinking that if he had not been absent he would have been able to protect her from being taken away by the disease. He regretted deeply having missed so much of his child's life. He really had only a year with her before going to the front, and then the awkward months in the hospital, when he was in no condition even to hold her. Since then his wife had become more and more distant, staying with her parents in the country weeks at a time. He had been given to understand that she thought his presence in the house was a poor trade for that of his daughter. He confessed he had no idea how this state of affairs might be repaired.

I agreed at this second meeting to see the patient every few days, as frequently as our respective duties would permit. At the conclusion of this meeting he asked for "something more powerful" to help him through the night, and I agreed on the condition he make an effort to reduce his drinking and on no account to take brandy or any other alcohol at the same time as his medicine. I prescribed one dram of laudanum so highly diluted as to convey only the hint of an effect. To this he readily agreed. He seemed quite satisfied and bade me good-bye in a much more relaxed state than when he first appeared.

As it was evident that this officer had repressed a long war's worth of traumatic memory, my plan was simply to release those memories by revisiting his experiences. His illness was compounded substantially by the loss of his arm, the physically dramatic aspect of which had served to mask his psychological state from view so that his mood and behavior, if remarked upon at all by friends and family, were attributed to it rather than to his mental state. To his wartime complaints were added, at precisely the time when all his reserves were occupied by his physical pains, the very substantial depression brought about by the death of his child. I doubted very much his own version of the domestic events he related and suspected he had attempted to bury this great mental pain alongside all the others he was experiencing. I suspected he was himself the remotest figure in the house, not his wife. All these experiences in combination served to produce the most profound feelings of guilt, which I determined to relieve by means of providing him with a situation in which he could talk about his worries without fear of judgment.

The patient's vague recognition of his difficulties had brought him to me. He had, he said, gone a long way toward adapting himself to the random cruelties of the war, but as the war had gone on so long his toughness, which he considered substantial, had begun to give out. He felt that by the time of his most serious wound—he had been wounded less seriously several times before but had refused evacuation—he was completely worn out, no good to anybody, and had become in fact a poor officer. He had become increasingly concerned he would let his men down and that he could no longer effectively protect them. It was at this very time that he was hit by shellfire during the German attack in '18 that had been so disastrous for our side. He had been out in the open trying to organize evacuation of several dangerously wounded men when a very-large-calibre shell had landed nearby and nearly buried him completely in an old shell hole whose bottom was composed of glutinous mud. When he came round, he was choking on account of his mouth being filled with this mud. He felt he might drown in it but was eventually pulled from his near grave by a soldier who was himself then killed by another shell. Only when he was clear of the hole and in the protection of the trench did he realize his arm had been mangled beyond repair. Although still addled from shock and in great pain, he put a tourniquet on what remained of his arm and attempted to carry on until he passed out once more. He awoke in a Casualty Clearing Station some time later to learn that nearly everyone in this sector of his trench had been killed and that the whole battalion had been forced to retreat from the attack. He believed his own survival had been nothing less than a miracle, and not an altogether just miracle because so many had been killed.

When, during his subsequent stay in hospital back in England, he was told he was to receive the Distinguished Service Order for his actions, he refused at first, saying that losing an arm was in no way to be celebrated or admired. But the colonel of his regiment called upon him in hospital and prevailed upon him to accept the medal on the grounds that England needed every hero she could get at the moment. Contradictorily, he also implied that the patient should put the war behind him, not only for his own sake but also in memory of those with whom he had served, and who had served him so well. The colonel of the regiment also said that it was the patient's duty, as it was every officer's, to set an example by carrying on. The patient finally agreed, not altogether willingly, and not because such arguments as the colonel had made were convincing, but only because he hoped that by doing so he would not be forced to take up again such an unwelcome subject. That was why, during our first meeting, the patient did not refer to his DSO. Indeed, he had never put the ribband on his tunic, preferring instead to wear only his Military Cross, which he'd won, he said, during "happier times" earlier in the war when he was a carefree junior officer.

The circumstances of his wounding, and the events that subsequently transpired, excited considerable anxiety in the patient. By refusing the DSO at first, he was concerned now that his standing in the regiment, which he was most interested to preserve, might in some way have been damaged. He did not wish to be thought of by his fellow officers as in any way a complainer. He feared he had given the impression, too, that he had "given in" to bitterness about the war or his part in it. That was all right for the wartime officers, he said, but it was just not on for a regular. And, with war's end and the demobbing, one's standing was all the more important. A great many officers had been pushed out of service. Every day he read in the papers of former officers appealing to the public for assistance. What with an arm gone missing, he feared, his chances of ever seeing really active service again were bound to be quite small and his future in the army thus jeopardized. He wondered, indeed, whether he would even be permitted to remain in the army. He had a small private income, he said, but not really enough for more than a meagre existence for him and his wife in some village. The prospect of such a life filled him with dread. He used the word "barren," a word that took on greater significance when he revealed that his wife had told him she would have no more children even if she could. Because of all this, he said, he felt the world closing in upon him from all sides and sometimes wished he was back in the trenches when at least "life was simple and straightforward."

Our conversations developed along these lines over the course of several visits. He reported finding it easier to sleep through the night but would not hear of leaving off taking the laudanum, which he reckoned was the reason for his improvement. He said he was taking far less brandy and also that he'd recovered his appetite, though not to the degree of the "old days." His wife's mood, however, had not improved at all. Indeed, she seemed more distant than ever. He began taking long walks in Hyde Park and had recovered some of his old fondness for watching cricket, but he no longer had any use for the riding which had so enthused him as a young man. He said that when he looked at horses now, memories of their slaughter during the war came rushing back to him.

After a month, the patient abruptly ceased calling upon me. He sent a note, explaining that his duties at the War Office were very pressing as the committee was concluding its work and was in the throes of preparing its final report. He said that in a curious way participating in the proceedings had helped him to understand his own situation much more clearly than before. He promised to call upon me again when the press of duties permitted.

A fortnight later, notices appeared in the press of the patient's death by his own hand in the room of a commercial hotel near Euston Station. No one having heard the pistol's report, some time had passed before his body was discovered. On the writing table he had left a note, which only read "Rain stops Play."

  W. H. R. Rivers

11

THE FINAL WAR

Battle slowly releases its grip over the world of war in the twentieth century. Dreams of martial glory decay. War is no longer an affair of clashing arms. Mere victory is no longer the object of war. War has gone in search of a new shape, struggling against the restraints of custom or law. Now war can be aimed at the destruction of nations and peoples. Here, a contest between law and the new shape of war is fought in an old general's country house.

Tokyo, Japan, March 16, 1946
International Military Tribunal for the Far East
International Prosecution Section, Meiji Building
Memorandum for Mr. Keenan, Chief of Counsel and Section
From: Major Lewis Popper, Judge Advocate General, U.S. Army
Deputy Investigator, International Prosecution Section
Subject: Investigation of Ishiwara Kanji

Sir: The purpose of this memorandum is to obtain your permission for an investigation of one Ishiwara Kanji, Lieutenant General, Imperial Japanese Army, now retired. Certain intelligence, supplemented by our preliminary inquiries, suggests grounds for a formal investigation of this individual.

Our findings show this individual to have been in official proximity to several of the leading Class A and Class B suspects charged with war crimes by IMTFE. Inasmuch as IMTFE has commenced formal proceedings, it is imperative, given our difficulty in discovering documentary evidence, that we develop every line of investigation that promises an opportunity to supplement our case against the principal defendants.

Our findings indicate that almost from the outset of Ishiwara's long military career (1909–1941), he exercised considerable influence within and even beyond the Imperial Japanese Army. He is regarded as a man of formidable intellect who is also, for a Japanese, something of an individualist, perhaps even an eccentric. Toward the latter part of his active military service, he stood in direct and often rather public opposition to Prime Minister Tojo. After his retirement from the army, his public criticism of war policies led to his being placed under close surveillance by the Kempeitai. Several of our sources agree that although Ishiwara and Prime Minister Tojo have known one another virtually their entire careers, the deepest possible animosity exists between them, and that for his part Ishiwara has never been reluctant to express his personal feelings.

Thus, it is all the more puzzling why Tojo did not order Ishiwara's arrest when Ishiwara gave Tojo more than sufficient reason for doing so, and when many others who committed lesser offenses were jailed by summary executive order during the war. So far as can be told at present, Ishiwara's personal standing in the army has not been exaggerated.

To this must be added his popularity beyond the army, especially among the rural classes in his native Yamagata Prefecture but also well abroad in the nation. Ishiwara's father was a leading figure in a certain Buddhist sect, and after his father's death Ishiwara appears to have inherited his father's followers. Whatever the reason, there is little doubt of Ishiwara's popularity today. Until Ishiwara was officially proscribed from public activity by Supreme Commander

Allied Powers (SCAP), our field operatives reported that he routinely attracted audiences of 10,000 or more when he gave public lectures on Japan's postwar future. At a time when the dispirited Japanese public is more than willing to criticize anyone tainted by official association with the wartime powers, Ishiwara's standing is worthy of note.

If all this makes it seem that Ishiwara was in any way opposed to the rise of militarism and Japan's consequent imperial expansion, it is an impression far from the truth. Far from opposing Japan's advances in Manchuria and China, Ishiwara was at the forefront of those officers who relentlessly preached the necessity for an expansionist foreign policy. His differences with Tojo appear to have turned upon the means, not the objectives, of aggression. Further, Ishiwara's official positions at critical junctures in Japan's prewar history appear to implicate him in several cases in which charges are being brought against other Class A defendants. Others may have promoted aggressive imperial expansion, but Ishiwara appears to have made a philosophy of it.

There is some suggestion, however, that Ishiwara's views changed after it became clear that the Pacific war was lost, that is, after Tojo was ousted as prime minister. We have reports that Ishiwara began calling for the restoration of the Diet, the rejuvenation of the system of political parties, and even free speech. Inasmuch as SCAP will soon promulgate Japan's new constitution, the uncertainty of Ishiwara's position is of even greater importance. He might be the one figure from the old days who has any public or official credibility remaining. If for no other reason than this, IMTFE should arrange to interview him.

Assuming further investigation warrants testimony from Ishiwara, his actual appearance before the Tribunal is at this point problematic. Our sources indicate that Ishiwara recently was diagnosed during an extended stay in hospital here in Tokyo as suffering from a form of cancer which he is unlikely to survive. Since his discharge he has repaired to Sakata City to convalesce, and this place would likely be the venue of any deposition we might require of him.

In view of the foregoing, I recommend the authorization of a preliminary interview of Ishiwara Kanji and, should discovery of fact so indicate, the taking of a deposition which bears upon the facts of the cases being prepared against the principal war crimes suspects now in custody. The question of whether charges should be brought against Ishiwara directly should be reserved until the results of our investigation, if approved, are examined by the International Prosecution Section.

Lewis Popper, Major, JAG, U.S. Army

April 16, 1946
International Military Tribunal for the Far East
International Prosecution Section, Meiji Building
Memorandum for Mr. Keenan, Chief of Counsel and Section
From: **Major Lewis Popper, Deputy Investigator**
Subject: **Ishiwara Kanji**

Sir: Pursuant to your approval and guidance of March 21, I traveled to the Yamagata Prefecture on April 4 to conduct an initial interview with Lt. Gen. Ishiwara Kanji, now retired. The interview took place in Sakata City that day. A true copy of the interview transcript is attached herewith.

The entire transaction, including formalities, required less than an hour. The general seemed less fond of ceremony than one might expect. He appeared to be most anxious to get on with the interview. He seemed to relish the prospect of discussing matters he considers truly important. At present he is surrounded by a most obliging and attentive entourage, one that is unlikely to test the acuity of his ideas or his mind. General Ishiwara was therefore all the more disappointed to learn how little I know of Japan.

The suspect's physician was in attendance, although not immediately present during the interview. A subsequent discussion with the physician revealed a hopeless prognosis. Upon returning to Tokyo, I consulted further with American medical authorities, who confirmed the prognosis once they had read a translation of the physician's last report on his patient's state of health. When I inquired whether an independent medical examination would be necessary to establish the general's state of health for the record, I was told there was no need, that if the general's doctor was only half right, nature would soon take its course.

We therefore have at hand a dying man who was an important figure in significant events comprising the basis on which several of our Class A suspects will be indicted. It is almost certain that he was the principal author of the deception that served as Japan's pretext for the invasion of North China and the establishment of the puppet government in Manchuria. He may well have been involved in the assassination of the Chinese warlord Chang Tsu-lin in 1928. Almost as soon as he arrived in Manchuria as an operations officer, Ishiwara was in direct day-to-day contact with the notorious Colonel Doihara (now, of course, indicted as a Class A war criminal and in custody at Sugamo). We have evidence, too, that Ishiwara was directly involved in the so-called Young Officers' Revolt against the central government in early 1936, a revolt which, though unsuccessful in achieving its immediate aim, is now regarded as the inaugural event of Japan's slide toward totalitarian militarism.

Exactly why this man was spared the censure to which every other wartime critic was exposed is unclear at this juncture. His immunity from official retribution may well derive from the protection of very highly placed patrons. After Hirohito's surrender broadcast, Ishiwara was summoned by the palace to serve as an imperial counselor to the emperor. We suspect that this was by no means his first direct association with the throne, but the very nature of the Japanese political elite makes it almost impossible to be more precise.

He is even now routinely described as an important "moral" and "philosophical" influence in certain militaristic circles, although whether his intellectual gifts alone were sufficient protection must be regarded at the moment as highly problematical.

Lewis Popper, Major, JAG, U.S. Army

APRIL 30, 1946
International Military Tribunal for the Far East
Exhibit no. 33082c: Transcript of Preliminary Interview of Ishiwara Kanji, Lieutenant General, Imperial Japanese Army, retired
Principal investigator: Major Lewis Popper, U.S. Army, International Prosecution Section, IMTFE
Principal translator: Mrs. Kazuko Mitsui Nordstrom

LP: Let the record show that this interview is being conducted in Sakata City, Japan, on April 4, 1946, at the subject's residence. Present in the room are myself, three official translators, and one court recorder. This interview is being conducted by authority of and under the terms of reference specified by the Proclamation by the Supreme Commander for the Allied Powers, January 19, 1946, and the Charter of the International Military Tribunal for the Far East, April 26, 1946. For the record, sir, please state your name and current residence.

IK: Ishiwara Kanji. I live here now.

LP: Please state your military status at the time of the surrender of the forces of Imperial Japan.

IK: I was retired at the rank of Lieutenant General, Imperial Japanese Army, in March 1941.

LP: You are, then, a professional army officer?

IK: Yes, of course.

LP: Will you summarize your military career?

IK: I received my commission in the infantry in 1909 after my military schooling . . .

LP: Excuse me. You attended the military academy?

IK: Yes.

LP: Please continue.

IK: From 1909 to 1915 I was on regimental duty with the 65th Infantry. From 1915 to 1918 I attended the Army Staff College, after which I returned to my regiment until I was attached to the Department of Military Training with the Army General Staff. From 1920 to 1921 I served with the Central China Garrison at Hangkow, after which I was appointed lecturer at the Army War College in Tokyo.

LP: Was assignment to the faculty at the War College the usual path of advancement for an officer of your rank?

IK: I suppose not. I had graduated second in my class at the academy and also at the War College. Assignment as a lecturer was regarded as a mark of distinction.

LP: Did you regard it so?

IK: Yes, of course. I began to think seriously for the first time.

LP: What were your duties at the War College?

IK: I lectured on strategy and military history for one year. In 1922, I was sent to study in Germany for two years.

LP: What did you study in Germany, and where did you study?

IK: I studied at the Kriegsakademie in Berlin. Military theory, strategy, history, operational planning, logistics, tactics, the usual. I also studied the German language. Then I returned to duty at the War College in 1925, where I remained for three years as a lecturer.

LP: By 1928, what was your rank?

IK: I was promoted to lieutenant colonel that year.

LP: And then?

IK: I was assigned as an operations officer to the Kwantung Army Staff in Port Arthur, where I remained until 1932, when I was temporarily assigned for several months to the delegation to the League of Nations in Geneva. From 1933 to 1935 I commanded the 4th Infantry Regiment in Sendai, and in 1935 I was appointed chief of the Operations Section of the Army General Staff in Tokyo. Two years later I was promoted to major general and served as the chief of the Operations Division . . .

LP: Just a moment, please. The Operations Section and the Operations Division, these were different?

IK: The Operations Section was one of several sections overseen by the division. I took over the division in 1937.

LP: And then you returned to China?

IK: I was appointed vice chief of staff of the Kwantung Army in Manchuria, not China. I served there, in that capacity, until the end of 1938, when I returned to Japan. Manchuria then was Manchukuo, a [pause] client state of Japan's.

LP: What were your duties when you returned to Japan?

IK: As I was out of favor with the ruling clique, I was given insignificant duties, command of depots and such, until I was ordered to the retired list.

LP: So, for the whole of the war you were inactive?

IK: I was retired from the army, but I was not inactive. I continued my writing and lecturing. After leaving active service I was appointed to the faculty at Ritsumeikan University in Kyoto, and I engaged in certain political activities.

LP: Are you still engaged in academic and political activities?

IK: I resigned my faculty appointment after one year, a resignation that was required because of my political activities. I continued to speak before public gatherings until my work was proscribed by the occupying powers.

LP: How would you describe your political activities during the war?

IK: I opposed Tojo's policies and spoke out against them from 1938 onward. From that time, perhaps even before, I was under official surveillance.

LP: By whom? By whose orders?

IK: By the Kempeitai, of course, who else? I imagine Tojo or one of his stooges gave the order, I don't really know.

LP: So your ideas and Tojo's are opposed?

IK: Tojo has no ideas. He only has policies. I never knew him to have ideas of any kind.

LP: But Tojo was prime minister, he ran the war.

IK: Tojo ran the war. Tojo was simply a dangerous mechanic.

LP: What do you mean by that?

IK: He believes only in mechanics. All life comes down to simplicities. If life can be well organized, that is all he wants. Organization, not ideas, that is the true foundation of his behavior. Tojo has no real ideas because he believes all ideas are worthless. His is truly a corrupt mind, a mind that denies itself.

LP: If you spoke out against Tojo as you say, why were you not arrested along with others who opposed him?

IK: Ask Tojo. I can only surmise that he did not wish to bring criticism upon himself from certain quarters.

LP: What quarters?

IK: In the army, among the younger and field grade officers, and, at least for a time, I enjoyed supporters in the Kwantung Army.

LP: And what was the basis of your reputation? Your opposition to Tojo?

IK: No. That was merely the logical manifestation of my views. My opposition was logical, derived from knowledge I had acquired as the result of two decades of study. Those who understood my views understood the value of logic, unlike Tojo. He was oblivious to logic. That must be clear now.

LP: Is it true that you were known as "the genius of the army"?

IK: The ignorant are impressed by titles, slogans, signs. Those things mean nothing. They are substitutes for thinking for oneself.

LP: Your studies, did you write?

IK: Yes, of course.

LP: Has any of this writing been translated? Into English, that is? Or any other Western language?

IK: No. I read Western languages. Why do Westerners not trouble with Eastern languages?

LP: Many do. I only have French and German myself.

IK: I think Westerners do not believe Eastern languages important. Westerners believe the world will eventually belong to them. You Americans believe the world should belong to you.

LP: Americans have no imperial ambitions, not like . . .

IK: Come now. You have your empire, and it is growing, flourishing, I might say. You deny to others the right to do what you have done.

LP: We did not start this war. Japan did.

IK: You did start it. You started it well before 1941. You started it with your diplomacy, with your immigration laws, with your embargoes, with your League of Nations. You, and the Russians.

LP: The Russians? You mean the Communists?

IK: Yes, the Russians, the Communists now, who are only Russians dressed up with Marxist ideas. They are still dreaming of their empire, and now they want a world empire. They may well get it, if you are not careful. And in the contest between your empire and theirs, you will find that you need Japan on your side.

LP: Under the circumstances, I fail to see how Japan could be of help to anyone.

IK: All this will pass. History will go on, according to its own pace and purpose.

LP: Karl Marx would agree with you.

IK: Perhaps in general. Not in the particulars. But I have explained all this in my writings, which you cannot read, of course.

LP: We must come back to the particulars. State exactly your position on the Kwantung Army staff from 1928 to 1932.

IK: I've said already that I was in operations, the G-3, you would call it.

LP: You were not merely in operations, were you? You were operations, for all intents and purposes, were you not?

IK: I was the principal deputy to the chief of operations for the Kwantung Army.

LP: The name of your superior?

IK: Itagaki, a colonel at the time.

LP: Is this Itagaki Seishiro, now general, who is in Sugamo Prison on war crimes charges?

IK: Oh, well, he has been charged with a crime then? I knew only that he was in prison.

LP: Yes, I mean, no: he is being held on suspicion of having committed war crimes. So are quite a few others. So is Doihara Kenji. I understand that you and he were in Manchuria at the same time. You worked with Doihara, did you not?

IK: He was not a member of the headquarters staff. His duties lay elsewhere.

LP: I should say they did. We know that he was an intelligence officer, of course, and an agent provocateur and an assassin besides. We know he commanded the Special Intelligence office in Port Arthur. And we know that he was behind almost every nefarious deed perpetrated in the Far East during those years.

IK: He never seemed busy to me. An assassin too! Those are the charges against him?

LP: Some of them.

IK: You mean to hang Doihara, do you not?

LP: If the court so pleases.

IK: Oh, I am certain the court will so please. How convenient for the Allied Powers to have these courts. Official murder can be made legal. What a wonderful idea!

LP: You are hardly in a position to be sarcastic, you know.

IK: I am in the best position of all to be sarcastic. I am dying.

LP: Was Doihara ever present when you performed your duties?

IK: Not often. Men who do his sort of work lead very irregular lives. And his addiction to opium did not contribute to his reliability.

LP: Doihara was addicted to narcotics?

IK: You didn't know. Yes. He was quite enslaved by it.

LP: Just as he meant to enslave the Chinese.

IK: The Chinese have been telling their old stories.

LP: We have evidence Doihara did all he could to flood Manchuria with narcotics, as a way of enfeebling the populace. We have evidence that you assisted Doihara in this campaign.

IK: From Tokyo? From Sendai?

LP: What?

IK: These were my last postings before I left active service, as I have told you.

LP: I did not say when Doihara undertook this work.

IK: Doihara conducted no such operations while I was in China.

LP: Are you denying any part in these operations?

IK: I am denying that Doihara had any part in such a program. Doihara saw Manchuria as a future colony, a bulwark against the Russians. If all the Manchurians were besotted with opium they could not have served such ambitions as Doihara had.

LP: You have logic. We have evidence.

IK: Perhaps you have misunderstood Doihara. He was always rather [pause] unruly, willful, if I may say so. And, as I have said, the Chinese . . .

LP: Yes, telling old stories.

IK: Exactly. The Chinese were always quick to complain when we protected our colonists from being murdered by their bandits, and they would always pretend their bandits did not exist. I was amazed that the world was always so ready to listen to the Chinese and so ready to deny the truth when Japan told it. When the Lytton Commission made its report, we realized we would never convince the world that our view of China was the correct view. We realized that we alone would have to correct matters in China.

LP: Was this your belief when you served as a member of Japan's delegation to the League of Nations?

IK: Almost every member of our delegation felt the same. And our instruction was that if the League accepted Lord Lytton's report, we were to withdraw altogether from the League. We would not be bound by the rules of those who refused to acknowledge our inter-

ests and our rights in our own region. To do so would be tantamount
to surrendering our national freedom. Our interests required that we
address China's disorderly condition; the other great powers denied
us that right.

LP: The right to deny China the same right you claimed for yourselves? I should say so.

IK: The West will never understand the East. The West will never
understand China. The West will never understand Japan.

LP: You and the other China ronin went further. You were sure the
West would never understand about China, but you were also sure
that your own political superiors in Japan would never understand
about China. You refused their orders when you were told to desist
from any more operations against the Chinese.

IK: Of course we were not ronin. In our tradition, the field commander is permitted to refuse unrealistic orders from afar. It is his
duty.

LP: You considered Tokyo's orders to cease fire unrealistic?

IK: We did. We had made gains and would make many more before we could give up our operations. We would not quit success.
That only made sense to us.

LP: In our army, such behavior would have led to a court martial.

IK: I don't believe you. Your army is not so highly disciplined.
You would never discipline a successful officer for misbehavior.

LP: Have you ever heard of General Patton?

IK: No.

LP: So even if an officer were successful, your army would have
disciplined him if the facts of a case so warranted?

IK: Yes. We executed several of our own officers for the so-called
Young Officers' Plot, if you will remember. And perhaps you did
not know that the survivors of the mutiny were very tough. They
were punished but they did not die easily.

LP: Let the record show that at this time the interview was interrupted by the subject's physician, who insisted on his patient's rest.

JUNE 1, 1946
Confidential, Mr. Keenan's Eyes Only
Memorandum for Mr. Keenan, Chief Counsel
From: Major Lewis Popper, Deputy Investigator, IMTFE
Subject: Ishiwara investigation and Emperor Hirohito

Our brief conversation after this morning's staff call moves me to write in some haste. I had not realized our pretrial preparations were so well advanced. I apologize if my outburst caused alarm or gave offense. I certainly meant no disrespect to you or anyone else in the chain of command.

However, if your forecast is correct—that SCAP will soon announce a decision not to proceed against Emperor Hirohito—I cannot urge too strongly that the results of my investigation, tentative though they are, be taken into account before a final decision is reached. I am convinced that any decision taken in their absence would be fundamentally flawed.

As the attached interview transcription shows, Ishiwara Kanji was one of the most influential army officers in the two decades immediately before Pearl Harbor and was intimately involved in many of the events we can now show contributed to the rise of Japan's militaristic imperialism. Indeed, it is difficult to imagine very many significant military developments in which Ishiwara was not involved, if only indirectly. Allow me to enumerate only some of the more important of these developments.

One Colonel Komoto, of the Kwantung Army's Operations Division, was directly implicated in the assassination of the Chinese warlord Chang Tso-lin in 1928. When Komoto resigned under pressure from Tokyo, Ishiwara was the officer sent to replace him. Ishiwara took up Komoto's mission: to wreck Chinese resistance in Manchuria by any means and to pave the way for the establishment of a puppet state in Manchuria as a buffer against further Russian expansion from the north.

Once in place, Ishiwara did not disappoint his superiors' faith in him. He conspired with Colonel Doihara himself, then in charge of the secret intelligence service in Port Arthur, against Chinese sovereignty. We have some evidence, poorly developed thus far, that Doihara and Ishiwara were at the forefront of Japan's "narcotization program," aimed at using opium addiction as a weapon in their campaign to colonize Manchuria.

There is no doubt at all, however, that Ishiwara was the mastermind behind the so-called Manchurian Incident of 1931, a piece of sabotage against the South Manchurian Railway, staged to seem as though carried out by the Chinese. As Ishiwara planned, this poorly disguised bit of theater served well enough as an excuse to send even more Japanese troops from Korea and from Japan itself onto the mainland. Although the initial sabotage was carried out by a Captain Kawamoto, Ishiwara himself is reported to have participated in a bombing raid on Chinese positions at Chin-Chou, north of Port Arthur.

When the international community protested these brazen acts of aggression, and political authorities in Tokyo ordered a cessation in the fighting, Ishiwara and his fellow army officers refused these orders, citing the supremacy of operational expediency over national policy in time of emergency. No doubt it was Ishiwara himself who had the presence of mind to evoke this dubious principle. Even as the controversy raged, Ishiwara sent his agents into the towns and cities to create the impression of general lawlessness. Faced down by Ishiwara and the other so-called China ronin, the moderate cabinet of Prime Minister Wakatsuke was eventually forced to step down.

Far from damaging Ishiwara's reputation, the Manchurian Incident made Ishiwara a respectable figure in political-military circles. Among the extreme militarist cliques, Ishiwara was well thought of. As if to prove so, Japan dispatched a delegation to Geneva after the Lytton Commission censured Japan's actions in China and Manchuria. Ishiwara was one of the delegates. Significantly, this was the delegation charged to arrange for Japan's withdrawal from the League.

In 1936, during the most dangerous period of the so-called Two Twenty Six Revolt, Ishiwara was placed in command of martial-law headquarters in Tokyo. Although the young officer-revolutionists argued that they only meant to save Hirohito from corrupt advisors and civilian bureaucrats, the danger to the emperor was real enough. That Ishiwara was one of the officers chosen by the military establishment to restore order in the imperial capital is indicative of his professional standing at the time.

Paradoxically, his standing was increased by his opposition to expanding the war in China after the Marco Polo Bridge incident in 1937. Although his position seemed a reversal of his views six years earlier, he had not become less aggressive. He now argued only that Japan needed to avoid further entanglements on the mainland in order to build up even greater strength for the final war with the great Western imperial powers. By 1937, he argued, China was to Japan as Spain was to Napoleon's France—an "ulcer," in which little could be accomplished by fighting a war of points and lines. My suspicion is that from this point on his relations with Tojo, never cordial, worsened.

Nor was Ishiwara's standing diminished by his subsequent opposition to Tojo and his wartime policies. Immediately after the surrender, Ishiwara was invited by the palace to serve as an imperial counselor. Perhaps palace officials were merely trying to realign the imperial household with more "moderate" elements in national life. So misshapen is Japanese national life at this juncture, Ishiwara can be made to seem like a moderate. He has shown that he is anything but that.

As I have tried to show, Ishiwara's activities intersect substantively with the very highest levels of politico-military policy and action. He is now one of the few former military officials who is capa-

ble of articulating clearly and unapologetically the ideological basis
of Japanese aggression, a talent all the more important after one
hears the nostrums offered by Tojo and his gang. Most important,
however, Ishiwara could be compelled by the court to testify directly upon the precise nature and character of imperial power and
to provide concrete examples of how it was expressed during the
critical period from 1931 to 1945.

After having interviewed Ishiwara and studied our transcription,
it should be clear that palace officials are trying to protect the emperor behind a cloud of misinformation, distortions, and outright
lies. Ishiwara's testimony of course would bear directly on the question of Emperor Hirohito's culpability and would go a long way toward preventing further attempts to obfuscate. SCAP might welcome the elaborations on recent history that Ishiwara could provide;
and there is no doubt that SCAP's final decision would be a good
deal more informed than one made now.

For these reasons, I respectfully urge you to petition SCAP for a
deferment of his decision until such time as our investigation of
Ishiwara Kanji is completed.

Lewis Popper, Major, U.S. Army

JUNE 2, 1946
[True copy of handwritten note attached to transcription]

Dear Major Popper:

I have your memorandum, dated June 1, in hand. The case you
discuss therein shall, in my opinion, be settled before very long. I
believe I indicated as much during our staff meeting, and I would
ask you to treat this information in the same way as all other pretrial
information, as privileged and confidential. You might well imagine
the consequences of a breach in our security at the present time.

I am sure I do not have to convince you how precarious is the situation in Japan at the moment. The nation is a perfect wreck. Only

the Allied Occupation forces stand in the way of Japan's utter collapse. At the same time, important and persuasive voices are being raised back home which argue for the complete dismantlement of Japan's ancient culture and the completest possible subjugation of her population. Our duty lies in assisting General MacArthur to steer between these dangerous reefs to a fair shore.

Aside from ensuring a modicum of public order and support, SCAP is in the midst of drafting an entirely new constitution for Japan—a constitution that will enjoy many unique and quite progressive features. It is General MacArthur's judgment that only under a constitutional aegis will Japan be able to bring herself to a point of reconstruction in which true progress is possible. Here is where our own welfare and that of Japan are conjoined, for a subservient or perpetually weakened Japan would be all the more defenseless against the ideological forces we now see gathering against world peace. I do not think I need say more here.

However, it is within this context that I hope you will see the path which has been chosen with regard to His Majesty. Only by seeing the longer run, by fixing our eyes on the future rather than dwelling unnecessarily on the past, may we succeed as God has given us the right and wisdom and strength to succeed. Under the present circumstances, therefore, I hope that you will confine your investigation to the immediate suspect and his liability to further charges. I look forward to reading your final report. We have much yet to do. I would not want to expend too much of our limited resources upon only one suspect.

     Yours truly,

     [Unsigned]

     Keenan, Chief Counsel, IMTFE

JUNE 1, 1946
International Military Tribunal for the Far East
Exhibit no. 47739f: Transcript of an interview of Ishiwara Kanji,
Lieutenant General, Imperial Japanese Army, retired.
Principal investigator: Lewis Popper, Major, JAG, International
Prosecution Section, IMFTE
Principal translator: Mrs. Kazuko Mitsui Nordstrom

LP: Let the record show that this interview is being conducted in Sakata City, Japan, on May 22, 1946, at the subject's residence. Present in the room are myself, three official translators, and one court recorder. This interview is being conducted by authority of and under the terms of reference specified by the Proclamation by the Supreme Commander for the Allied Power, January 19, 1946, and the Charter of the International Military Tribunal for the Far East, April 26, 1946.

LP: Good morning, General.

IK: And to you as well, Major. You have been offered refreshment?

LP: I [pause] yes, thanks. I should like to ask whether you have been interviewed by anyone else from the occupation authorities since my last visit.

IK: I am told I was visited by two Americans, but I was unable to receive them.

[*Investigator's note:* We have been unable to ascertain the identity of these two men. We suspect they were journalists. I have ordered the house guard to detain them should they reappear.]

LP: Because of your health?

IK: Yes.

LP: General, I must ask you to regard yourself as under house arrest from this moment. You may not travel or receive guests. You are permitted no official visitors unless specifically approved by me.

You are not permitted to communicate with the public in any way or by any means. If you wish, you may engage legal counsel.

IK: May I ask the reason for my arrest?

LP: You are placed under arrest because you are suspected of war crimes. A formal document in your own language will be delivered to you later today.

IK: Do you know the specific crimes I am suspected of committing and are you permitted to discuss them with me now?

LP: Yes, of course. You are under suspicion of conspiring to plan, prepare, initiate, or wage aggressive war.

IK: Yes, well, it does not appear to have been sufficiently aggressive after all.

LP: I see you still will not take this seriously.

IK: I beg your pardon. I have no wish to be impolite. But I must say that this tribunal of yours seems rather dubious. If you wish to kill those whom you have vanquished, why not do so promptly? There is no law against war. What authority would make such a law? And what authority is there to enforce such a law? Therefore, a trial is superfluous. I should think firing squads would serve your purposes equally well without all this tiresome play-acting.

[*Translator's note:* A brief discussion follows between the suspect and the translator over the best way to render the Japanese phrase for "play-acting."]

LP: My purpose here is not to debate international law with you. We claim the precedents of the Hague Convention of 1907 and the Red Cross Convention of 1929. Japan was a signatory to both of these and furthermore agreed *mutatis mutandis* to the Geneva Convention of 1929. You may accept or reject these as you wish, but whether you approve of our legal standing is quite irrelevant to these proceedings.

IK: I see several difficulties, if you will permit me to say so. You may well claim these precedents, but the international bodies that gave them life are now defunct. This is not merely a theoretical question, you see. I take one of the functions of a law-giving body as creating and building a system of laws and procedures by which it works—the rules governing its conduct, rules so that the law may not itself tyrannize those whom it is supposed to protect. Obviously you mean to argue that the alliance you represent serves as the defender of these imaginary principles of international law. But that is not the whole matter, for there remains the question of the law under which you mean to have these trials. Under whose rules, I would ask, and by whose philosophy of law will you conduct these trials?

LP: I reject categorically your line of argument. If, as you say, we may do what we please by right of conquest, I say that by right of conquest we propose to conduct a trial of those who have committed crimes against humanity by means of aggressive war.

IK: Yes, you now have the power to amuse yourselves as you please. But please do not ask us, the victims, to believe that you are genuine or sincere. If, at some point, you do wish to retrieve your principles, you may wish to recall an ancient principle of your law, handed down by the Romans—where there is no law there is no crime; where there is no crime, there is no punishment. Waging war, even aggressive war, is not a crime.

LP: Fortunately for you, General, I am not the one to be convinced. However, I am quite sure the court will be unsympathetic toward your claim to be a victim here. In any case, these are matters for your lawyer to consider. On questions of law, you are clearly beyond your ken.

[*Translator's note:* The interview is interrupted by a discussion between the suspect and the translator over how to render the English word "ken," which in Japanese serves as the term for Japan's prefectures. Here follows an extended discussion—in Japanese—on this coincidence of language until Major Popper intervenes.]

LP: If we might remember why we are all here, perhaps we could move on? Very well. I am particularly interested in your role during the so-called Marco Polo Bridge affair in the summer of 1937.

IK: During the business at Lukouchiao I was in Tokyo. I don't know that I had a role.

LP: You were on the Army's General Staff at the time. Of course you had a role.

IK: You may be surprised to learn that merely being on the Army General Staff was not itself a guarantee of being at the center of every event.

LP: But you must have known what was happening at the time. What was your relationship to these events?

IK: I did know. The local command informed us as soon as the skirmishing with the Chinese garrison began, and we ordered them to solve the problem locally.

LP: But they did not solve the problem, did they?

IK: There, at Lukouchiao, and in Tokyo, of course, different opinions prevailed. After a few days, we did manage an armistice, but fighting began again.

LP: This incident began your war with China.

IK: Relations with the Chinese had not been favorable for quite a long time.

LP: And in fact the General Staff saw this incident at the bridge as an excellent opportunity to expand further into China, did it not?

IK: You must not see the General Staff as completely in agreement with itself on this question. Several of us believed that the way in which we responded to the business at the bridge was the wrong way. We believed Russia was far more dangerous to us than China. China was attractive but it was a strategic distraction. Throwing our army toward the Chinese meant that much less protection from the Russians. That seemed self-evident to me at the time.

LP: Did you voice these opinions in official circles?

IK: I did.

LP: And how were your opinions received?

IK: The General Staff directed the immediate reinforcement of the Kwantung Army, so one must suppose my advice was rejected.

LP: How long did you then remain on the General Staff?

IK: Shortly after this incident I was transferred to the Kwantung Army.

LP: In what capacity?

IK: I've told you already: I was assigned as the vice chief of staff of the army there.

LP: Was this a demotion? Were you officially disgraced?

IK: I was promoted to major general.

LP: Just a moment. You took a line opposite to the one adopted by your government, and adopted by your colleagues on the General Staff, and for this you were promoted and made one of the senior officers responsible for the very operations you opposed?

IK: Yes.

LP: How do you account for this?

IK: I don't account for it at all. One could speculate, but I have no way of knowing why this happened. I was a senior officer. I had a certain amount of experience in China.

LP: A certain amount of experience in China? I should say so. When you reached China, er, Manchuria, or Manchukuo as you called it, were you able to moderate the army's reaction to the incident?

IK: Not noticeably, but as relations with the Russians along the Manchurian frontier were worsening, and as our own people were being killed by Chinese terrorists, the whole matter was becoming so serious we were busy with operations.

LP: Did the emperor exercise command over Japanese forces in Manchukuo?

IK: The General Staff exercised overall direction, but day-to-day actions were impossible for them to keep up with. We directed those.

LP: Did the emperor exercise command over the General Staff in Tokyo?

IK: If I understand your question, then, no. The General Staff exercised broad control over all field commands on the basis of direction from the army minister. Of course the whole government answered to the emperor, but the emperor was not an executive of government in the way I think you mean.

LP: Could one say that the emperor exercised influence, then?

IK: Yes, of course.

LP: A great deal of influence? Very little influence? How much?

IK: The emperor is the embodiment of our national soul. [*Translator's note:* I have rendered the Japanese word *Kokutai* as "national soul."]

LP: And in 1937, the national soul aimed to make war on China and dominate Southeast Asia and the Southwest Pacific all the way to New Guinea and westward to include even India itself?

IK: Not to make war. The China incident arose originally because China's relationship to Japan was improper. It happened that force was occasionally required to establish a proper relationship. You must understand that China had been in a process of disintegration for a long time. China had no real government, no social order. Banditry and terrorism ruled the villages, which were helpless in their poverty. Look then at Japan during the same time. Japan showed the world that it was capable of correcting China's decline, but because of China's disorganized state Japan had to play the role of the big brother, to impose some discipline on China. That meant our presence was required, would of course be resisted, and would of course require highly disciplined military action if our goals were to be accomplished. I have said already that the means of extending Japanese influence were a matter of dispute. There was little disagreement that Japanese hegemony was inevitable. As to the matter of whether the emperor commanded events, I do not think the emperor was pleased with the army. After a certain point, he had little choice but to agree with the course of affairs.

LP: What certain point?

IK: When the army minister and the army's chief of staff assured him the situation could be cleared up in a short while, we committed more troops in Shanghai. Then it became clear that the situation was only getting worse. What could anyone do after that? Then we were victims of our own miscalculations.

LP: Did anyone completely oppose your operations in China? Did anyone argue that Japan had gone too far in China? That Japan should leave China alone?

IK: To leave China? No. Perhaps the communists, or other enemies of the Kokutai.

LP: Kokutai is your expression for Japanese nationalism, isn't it?

IK: Kokutai is how our nation follows the imperial way, the essential, spiritual character of our way of life as a race. We believe that way expresses the highest spiritual achievement of our race.

LP: You believe the Chinese would have been well served by following your example?

IK: Yes. We believe our way is worthy of emulation by any moral people.

LP: You believe Japan was so "worthy of emulation" that it was worth making war on people who did not agree.

IK: In my experience, armies are not the best means of spreading spiritual ideas, but as I have already explained, force is sometimes required in a lawless situation.

LP: Do you understand the concept of "crusade"? Would you characterize your operations as being in the line of a crusade?

IK: Perhaps. And, as with all the crusades, the understanding and the motives of those who took part were by no means the same. Some sought to spread their ideas. Some were on a quest for power, or wealth, or some other advantage. Some wished to affirm their superior nature over others.

LP: But Japan's expansion in Asia served all these purposes.

IK: Yes, to a certain point. Sooner or later, those who were insincere were revealed.

LP: But that did not prevent Japan from going on. In the end, that did not prevent Japan from widening the war against China.

IK: The fundamental principle was unaffected by these developments. The Asian way will be better for the world than the Western way. History will show this to be true. For the moment our way has been defeated, but defeat is not a permanent state of history. You did not have as much to do with our defeat as we did ourselves. We were not worthy of victory. We believed our way was worthy of imitation, but we were not so morally advanced as we believed, and so we failed. But our failure will be overcome by our moral progress. When we have attained complete moral power the world will enter a new, higher stage of development. History looks eagerly toward our regeneration.

LP: So history is on the side of the war criminal?

IK: You must not allow yourself to be blinded by the present. The crimes, as you call them, of this war and all wars can be left behind when we achieve the next stage of civilization.

LP: We may yet transcend our shortcomings, then?

IK: You need not be so smug. The ultimate stage of democracy is chaos, spiritual destitution. Perhaps I will not see it, perhaps you will not see it, but there will be another war, a final war, between Asia and the West. And we will emerge from the destruction as the ultimate moral power on earth.

LP: We've heard all this before. Just like the Thousand-Year Reich, isn't it? The rest of the world is soft. Decadent. Doomed. You chosen ones, you are stern, hard realists, unsentimental. You claim you own the future. Oh, you'll have to set aside morality for a minute, just for the sake of the future. But, don't worry, trust us! Once we've burned your books, once we've cleaned out the population, when everything is sorted out for the New World Order, we've done as much as redefine the future.

You guys. Nazis, Marxists—doesn't matter, one religion's like any other. You guys have got yourselves organized just to shape me up. Well, General, I've just spent the last five years in the army, and I'm just about as shaped up as I ever want to get. You guys should have saved yourselves the trouble. I'm with the rest of the world: I'll take my future straight, no ice, no chaser. I don't mind if life is messy.

But I'm curious now. This apocalyptic future of yours: you decided on that long ago, I'd bet, long before you became a student of war. So all your books, all your studies—they were only meant to provide the argument for your conclusions, weren't they? No wonder you weren't permitted to go any higher. Did your colleagues regard you as radical? How about Tojo? Or even the emperor? Where did he stand in your ultimate world?

IK: Perhaps you want to know if I am a fanatic? If Tojo is a fanatic? If the emperor is a fanatic? I think I have the right word. Is that how your superiors see us? Merely as a nation of fanatics? Will you put all of Japan on trial? Line up all of us to wait our turn at Ichigaya?

I wonder if you would agree that your President Roosevelt was a fanatic? To us he was. He would not see reason. He drove us into this war. He could not accept our growing, rightful power. He made an unnecessary war on us. He encouraged our enemies in China, and even the Russians, to attack us. He commanded the destruction of our cities. Do you realize that reports of cannibalism are reaching us from the country districts? We can no longer feed ourselves.

Is this the work of a righteous nation? No. You are already victims of your power. You do not know where and how to show your strength. Your mistakes do not matter at the moment, when you are so much more powerful than all other nations. But one day, your mistakes will be dangerous.

LP: I've had enough of your sermons for today. You were a leader in an army that massacred hundreds of thousands of innocent people for no reason other than you could. Even the Nazis professed a purpose for their murders. You murdered innocents for the pleasure of it. You were a leader in an army that stole its own nation, and then turned that nation over to a gang of militant imperialists. You have shamed your ancestors, you have defiled centuries of rich and noble tradition. No excuse, no justification could erase your crimes.

You must continue to regard yourself as under house arrest. The military police will not allow any visitors without my permission. This concludes the interview. Good-bye.

IK: I look forward to our next meeting, Major.

OCTOBER 19, 1946
Top Secret, One Working Copy Only of _____ Copies
International Military Tribunal for the Far East
Investigator's File
Subject: **Ishiwara Kanji**
Transcript of an interview of Ishiwara Kanji, Lieutenant General,
Imperial Japanese Army, retired
Principal investigator: **Lewis Popper, Major, JAG, International**
Prosecution Section, IMFTE
Principal translator: **Mrs. Kazuko Mitsui Nordstrom**

LP: Good morning to you, General.

IK: And to you, Popper. I thought I would not see you after the trials began. Those of us in the country, so far away from Tokyo, must survive on rumors from the wider world. Have the trials indeed begun? What of the imperial house? We heard that His Majesty might abdicate, perhaps in favor of Prince Chichibu.

LP: Yes, General, I can see how you are rusticating here. Aren't you still an imperial counselor? Are you of Chichibu's party, or do you still favor Hirohito?

IK: I favor only Japan, and I am now and evermore the servant of my emperor. The affairs of the imperial household are beyond my [pause] ken.

LP: I've come this morning, General, to clear up a little mystery. I hope that you might assist me. When we last met, I asked if you had

received any other Western visitors and you said that two men had
come, but that you had not actually seen them. Do you remember?

IK: I do remember.

LP: Were these men in uniform, do you know?

IK: Yes, I saw them waiting for me in the garden. I had the impression they were officers. You know how officers look in normal
attire. Very few look comfortable. These two did not.

LP: Did you notice anything else about them?

IK: My eyesight is not so good at that distance. I could not see
their faces. One was older, one seemed quite young. The younger
deferred to the older, as usual.

LP: What if I were to tell you that the older man was General Fellers, one of the most influential members of General MacArthur's
staff?

IK: I have met this general. I do not think this was the same man. I
would have recognized him, I think.

LP: Where and when did you meet General Fellers?

IK: Earlier this year, once in Tokyo and once here.

LP: I'm afraid I must ask what was the subject of these meetings?

IK: Why not ask General Fellers?

LP: I shall. But now I'm asking you.

IK: General Fellers was interested in the emperor's activities during the [pause] incident.

LP: Why must you use this term? If you mean the war, why not
say so?

IK: Yes.

LP: So: which activities during the war?

IK: General Fellers was interested in knowing how much His
Majesty had to do with the routines of directing the war. What were
his habits of rule as the war was concerned. What were his relation-
ships with the prime minister, the army and navy ministers, and
other members of the cabinet at various times. Those kinds of
questions.

LP: And was General Fellers satisfied with your answers?

IK: He said he was. He seemed very anxious to be satisfied. He went on for some time about how it was important to clarify the imperial relationship with the government.

LP: What seemed most important to him when he spoke about this matter?

IK: General Fellers seemed to be interested in emphasizing that His Majesty did not direct the war. He wanted to be certain of what would be said during the trial. We spoke for some time about the [pause] complex connections of His Majesty to the government. He thought it was important to show that His Majesty stood above such ordinary matters, that he concerned himself with ordinary matters only at extraordinary times.

LP: Ordinary matters at extraordinary times. I've heard this expression several times of late. Did General Fellers say this?

IK: Yes. I thought it was an excellent description of the emperor's way.

LP: So, you and General Fellers were fundamentally in agreement about the emperor's role in the conduct of the war?

IK: Yes.

LP: And will you be testifying?

IK: Yes, of course. Did you not know?

LP: It often happens that one part of the Occupation does not know what another part is doing.

IK: And you are not of very high rank.

LP: A fact often pointed out to me during my association with the army.

IK: You do not like being in the army, do you?

LP: Of course not. I wonder how anyone could like being in any army.

IK: The life of an officer is not to everyone's taste. To everyone's taste, that is the phrase?

LP: Yes, not to everyone's taste. Will you be seeing General Fellers again?

IK: Yes. I expect I shall see him again before I testify.

LP: I wonder—did the general say that he had talked with others about this?

IK: I do know that he had already talked with Tojo Hideki.

LP: About the emperor?

IK: Yes.

LP: And?

IK: The same matter that interests you—the relations between His Majesty and the government.

LP: What is Tojo's position? What did Tojo say?

IK: Tojo assumed complete responsibility for the direction of the war.

LP: The emperor is, or was, *genshu,* he is *daigenshui.* Tojo had no such power. The emperor is hiding behind Tojo. If he is head of empire and supreme commander, how could a mere prime minister assume full responsibility? Hirohito can't have it both ways—he can't assume power only when it suits him and evade its responsibility when it doesn't.

IK: I see you have been making a study of us. Are you attempting to trick me with a lawyer's play on words? Is this what I have to look forward to when I testify?

LP: I don't know that you will testify, despite what you've been told. It seems the verdict is already in. Perhaps you will have heard that your emperor will not stand trial either?

IK: Yes. General MacArthur himself said so, I am told.

LP: A new shogun.

IK: Your voice tells me you do not intend to compliment your general.

LP: By the way, how are you enjoying your house arrest?

IK: I knew you were merely pretending to be angry. I have done so myself, many times, when I was on active service. I also knew that your authority was not greater than General Fellers, who sometimes also enjoys the authority to speak for a higher-ranking officer. In any case, your rank was not so high, so I merely ignored your order. In any case, my state of health will not permit me to abuse my freedom.

LP: I see. Fellers was not the older man who came to see you. MacArthur. It was MacArthur who came to see you. No. Don't say anything. He and Hirohito are much the same. Power without principle.

IK: Power is the right way, but we can see how power leads one into darkness if it is not used with discipline and wisdom. We are inevitably brought to clash with one another because of it. The world will find peace only when power is put in its cage, when all eight corners of the world are under one roof.

LP: General, I must say good-bye. I leave Japan tomorrow.

IK: Tomorrow? Such a hasty departure.

LP: I have resigned my position and my request for release from active service has been granted. I am under orders not to speak with anyone about the findings from my recent investigations.

IK: Have you just been violating those orders by speaking with me?

LP: Most assuredly. I am considered politically unreliable and my superiors believe I can no longer be trusted to deal officially with matters of high-level importance. They would be very upset to learn that I had come to see you today.

IK: You believe the emperor is guilty of war crimes and have said so officially.

LP: Yes.

IK: You believe your superiors have conspired to suppress evidence and corrupt the proceedings of the Tribunal, and you have said so officially.

LP: Yes.

IK: And now you know the consequences of your beliefs.

LP: Yes.

IK: But you have honor, even as you fail.

LP: Yes.

IK: I bid you farewell, then, Major Popper.

LP: Good-bye, General.

IK: Major Popper?

LP: Yes, General?

IK: You could be Japanese.

12

AT THE FAIR

Is global hegemony a nation's most perilous state? A superpower displays its wares and its ideas in a modern marketplace.

Narrator: Each year the Association of the United States Army holds its annual convention in Washington. All the largest defense corporations in America are represented, and a few foreign companies as well. Even some smaller companies manage the expensive exhibitor's fees too, hoping to land a major deal with the Pentagon. For some of these exhibitors, a deal at the AUSA meeting could be a make-or-break proposition.

Intermingled with the corporate vendors—as they are called sometimes—are exhibits sponsored by the army itself. Information booths from various commands, units, and organizations from around the army are put on display for the corporate vendors and the 30,000 members of the official and quasi-official public that tour the convention—politicians, officials from other parts of the government, businessmen from other industries, and high-ranking military officers from the army and the other armed forces.

As with any trade show, this one is punctuated by live music, ceremonial dinners and speeches, attractive announcers, as well as those who could be regarded as the ultimate customers of the many crafts represented here—soldiers, fresh from America's battlefields, ready to tell their own stories.

Those who attend this convention can be expected to have certain views in common, and in their own way represent the state of American official thinking about war and peace at the beginning of the twenty-first century.

Convention Manager Max Schelling: This is one of our most important conventions here at the Washington Convention Center. It'll take up more space than the boat and car shows. Military equipment is really big stuff—I mean, not many boats are as big as the Abrams Tank. We've even got a V-22 in here and that belongs to the Marines.

Interviewer: Didn't the Marines have some trouble with this plane? Lots of crashes and that sort of thing?

Schelling: Yeah, I guess so. It's here now, though. We have more than 500 exhibits here today, lots of the defense companies and then the rest from the army. But even Homeland Security has a big exhibit, all about fighting the G-WOT.

Interviewer: G-WOT?

Schelling: What? Oh, I see what you mean. Yeah, that's the Global War on Terror. Or terrorism. Can't remember which.

Interviewer: How about Amnesty International? Do they have a booth? Doctors without Borders? U.S. Institute of Peace?

Schelling: [chuckle] Very funny. No. I can see where you're going with that. This is not a political meeting, you know. Say, are you sure you and your crew are accredited with the convention press authority?

Exhibitor video: The Super Chief XC 5.56x45mm lightweight modular weapons system is a follow-on to the earlier CXC variant

VI that developed a combinatorial weapon system based on a standard platform using separable KE (Kinetic Energy) and IIE (High Explosive) modules. Leveraging Boeppler and Bloch GMBH's world-class experience in small arms, the XC 5.56x45mm is currently in a limited redesign phase that will terminate with Limited User Testing (LUT) in late 2005 or early 2006. This weapon system, when finished, will optimize soldier firepower in close-in expeditionary operations, especially in the urban environment. B&B's objective is to provide a platform that offers rapid user alterations (in less than five minutes) under field conditions, even under fire, from the standard shoulder-fired rounds for intermediate ranges to the carbine version for use in highly confined spaces to the longer-barreled precision required for sniper action. The B&B Super Chief is the perfect soldier weapon for the future operational environment. Several world-class armies are considering a wholesale adoption of this weapon system.

Exhibitor: Here, pick this baby up. Sure. Go ahead. There you go. Pull that lever. See? We have five different models. You can fix it up with different barrels. Twist that. One barrel is for close-in stuff. There's another for high-volume shooting, hundred rounds at a time for suppressive fire.

That? Why that's your grenade launcher. 40mm. Hell, you can turn this thing into a shotgun in about a minute if you want to.

You can change out the sights too. You got your basic iron sight, you got your close combat optic, your infrared point and aim lasers, your thermal. Man, you can just about see around corners with this baby.

We're pretty sure we're going to get the contract for the army. Technology's just way past that old gun. This is not just a gun, this is a system.

Interviewer: How does this system compare with the AK-47?

Exhibitor: The old Kalashnikov? Hell, there is no comparison. Trouble with the K is, everybody's got 'em. Must be zillions of 'em around the world. The communists saw to that. World'll be a better place when there aren't any more Ks out there. But, I'll tell you this. The XC is worth about five Ks when you consider the firepower you can put out. And that's what the soldier wants: firepower. Stand the two up against one another, the XC will win the fight every time.

Interviewer: In your experience, does that happen very often? One on one?

Exhibitor: Naw. Not if you work it right. You just want to drench the bad guys with fire if you can. Man, I wish I'd had this in Nam. We could've really done some damage.

Narrator: A recent report from the General Accounting Office shows that the percentage of high-ranking military officers who retire and find employment in the defense industries is on the rise. Often these officers do exactly the same work they did in uniform. All evidence suggests that the relationship between the defense industry and the armed services is far more intimate than when President Eisenhower first warned of the "military industrial complex" in the 1950s.

Conventioneer: [overheard in conversation] So I said, I said, you don't know who I am, do you? And then they said, oh general, I didn't recognize you there for a minute. After that, it was all sweetness and light. Before, they wouldn't have given me the time of day, but then it was like I was still on active duty. I got a car to take me around, and everybody was happy to brief me out on the latest developments, show me the statements of work they had going. It's a real advantage, especially with friends still on active duty. And I think that's the best way to do business. Doesn't everybody benefit?

Exhibitor: Here at Maximcorp we provide services to the army that would otherwise take them away from warfighting. The warfight is what we are all about. You don't want your soldiers worrying about laundry. You don't want 'em thinking about pulling KP at the mess hall, like we did in the old days. You don't want your soldiers doing that kind of housekeeping stuff, which really doesn't have anything to do with fighting. You want 'em doing what they're trained to do—the warfight. So we do their laundry, feed 'em, put up their camps and maintain 'em, make sure they have recreational facilities—you know, basketball courts, weight rooms, movies, a PX, that kind of thing. We want everybody to keep his mind on his business in the field, and we can make our business out of that.

Interviewer: When you say "in the field," is that everywhere, around the world?

Exhibitor: Everywhere. We've got contracts from Romania to Korea and every place in between.

Interviewer: But we aren't at war in Romania or Korea.

Exhibitor: The soldiers have their jobs to do everywhere, even if there's no fighting where they are.

Interviewer: So the days are gone when soldiers have to set up and maintain their own bases?

Exhibitor: Look. Two things. First, today's soldiers are different. They aren't draftees you can just jerk around. They're volunteers. They won't put up with the shit we took when we first went in the service. Second, we don't have enough of 'em to go around. So you pay people to come in and do noncritical jobs.

Interviewer: In places that are hot, your employees are put in the middle of it too, aren't they?

Exhibitor: Well, sometimes you just can't avoid getting caught in a fight. The other side always gets a vote, they say. So, yeah, some of our people have to be armed, for self-protection, you know? So if things really get hairy, they can defend themselves and maybe even help out the soldiers.

Interviewer: Is there, is there a line somewhere that you can't cross? I mean, you hire people to build and maintain bases, do the laundry, and run the messes and so on, and sometimes you fight too. What's to keep us from just hiring a private company to do the whole war? That's happened before, you know, and the result was not quite what the nation wanted.

Exhibitor: The United States did that? When?

Interviewer: No. But most of the Europeans did it at one time.

Exhibitor: Oh well, that's history. I wouldn't know about that.

Interviewer: These installations you're building and running: they sound a lot like the base camps we had in Vietnam.

Exhibitor: Yeah, but there was Vietnamese working there and you just couldn't trust 'em. Not to mention they were lazy. Now our company, we just use Americans. I think that's a good thing for the army and a good thing for the American economy.

Narrator: Most of the exhibits here use state-of-the-art presentation technology—multimedia light and sound shows, holographic displays. Many have trinkets to give away to people passing by. Grand Corporation has books to give away, but it appears not many of the conventioneers are interested.

Grand Corporation spokesman Douglas Trumbull: Grand Corporation helps governments around the world think through their most difficult problems. We've helped organize national elections in South America and Eastern Europe. We had a team of economists recently in a certain country, helping to level out its balance of payments problems. Using our plan, they'll cut their inflation by one-third over the next decade. We've even reorganized several governments and streamlined a few armies, mostly in Africa, where there's lots of capital from natural resources but no tradition of responsibility. Our budget runs to 1.6 billion a year and we don't make a single tank. We sell our expertise. And we sell good ideas, as everyone knows.

Interviewer: What does Grand Corporation do for the army? Why do you have a booth here?

Trumbull: The booth is here to remind everyone of the work we

do and how much they can get out of us for a very small fee, relatively speaking. Armies sometimes talk themselves into a corner, assuming every problem can be solved with firepower. Just solved, not
necessarily the best way. Have a problem? Call up the tanks, drop a
2000-pounder. I think we've learned enough from hard experience
to know firepower is just not a one-size-fits-all solution.

Interviewer: Would you say that's a sentiment widely shared in
the Pentagon today?

Trumbull: Our revenue has fallen off a bit in the United States.
Other countries seem to be more receptive to ideas in general these
days. If I had to say what change there'd been recently, that would
be it. Ideas don't seem to carry as much weight in certain circles as
they used to. Everyone thinks he has the answer, but that's not usually right. Business may be looking up, though. We're far enough
into this thing now. Even the Pentagon is looking for help.

Interviewer: By "this thing," you mean the war in Iraq?

Trumbull: Wars, I'd say. Make it plural. We seem to have several
going at one time now.

Professor Jacob Engelmann, Johns Hopkins University: Walking around these exhibits, you'd be forgiven for thinking the Cold
War was not over after all. All the usual players are here, just as
they were in the old days. Big defense contractors. Pentagon bureaucrats promoting their favorite project. All the army propaganda
booths. The generals, anxious to please everyone, hoping for a
postretirement job, secretly despising everyone not like them. Everyone sensitive to the slightest deviation from the ultimate message.

Interviewer: What's the message?

Engelmann: Everything's all right, just right. Not a hair out of
place. Everything's under control. But everything's not all right. See
that portable bridging unit? Wonderful piece of machinery. Lots of

training required before you can actually use the thing. When the hell are you going to use that? When did we use something like that anyway? World War II? Look at the other displays. You've got tanks so big the C-5 can hardly lift them. Impressive on the ground, but how many do you need in Grenada? Panama? Colombia? The Philippines? Afghanistan? Iraq? How many of these do you really need in a modern army, unless you're planning to fight someone exactly like yourself? How many mirror images of the United States do you see out there? I'll tell you: none.

Does that mean we have fought our way through all our enemies? Not by a long shot, because the number and kind of enemies we have today is far different from the number and kind of enemies we had during the Cold War. People with fifty-year-old guns and cell phones are spoiling our victory parades.

But here we are, fifteen years after the end of the Cold War and our military services really haven't changed. And they're quite comfortable with that. Our enemies should be too.

Interviewer: What is a best-selling author doing at the AUSA convention?

Peter Haywood, best-selling author: I was invited. In my latest book, *Deadly Horizons,* I imagine a chase scene through the convention center. The hero is after a rogue general that the establishment has protected, and he finally uncovers the general's scheme to sell nuclear secrets to Arab terrorists. I thought it would be fun to see the exhibits and see some of the people I wrote about.

Interviewer: You've been quite a friend to the military over the years. All of your books have dealt with them in some way. How are your friends taking this latest book?

Haywood: Oh, the reception's been terrific. They can always relate to my characters and the situations I put them in. It never fails that someone will come up to me and say, "I know a general or whatever just like that. Did you base your character on him?" I always do book signings on the shopping concourse at the Pentagon. The line this time stretched all the way past the barbershop. People at the bookstore say my signings draw a bigger crowd than Bob Woodward or Colin Powell. And that's really something.

I wanted to do something a little different this time, you know. Like, a little farther away from Tom Clancy and more in the direction of John le Carré, where the characters are a little deeper and everything isn't so obvious.

Interviewer: Le Carré's view of the world is a good deal darker and more complex than Clancy's, isn't it? Le Carré's been very critical of the United States in recent years. Is that where you wanted to go?

Haywood: No, I think Le Carré's gone off the deep end lately. Sometimes I think he'd be happy to see the U.S. suffer more than it has. His earlier books were better—*Spy Who Came in from the Cold; Tinker Tailor.* I didn't want to get on his soap box. I don't think my readers would put up with that. I have a lot of friends in the military, and they've given me a lot of help over the years. And I've tried to help them over the years, too. I think America has a lot to be proud of and I think we're going to need the military more than ever, what with the war against terror and everything that's happened since 9/11.

Interviewer: In your early books, the Soviets were always the bad guys. Now it's Arab terrorists. Do you find it more difficult to write about them?

Haywood: Not really. The names make it a little more difficult, but bad guys are the same all over. A Russian bad guy is just like an Arab bad guy. And they have the same goals, really. America's their target, and it has to be defended. I take the same viewpoint when I do op-ed pieces.

Interviewer: You've been doing a lot of those. One has the impression from your articles that the military has as many enemies in American politics as anywhere else.

Haywood: There's no question in my mind that the liberal politicians are good at getting us into trouble without figuring out how to solve the problems they create. And of course the military can't speak out, defend itself, so I speak out for them from time to time. They need someone to talk back to the politicians. And I think that's something I can do. I have a lot of friends in the political world too.

Interviewer: You're still welcome at the Pentagon and the White House, then?

Haywood: Sure, more than ever. It was the liberals that coddled the Arabs and never held them accountable for their actions. This administration isn't about to do that. These guys will stand up and fight, and I'm for that.

I do a lot of speeches these days. I'd say my op-ed pieces had more to do with getting invitations to speak than my books. Maybe that's because the people who ask me to speak don't get much of a chance to read books, but what I have to say in the op-ed pieces resonates with them. They'll take the time to read a few inches of newsprint. Not a book. I enjoy giving speeches so I go do that whenever I can. And from time to time I'm invited to come in to the Pentagon, get some briefings on current ops, that kind of thing.

Interviewer: Are you asked for an opinion?

Haywood: Yeah, I am. And it looks like they take my advice sometimes. I'll have a session with these guys, you know, and a while later something will happen and I'll go, hey, they're doing what I said to do. So that's gratifying. It's hard to prove, of course, because a lot of these ops are classified, you know, special ops, but, hey, there's this feeling that I'm having an impact, you know, doing some good. I've even done a few small missions for them, but I can't say much more about that.

Interviewer: So you don't see a conflict between your role as an author and Pentagon advisor?

Haywood: None at all. In fact, they go together real well. I spend a lot of time paying attention to military affairs, and I've learned a lot about all of it. Now I don't have a fancy degree from Harvard, but I've managed to teach myself what I need to know. And the guys in the Pentagon recognize that.

Interviewer: So in the Pentagon you're considered an authority on modern warfare?

Haywood: Sure, why not? My opinions are as good as some cheesy, antimilitary college professor making fifty grand a year, or some twerpy guy writing for the *New Yorker.* Everybody's a critic. No one's ever satisfied. They're ready to believe the worst about our military. They'll say anything. At least the military guys can see that I'm a friend. Listen, these people in uniform today are some of the finest people you've ever met, intelligent, decent, self-sacrificing. Real patriots. And I think that's a fine thing, and they deserve all the support we can give them, no matter what. This country's at war, you know. We've all got to stand up, make a contribution, see this thing through to the end. That's all.

Interviewer: You see an end?

Haywood: Of course I do. Just look around you, all this fantastic equipment, computers, weapons no one ever dreamed of a few years ago. So we can take all this stuff and beat 'em where they live, because if we don't they'll come back here to make war on us and do more harm to our country. And we *will* beat 'em too. There's no way these guys can beat us. We'll win. I'm sure of that. But it's gonna take a lot of sacrifice, and I'm not sure America's faced up to that yet. A lot of people seem to think the terrorists are just gonna fade away. I don't. There's no negotiating with these people. They hate Americans and everything we stand for.

Interviewer: If they can't win, why are they fighting?

Haywood: I just don't know. Hate does funny things to people. Makes 'em irrational. Doesn't make sense to get in a fight you can't win. Take the suicide bombers. Using your own life as a weapon. How does that make sense? You kill yourself, and you kill a lot of people, ordinary people, who aren't fighting you. Men, women, children, makes no difference, as long as there's killing done. And it really doesn't accomplish anything, like a real war. I don't call that warfighting. That's just the work of fanatics. I do know this: we'll have to keep fighting 'em and killing 'em, and then one day it'll be over and America will be safe again.

Interviewer: How about your next book? Working on one?

Haywood: Yeah, I've always got a book going. This one's got the President as the main character. This time, the Man himself is going to be at the center of the action. He'll really mix it up with the terrorists, you know, kind of like Harrison Ford did in *Air Force One.* That was something. So, I thought this would make a new kind of book for me.

Interviewer: You think John le Carré will like it?

Haywood: Naw, probably not. As I said, he's way past his good books. His day, you know, the old Cold War, that's over. People don't buy his kind of books anymore. It's a new world order out there, and whether the terrorists like it or not, it's our world order. America is the superpower and some people, like the French, just can't stand it. Well, as far as I'm concerned the French are some of the best friends the terrorists have, and if we're not careful we'll end up being like the French.

Interviewer: Like the French?

Haywood: Yeah, you know, decadent, more concerned with themselves than acting like real world leaders. I mean, after all, the French haven't won anything since World War I, and that's only because we were on their side. The French are really just living the good life, hiding behind our power like the Japanese, never putting in their fair share for world peace, taking the heat when it's necessary.

Interviewer: How do your books do in France?

Haywood: I don't have any sales in France. Too hard to translate, I guess.

Announcer at the Stryker Armored Vehicle Display: The Stryker Armored Vehicle, formerly the Interim Armored Vehicle (IAV), is the centerpiece of the army's newest fighting formation, the Brigade Combat Team (BCT). The Stryker represents a completely new concept in modern American warfighting. The Stryker is not a tank but a light armored vehicle (LAV), capable of carrying a complement of mounted infantry directly into the close-in fight and supporting them throughout their mission. It is powered by a Caterpillar engine and is capable of speeds up to 60 mph and a range of 300 miles. The Stryker rides on run-flat tires that can be inflated or deflated from inside the crew compartment, according to surface conditions in its tactical area of operations. Its armor protection can defeat 50-caliber bullets, and its overhead cover can protect the crew from 152mm airbursts.

Two different models are in production: an Infantry Carrier Vehicle (ICV), and a Mobile Gun System (MGS) which mounts a 105mm cannon. Until the MGS can enter the inventory, the Infantry Carrier Vehicle will be mounted with an Anti-Tank Guided Missile System which will be able to blast through reinforced concrete—an especially valuable capability on the modern urban battlefield. The army has contracted to purchase 2,131 Strykers at a projected cost of $4 billion.

Six Brigade Combat Teams will be organized around the Strykers in the next three fiscal years. Each of these brigades will have 300 Strykers and will be manned by 3,800 soldiers, including 1,400 infantrymen and 250 scouts, formed into three infantry battalions, a cavalry battalion, and an artillery battalion with M198, 155mm howitzers, and counterfire radar.

The Stryker BCT is unique among army units in that it points the way toward the future of American ground warfare. The BCTs pack a deadlier punch than traditional light units and are more easily deployed than heavier armored units. Command and control of the BCTs includes a fully networked digital command, control, communications, intelligence, and surveillance (C4ISR) system that integrates data through Force XXI Battle Command Brigade and Below (FBCB2) software from satellites, sensors, vehicles, and aircraft, including unmanned aerial vehicles (UAVs). No other unit in the army's force structure can match the BCT's fighting scope and lethal power. Moving soldiers and weapons systems more rapidly over greater distances to fight in the full spectrum of modern warfare, the Stryker Brigade offers a powerful new capability to American ground forces in modern warfighting.

Brigadier General Thomas Berrigan, U.S. Army Program Manager for Stryker Combat Development and Training: To be frank, we've been resting on our laurels. Warfare has changed, and we haven't changed with it. That's what Transformation is all about. We've got to leverage technology and fight smarter. We have to acknowledge the real world. That's really what Stryker is all about. It's a means to an end, and that's accomplishing the mission with speed, agility, and firepower. Have you read the Chief of Staff's new paper on Transformation? Very powerful. Very powerful. The Stryker is the army's answer to the new world of warfare. It's the centerpiece of army Transformation. You know we developed and fielded the Stryker in four years? The vehicle and the units that'll take it into the fight. That's a record for the Pentagon. Never been done before.

Interviewer: You mean like the atomic bomb? That took about four years.

Berrigan: Yeah. Exactly. Well, no. Those were simpler days. Ancient history really. We've got a much more complex world today. You've gotta be able to get to the AO ASAP with enough combat power to sustain yourself until the rest of the force closes. We gotta have heavy power out there, but with less weight. That's key. We want to throw Strykers on the plane and move 'em into the warfight. Set the terms of the engagement from the first. Halfway around the world if we have to. We can get the SBCT to the AO in 96 hours, and we can put a whole division on the ground in 120 hours. That's our goal. That's powerful.

Narrator: Late in 2003 the first Stryker Brigade deployed into Iraq's Sunni Triangle and early in 2004 replaced the 101st Airborne Division in northern Iraq. Staff Sergeant Carl Pettis of Tacoma, Washington, served in the brigade until he was wounded during a raid in Samarra. He is currently assigned to the prosthetic rehabilitation unit at Walter Reed Army Hospital. He was asked by his superiors to attend the convention and talk about his experiences.

Staff Sergeant Carl Pettis: I spent as much time in Strykers as anyone, I guess. Worked on it at Knox and later at Lewis. Then I went out with them. You understand I'm not with the exhibitors? So I've got a different opinion about the Strykers.

Interviewer: You've actually gone into combat with the Stryker. Does it live up to its publicity?

SSGT Pettis: No. Not even close. Look at the way it was developed. We got the things, and it was obvious the chain of command had decided it was going to be a success. We trained for the production tests. Trained and trained. So when the general came we could put on a good show, like everything was perfect. Those weren't inspections, really. All the glitches were just hidden, or we designed the demonstrations so they didn't come out. You know, the damned thing is really top-heavy. Roll over on you in a heartbeat. Supposed to be so light you can go anywhere, but you can't. Nineteen tons, base model. Drive it off pavement and you'll sink right into the ground. And they keep adding shit to it—sorry, can I say that on TV? Anyway, we're up to 42,000 pounds now. We had to hang more armor off the sides. And if you do that, you can't get it on a 130. The geniuses who designed it didn't know shit—sorry—about fighting in cities, so they didn't think it was necessary to protect against RPG-7s. We told 'em, look, everybody's got RPGs. Everybody. It's the weapon of choice in the Third World. Easier to use than an AK-47. A kid could use it. Did they listen? Hell no. Just drove on. I mean, it was clear to all the guys working on it that this sucker was going to be adopted, come hell or high water.

Interviewer: Did you fix the RPG problem?

SSGT Pettis: Yeah, eventually. Ended up putting a big cage around it, so the rounds would pre-detonate. You know, like the Israelis did in the '73 war. Except that they used barbed wire, mattress springs, shit—sorry—stuff like that. We told 'em about all that before, but they kept saying they didn't want to hear about the Israelis. Ancient history, they said. Well, the RPGs are ancient history and there are millions of the sonsabitches out there and they're all pointed at us.

Interviewer: The army says Strykers are perfectly suited to urban warfare.

SSGT Pettis: Well, excuse me sir, but that's just bullshit. In towns, you've got a 360-degree fight on your hands. You have to think differently than if you're just out in the country. In towns you're always in danger of being surrounded, and it can happen in a heartbeat if your enemy's any good. Look at what the Chechens did to the Russians in Grozny. Took 'em and their BMPs apart. Russian armor was good for the Chechens. Soldiers stuck close to their armor and got whacked, big time.

So, we got all kinds of blind spots on this thing. When you're buttoned up, hatches closed, crew's sitting there with all these computers, doing their e-mail, listening to the 'net, you can't tell what's going on 25 meters away. Don't get me wrong. Armor's good, better than a flak vest, but hell, you gotta dismount if you're gonna do any good in a town. Just riding around in these things, that's hopeless. Sure, you can lay down lots of fire, get up close, but sooner or later you gotta get out.

Interviewer: Our army is just so much more powerful than the resistance in Iraq. They can't possibly expect to fight you on equal terms.

SSGT Pettis: They don't have to. They'll just keep fighting until we're sick of it. They don't have anything but AKs and RPGs and HE, and they don't need computers to tell them where they are all the time. And they aren't afraid of us. They wait until conditions are right, and then they come after us. Usually they'd get off a few rounds and then we'd just hose 'em down. They weren't afraid of dying. And we sure helped 'em do that. But they'd keep coming as long as they wanted, and when they didn't want to come at us any more they'd just disengage, just leave. Stash their weapons somewhere and go have coffee at the market. And we'd just sit there, smokin'.

Interviewer: Are we winning?

SSGT Pettis: I don't see anybody givin' up. And you know, say we find a way to defeat the RPGs. They'll think up something else. Awhile back, the Palestinians blew up a Merkova in Gaza. Just blew a main battle tank to pieces. Killed the crew. And don't you think these guys know about that? You can blow up anything. If we defeat the RPGs, they'll find another way to come at us. I don't see us adapting.

Interviewer: Were you inside the Stryker when you were wounded?

SSGT Pettis: Naw. I was walking beside the vehicle. Dumb. Should've stayed away. The things draw fire. Say a guy who wouldn't waste an RPG round on a bunch of grunts sees one of these things, he's gonna take his shot. Our guys bunch up around vehicles, they take their shot and our guys on the ground take the collateral damage. Maybe everybody does it, bunch up like that. Hard not to do it. We lost two guys that day. Good guys.

Interviewer: Strykers cost about $2 million each.

SSGT Pettis: Maybe they're worth it. The design sucks, but its better than riding around in a HUMM-V. I'd rather have my arm than $2 million, though.

Deputy Assistant Undersecretary of Defense for Policy Melvin Graham: The United States is *the* superpower. We can go where we want, when we want, do what we want. You know what the French call us? *L'hyperpuissance,* the Hyperpower. And it's true. So the United States sets the terms of engagement. We may not even like it, in fact, I think many do not like it, but it is nevertheless true. Avoiding reality only postpones the unpleasant, if one thinks it is unpleasant. I don't happen to think so. I think America has a great opportunity at this point in history to expand the democratic universe in this world.

Interviewer: As we know, a great many people and places in the world are actively hostile toward America and indeed anything having to do with democracy.

Graham: Well, off the record, OK? Success breeds resentment, irrational resentment, hatred even. But democracy will not be denied. It's the wave of the future, and we will apply all the instruments of our national power to ensure that the future is safe for democracy. Some countries seem to insist on being poor, dysfunctional states. And that's dangerous for us. We have to contend with these dangerous states, in one way or another. Sometimes force is the only avenue of change for these states.

Interviewer: Would it be fair to say that armed force is now the primary tool in our foreign policy?

Graham: The primary tool, maybe not the only tool. But it is clear to me and to many others in office that a demilitarized foreign policy no longer works for us. The world is a very dangerous place. And we can't just sit around, waiting for our enemies to make the first move. We have to set the terms of engagement. That's why our new policy of preemption makes sense for us now.

Interviewer: Do we have more enemies now than ever before?

Graham: I think we do. Many small enemies. None as powerful or as dangerous as the old Soviet Union, but the new guys are ready to try things against us the Soviets would never have dared to try. Well, retaliation, you know, deterrence, doesn't mean as much today. How do you really threaten people who don't have much to protect in the first place? On the other hand, we have a lot to protect against these small enemies. That's why we have to take the fight to them before they bring it to us.

Professor Stanley Freeman, Boston University: Isn't that what happened on 9/11? I don't think the Pentagon gets it. I really think the whole problem is beyond them. Look. After spending trillions on defense after the Cold War, we aren't really defended. It's like asking a football team to play soccer. They can do it, but they aren't designed to do it, so their game is clumsy, full of needless mistakes. The Department of Defense, it turns out, doesn't defend us very well after all. Think about what happened as unemotionally as you can. A new global constituency of the disaffected is forming. The only common ground of this constituency is their enmity toward us and everything we symbolize. Anti-Americanism is now a global phenomenon.

One way to look at 9/11, however traumatic that day may have been for us, is as a strategic raid. An earlier raid—on the same target, by the way—didn't succeed. So, after years of reconnaissance, planning, putting together the necessary support in the target country and abroad, a new mission is launched. A team enters enemy territory undetected to carry out an attack that entails almost certain suicidal risks. Indeed, all of the direct-action team does die, but those who planned and supported the mission didn't. They're still planning, still supporting, and still sending out other missions, other raids. Officials in this administration will tell you they are taking the war to the enemy, but the truth is that we are still on the strategic defensive, and we will stay that way for a long time.

This is just the beginning of a global war. Our enemies are patient. They will fight on for decades if they must. The United States is a rich, soft target that offers plenty of opportunities. Our military power is unmatched now and for the foreseeable future, but our enormous power makes us intellectually lazy, complacent, and almost casual in how we express it. We do not know how to fully use the power we have. We act before we think, and when we use our brains later, it is only to condemn our earlier stupidity. We seem to be incapable of learning from our past. To those who have suffered because of our clumsiness, we look feckless at best, evil at worst. So the fundamental equation of war was set in place on 9/11, but because this is a new stage in the history of war we are slow to see how to fight it. We act, but we don't really know where this action is ultimately leading us. We are fighting to win, but we don't know what winning would mean. Until we do, our military power will lead us from one place to another, sowing hatred and resentment faster than we can uproot it.

Dave Bullion, syndicated columnist: What you are seeing around you here at this convention is a startling absence of perspective. The Pentagon has been trumpeting its transformation for the past three years, but critics have argued that the culture of the place has hardly changed. The army has always had a bureaucratic subculture that impeded any kind of change, or heaven forbid, progress. Now the bureaucracy is on top and the fighting army, as usual, is the dog's tail. My sources tell me that the political appointees are the worst they've seen since McNamara and maybe even worse than that. If the Pentagon were NASA, I'd say we're about to have another shuttle disaster. The building is like a black hole when it comes to genuinely new ideas: it just sucks the light out of every good idea that comes along. That's the tragedy.

Transformation, for all the publicity, isn't it, that's for sure. No one can even define it. Even its promoters won't bother anymore. It's become a catch-all phrase the bureaucrats use in order to spend more money on the same old programs, expensive weapons that are often counterproductive, and the rest goes to the tremendous waste. God, we just launched another submarine. Then there's the Joint Strike Fighter and the V-22, more troop transports, space-based radars, and of course there's the ever-useful national missile defense. That's to be used against all those Afghanis, Iraqis, Iranians, and North Koreans who have all those ICBMs.

All this would be less important if we weren't at war all around the planet. Yet no one can tell me or the rest of the American people what victory looks like. And when you bring up a subject like that at the Pentagon daily briefing, the secretary and his handlers behave as if asking it is somehow disloyal. But the public requires an explanation, and all they're getting now is "Trust me," just like Johnson and Nixon during Vietnam. Where in the traditions and laws of the United States does it say the public must trust its servants? The answer you'd get from the true believers here is, well, we are not really servants, we're the stewards of the public good. We're more committed, we're smarter, and we know more secrets than you, the general public, know. So you have to trust us. But we don't. We don't have to trust them, and we don't.

Eden Woodward-Lewis, Professor of History, Institute for Advanced Study, Princeton: I think war is breaking apart. It isn't cohesive anymore. I don't think it's possible any longer to see war as a monolithic social phenomenon, the way they teach it at West Point and the war colleges, all nice and tidy and bounded by rituals and consensus. What really scares the professional soldiers around the world is that they're being challenged by people who are refusing to play the old game of national war and are evolving new, nonstate, noninstitutional approaches that are almost impossible to defeat. In this new context, Sun Tzu's injunction takes on a renewed relevance. "War is a matter of vital interest to the State." You bet it is, because the state is no longer able to monopolize war. War is becoming public property again, reverting to its primitive origins if you like. We are seeing a real decline in the efficacy of national war. So now we have subnational, antirational war on a global scale. The old Westphalian boundaries have been breached. We're just trying to plug the gap now.

Interviewer: The army is about to expand, isn't it? We've heard reports of as many as thirty, maybe forty thousand additional soldiers over the next three years.

Army Major General [name withheld by request]: We need more soldiers, that's for sure. We've been promised three or four billion dollars, and with that you can buy 30,000 more soldiers. If we can meet our recruiting and retention goals, then that increase might see us to the end. Everybody believes in what he or she is doing. They're committed. They're proud. The critics said we'd never be able to hold back the resignations, to keep soldiers from leaving the service when their tours were up, but the retention and recruiting numbers are phenomenal. The quality is really high, higher than I've ever seen in the volunteer army. Then, we're going to recall several thousand highly qualified former soldiers in the Individual Ready Reserve. They'll come in behind the reservists we've called up for active duty.

But—and you didn't hear this from me—I think, ultimately, we'll have to reinstitute the draft. You might ask, if our numbers now are so good, why look to a draft? And the answer is that this nation isn't really convinced we are in a war, so this is a good way to convince the public. Then, when the public sees that we really are at war, they'll begin to ask hard questions about why we're fighting it. And if they don't get the right answers, the public will demand we all do a better job. The army can't fight this war by itself, you know, and right now, it is.

Interviewer: The end. When does the war end?

Major General: You'll know it when you see it. You won't need an announcement. It'll be evident to everybody.

Interviewer: Does that mean victory?

Major General: I think victory is an outmoded concept. We don't think like that anymore. When we complete the mission, it'll be over.

Narrator: Colonel Liu Hsun is the senior strategic counselor in the Higher Politico-Military Directorate of the Central Staff of the Chinese Peoples' Liberation Army. He is regarded as one of the more forward-thinking officers in his army, one with access to the highest levels of national leadership. He is a graduate of Beijing University and the London School of Economics.

Colonel Liu Hsun: A Western philosopher, Kant, I believe, first had the idea that peace was the normal state of world affairs. Since he wrote in the eighteenth century the Western world has pretended that war was an aberration, an interruption of peace. The history of the last century, and all the signs for this century, should have convinced the world that Kant was in error. Perhaps a hundred million people died in the wars of the twentieth century. The most violent century—in the West—since the Thirty Years War. Of course, Kant's misconception was never accepted in Asia, so reality has never disappointed us. Any analysis of the future must begin, in my opinion, with correcting this mistaken assumption. Struggle is normal. Peace is not. The world must reconcile itself to this reality.

Interviewer: Of course this view is completely at variance with the official view of the United States.

Colonel Liu Hsun: Oh, is it? The United States pretends so, but its actions speak differently. The United States is making war on the rest of the world, it seems. Has not the United States declared its right to intervene anywhere it chooses if it feels threatened? Not once since the United States attained world power has it accepted the situation as it is. No. The United States is ever striving to recreate the world in its own image. Now the world seems to be resisting. China has resisted this pretentious stance from the first, but then we have strengths the U.S. does not. China is a civilization, not merely a nation. If the United States were a real civilization, perhaps it would not be so insistent that others follow its path. Humility and patience are not virtues one finds in the United States. I mean no offense, of course.

Irwin Edwards, Contributing Editor, Bulletin of Concerned Scientists: Science can only do so much, and sometimes science—and our material strength—actually misleads us. You hear people talking on the convention floor about how fast we can get to the scene of a war now, but no one ever asks why getting into war quickly is a good thing. We're fixated on the material side of war, almost to the exclusion of everything else. And the everything else is the part that seems to mean more in the end these days. Now everyone has some access to dangerous science, even if they aren't materially rich. And with that dangerous science, they can do us great harm. This convention epitomizes our mentality, our assumption that if no one can match us materially, we will be victorious. This assumption turns the relationship of politics and war on its head. Political objectives take a back seat to military action. Tail wagging the dog. An American way of war, as someone said.

Interviewer: When does the war end?

Professor Stanley Engelmann: I don't—not in our lifetime. Not with all the AUSA conventions in the world. But there's something else.

Interviewer: What else?

Engelmann: We can lose this one.

13

THE DISCOVERY OF KANSAS

The story behind the first draft of a history of war.

The discovery of an ancient library at a site called "Kansas" was a singular event in modern history. It has already revealed a treasury of long-lost knowledge. All of the texts printed in this book were unearthed during the last decade from that excavation. Although these texts have added immeasurably to our understanding of the war, many more texts await restoration, a process fraught not only with technical difficulties but physical ones too. The war may be only a memory now, but Kansas is still regarded as a dangerous place to be.

When the work of excavating this site fell to me, I was not at all certain I was equal to the task. For some ten years I worked alone. My skills were certainly rudimentary, and my understanding more so. More than once, when I unearthed pieces of another book, I did not really appreciate the significance of what I held in my hands.

I had hoped to educate myself as I went along. I was sure I would not be disturbed in such a remote place. To me, Kansas was heavenly. I thought I could spend as much time as I wanted in my work. Surely, someone else would come along, just as I had, and take up my work when the time came.

361

Unfortunately, my situation took an unexpected turn, and so I have decided that I cannot delay assembling this little book until we have learned everything we can from Kansas. The reason is simple: the sheer size of the discovery is far larger than was thought at first. Originally, we assumed the library had only a few thousand books; now we suspect the site contained more than 300,000 volumes. We simply must begin learning now; the costs of waiting until we know everything are too high. Once before, we thought we had nothing more to learn, and we have seen where such pride has taken us. Now we must learn and dig at the same time.

So I have not been able to reconstruct the complete history of this war, and readers will have to forgive my ignorance about many events. Of one thing I am certain: this war was the greatest war ever fought in all of history. Some of the texts I have restored speak of ancient wars that were true cataclysms, and we may not doubt the sincerity of the writers who said so. However, in my judgment the past can call forth no war equal to ours in scope, duration, destruction, or violence. Our war was truly beyond precedent, so terrible it was beyond naming.

The beginning of the war, seen so long after the fact, was almost quaintly straightforward: a surprise attack was followed by a partial recovery, a violent reply, and then a steady escalation of attacks and replies in the usual way. Of course, the way the war began told us nothing about how the war would develop and certainly nothing about how the war would end.

If the beginning of the war was conventional, its causes were not at all straightforward. None of the world's many animosities seemed so serious that they would grow into the war we fought. Now we can see that a great reservoir of resentment against us had built up all around the world. Our enormous power was the reason for this widespread disaffection, but it was far from clear to us how such power had collected here. We had been victorious in most of our wars, but we had not been especially assiduous in our pursuit of national power. Compared to other empires, ours was different. After all, our power was usually benign, or at least not intentionally dangerous. If our power had been only of the crude military kind, all the resentments against us would have been easier to see. But our power was composed of many different parts: our cultural, social, economic, and even environmental power reached the world around. No corner of the globe was free of our influence—and most often our influence was decisive.

Perhaps this power was attractive simply because of its welcoming nature. Talents from every field and every nation came in our direction sooner or later. Nations all over the world believed that their own best interests were served by a close connection with us, even if they had to hold their noses when they professed loyalty to our interests too. Perhaps those who had most compromised their independence were most resentful. Their self-respect was challenged. No one likes to be reminded of his weakness, even if it is of benefit to him.

We demurred that too much was made of our power. We did not wantonly make war on anyone, nor bully our allies, nor manipulate the wealth of the world for any reason but the global good. Anyone could see that; and allowing for a measure of overstatement, we thought most people agreed. This made some people all the more resentful. They suspected the reasons for their animosity were hardly reasonable at all. Slowly, the world's various little jealousies— which we had always dismissed as petty and harmless—grew into a general feeling. We did not notice.

Now certain parts of the world had always been dangerous for outsiders and even for the people who lived there. In those days, when schoolchildren studied their geography, areas that were commonly seen as dangerous were colored pink. Friendly areas were always green. For a long time, the pink covered large tracts of old nations in regions known as Eurasia, Africa, and South America. The greens were prosperous and safe; the pinks were poor, and everyone knew poverty was dangerous as well as embarrassing.

But our enemies came from every part of the globe, the pink and green parts alike. Even after the war started, we could not comfort ourselves by saying that this or that nationality was responsible for the misery. Consequently, the war could be said to have been global from the beginning. Our enemies believed their grievances against us transcended mere locality; they could only be understood with reference to the entire world.

Naturally enough, some parts of the world had remained resolutely poor despite global prosperity. Global strategists had come to think that some as yet undiscovered characteristic impeded development in these parts. Whenever one of these regions declined to a certain internationally agreed level, the general world reaction was merely to render them less poor than they had been. When the people of these regions complained that this policy did not address their more fundamental problems, the complaints were dismissed as bad manners, ingratitude. We had done them a favor, the strategists said, and now we should suffer abuse because of it?

The world's highest authorities adopted a medical analogy that seemed quite handy: these unfortunate parts of the world were suffering from a kind of infection. To eradicate the infection, an infusion of wealth was the preferred form of treatment. Should that approach fail, a more direct, systemic treatment was warranted. Often, that required the deployment of a small army. Even if the patient died, the infection would be prevented from spreading beyond its original site.

We might say it is obvious now that "the movement" started in the poorest parts of the world, but that was not obvious at the time. The evidence we have now points to the *favelas* along the boundaries of the ancient city of Rio de Janeiro. The *favelas* were densely populated, lawless slums, a place as dangerous to humans as a battlefield. Whether or not the movement began here, Old Rio was reduced to one of the most highly poisoned zones in the world. Today, the region is inaccessible, as are all the old dead cities. But that all happened later. The early infection did escape its original confines. As it spread, its character changed. To conclude the analogy on an unfortunate note: the infection metastasized.

One can see, therefore, how the global character of our enemy made problems for us from the beginning. The enemy's leadership was composed originally of those who could invent attacks that would create the profoundest possible effect. Too, as the war began we had some difficulty clearly seeing the enemy. The enemy seemed to have no primary base of operations. They took care at first not to collect themselves in numbers that would attract our attention. They concealed the identity and locations of their political and military leaders, who were happy to remain anonymous even to those under their command. Certain nations that had proclaimed fast friendship with us had secretly allowed the enemy to take up residence, and some countries had even provided important technical and material support. But we did not know this at the time. Without really understanding that our enemy was around and among us, our frustrations drove us to a nonsensical policy.

As for the enemy's policy, that was just as hard to understand. One could start an argument today by saying that ideas gave the movement its power. I think most people still believe just the contrary, believe the beggars dressed up in evening clothes, as it were, to justify the crimes they were planning. Most people say the world had naturally divided itself into those more or less fortunate. Perhaps this was true, for the movement and the countries that fell under its control defined themselves not by what they were but by what they were not. Was that why the movement found friends everywhere? Apart from their hatred of global power, they shared little else, except for a certain worshipful view of the old ways of life. One might think they would have been content with life as it was then, but that was profoundly not the case. They actually believed they could return the world to the way it had been, reversing history itself.

So we could not change, and our enemy could not leave us the way we were.

The enemy's power had real limits. They could not hope to fight us on anything like equal terms. No one could. In theory, only a few nations could have formed an alliance capable of meeting us in a war of our own choosing. That was why the enemy began the war with clandestine attacks. He aimed at civil targets and ignored our armed forces altogether. An enemy strategist taken prisoner much later said that he and his comrades had decided ordinary armed forces were no longer relevant. As far as they were concerned, their essential target was the nation itself—as he put it, the source of great power, not merely its armed manifestations. We possessed a huge military establishment furnished with every imaginable weapon, but it was so ponderous as to be quite unsuited to defend us, and until emergency adjustments were made, unable to uproot itself from its cherished traditions. From all the evidence I have seen, that proved to be true of our government generally. We were certainly unprepared for what lay ahead.

Only an unnatural foresight could have predicted the war. So profound was the surprise, and so deep was our disappointment, that the nation mobilized its shock into a bitterness toward the world at large. What was worse, our bitterness hardly discriminated between our friends and our enemy. Only the longest standing affections kept our friends from deserting us during this ugly time. Just when the power of thinking clearly was needed most urgently, it seems to have deserted us.

So what one might think of as a general devaluation of knowledge occurred as the war began. There arose the curious notion that reason was not practical now, and that only pure action could defend us. From the outset, any hope of moderation or forbearance was crushed by official and popular weight. Gratuitous violence, death in every shape and form, was about to fall upon the peoples of the world. All sides would enter the fight with no thought but the abject destruction—indeed, the extinction—of their enemies.

In the end, I think, we were almost as dangerous to ourselves as was the enemy. We had arranged our national life in a certain way for so long that we no longer saw its vulnerabilities. We thought of our society as a great machine with many parts, fitting one into the other in vast combinations of complexity. And we spent much of our time attending to the proper functioning of this machine. Naturally, some parts of the machine were more fragile than others; some, by themselves, seemed of little moment. Their importance became clear only when one saw them as part of their larger whole. If the old social machinery seems cumbersome now, in those days it was nevertheless manageable and strong enough to withstand normal stresses and strains.

The enemy's genius was to understand us better than we did ourselves. Our system was certainly capable of performing under stress, but only so much stress. As we were to see, there came a time when the system could no longer answer the stress the enemy applied. Then, in a manner of speaking, the machine stopped running.

The enemy's first strikes were notable for their technical crudity. Nuclear, chemical, energy, and environmental weapons were employed. Not one of their weapons had been produced in the last generation, but the enemy used them quite inventively. As the attacks unfolded, seemingly unstoppable, even the hardest of military hearts on our side managed a nod of professional approval.

We think there must have been about a hundred nearly simultaneous actions. No one can say for sure because all the attacks were designed to be impossible to trace. Other actions were so finely co-ordinated they seemed to be just one attack. In the literature we have remaining, the question is complicated further by the persistence of the term "battle" to describe these actions. Battles, they certainly were not, if by that term one means some measure of exchange between combatants. No, these actions were more properly attacks, aimed to produce specific results. In turn, the attacks were designed—and it was this quality that elicited the greatest admiration from the professionals—so that their effects would cascade, one on top of the other, producing what one might call a "singularity." Singularities were those effects from which we would find it difficult if not impossible to recover. That, at any rate, seems to have been the enemy's theory so far as I can reconstruct it.

Those who survived to remember the attacks agreed on how ordinary the day seemed. News from everywhere was unremarkable. No domestic or foreign crises were in view. The imperium hummed with its routines.

At 0900 hours local time, the enemy detonated an extremely poisonous radioactive device in Washington, near the Capitol. Within minutes, the enemy detonated several other similar devices in lower Manhattan. Among some sources, there is the suggestion that communications systems were left alone in both places just long enough—about an hour—to transmit news of the attacks around the world. Afterward, however, the enemy tried to "starve" developing news, assassinating journalists who attempted to report from near the dying cities. At the same time, attacks on the national communications infrastructure commenced and did not abate until the system collapsed under the excessive loads created by the emergency. The psychological effect on an already shocked population could not be overstated.

The "battle of the cities" inaugurated the enemy's campaign, but those attacks could hardly be separated from the attacks associated

with the "battle of the airports." Passenger terminals and control facilities in forty-four of the nation's largest airports were attacked by
enemy units. Most of these attacks were carried out with high explosives, although in certain special cases smaller radiological devices
may have been employed.

The enemy had thought through the first attacks, and successive
attacks, with special care. In the now well-known case of the
Bethesda Massacre, police and medical services attempting to rescue the injured from the grounds of the National Institutes of Health
were killed by what appeared to be a combined chemical-biological
attack. The attacks seem to have been carried out by two enemy
fighting groups that did not know of one another's mission. Evidently, the same methods were used in the Chicago Loop attacks.
As in all the other attacks, the enemy's objective was not merely
functional—our physical destruction was less important to the enemy than our psychological destruction. Put another way, the enemy
wanted nothing less than the eradication of our identity as a nation.

After the first day of the war, the question of what came next was
on everyone's mind. Surely the enemy would try to sustain his strategic momentum. And indeed, this is what happened. Our friends
were attacked next. We had suffered enormous damage, but we were
considerably stronger than some of our allies. When the enemy
turned on them, the effects of their attacks were more profoundly
felt. The enemy had clearly tailored attacks to take advantage of
each nation's vulnerabilities. In Japan, for example, the congested
Kanto Plain contained more than fifty million people. More than in
any other place in the world, the people of the Tokyo agglomera-
tion—especially the fifteen million who moved in and out of the city
each day—depended on one another to help make their world work.
The enemy attacked this intricate system with particular savagery,
immobilizing whole rail and subway lines with chemical detona-
tions. Tens of thousands of dead and dying commuters were sealed

underground when authorities concluded there was no other way to arrest the spread of chemical poisoning. Unfortunately, these measures were of no help, for while the authorities were trying to deal with the immediate emergency, the enemy was free to poison the entire Kanto Plain, detonating weapons exactly placed for the greatest effect. My best estimate of the elapsed time required for all these operations was two hours. Certainly by the end of the second day of the war, the general vicinity of Tokyo was dying. Life on all the Home Islands has been gradually less tenable ever since. Once a vital, thriving, and productive people, this nation has now almost wasted away, mortally wounded by weapons that were considered ancient when most of its present population was born.

Tokyo was one of three hundred cities around the world to suffer in this fashion. A dreary litany of results would accomplish little. One need only understand that by the time the enemy's first campaign was over, our way of life in the world had changed.

We felt we were under siege. When we reestablished a semblance of national government at one of our alternate command centers, an enemy strike eliminated the entire complex. Although we did mount counterstrikes here and there, in reality our offensives were good only for relieving our anger. Not one of them changed the strategic situation an iota. All during the long early days, we truly were under the hand of our enemy. Some even wondered if we were losing the war.

If all this were not enough, we injured ourselves. Driven by a people gripped with fear, our national authorities raised a huge new army for internal uses. Rather than deploying our regular armed forces for this purpose, the government turned to what was then called "social mobilization." The idea was to invest some limited legal authority in organizations known to be especially supportive of the government. Ex-soldier's societies were held up as models, but as the scope of social defense was so huge, many other groups were mobilized too. Uniforms of every description appeared everywhere.

Soon, news leaked out that groups were being organized especially for the purpose of being deputized by the authorities. Still other groups did not bother with obtaining legal approval. In keeping with the public's desire for the resumption of national order, any legal objections to these private armies were waved aside. Most of our citizens were in no mood to question national policies.

Even in the extremities of national danger, it seemed, humans could not deny petty impulses. The war transformed narrowness of mind into a social virtue. Every one of these comic-opera organizations, full of their elevation in status, soon took to announcing their own laws, rules, procedures, and standards—all founded, it must be said, on exceedingly dubious authority. Unfortunately, the manic activities of these pseudo-legal societies gradually influenced the behavior of our elected representatives. After several years of war, even our real laws became progressively more authoritarian, imitating the so-called "social emergency laws," dating from the early days of our panic. Our ancient liberties were slowly, casually erased.

A newfound passion for conformity descended on society. Citizens were naturally expected to unite against the common danger, but the nature of our common cause was more exactingly defined with each passing day. The range of permissible opinion gradually narrowed until any discussion was rendered irrelevant by official pronouncements. Discussion became unpatriotic because of the danger that talk might veer toward different points of view. Any hint of subtlety, nuance, or discrimination in public speech brought on the most savage denunciations.

Thousands were arrested and detained after being secretly denounced by their fellow citizens. Self-appointed civic and social guardians tormented others who for one reason or another were not arrested. Instances of this sort happened most often where laws had been upheld casually even before the war. Once the war began, society in these places devolved to near-tribal behavior. People who were unconvinced by propaganda and who resisted conformity placed themselves in danger of civic attack. Inevitably, innocents were killed or driven to the despair of self-destruction. Still others fled, collecting with their own kind on the dangerously poisoned fringes of the old cities. Eventually, even these settlements wasted away.

The first several years of the war, then, marked a time when no revenge would relieve our anger. We were unsure of where we might attack because so many of our enemies came from so many places. Our first responses were notable for a lack of focus. In truth, we just lashed out at any suspicious concentration of people, no matter how small. The destruction of Rio de Janeiro was a special case, but predictable. Seized by a perverse civic pride, that city had proclaimed itself the birthplace of the movement just after the war began. City leaders clearly assumed we would ignore their bravado. The members of our war cabinet were hardly so forgiving; reflecting our own national sentiment, they demanded a prompt, ruthless attack against Rio. Their wishes were granted. Twenty-seven million citizens of Rio perished. Unexpectedly, instead of satisfying the public's anger, still more attacks were demanded. The word "extermination" was used for the first time in public speeches. Plans were thus set in motion for a much grander affair.

The avowed purpose of the first Grand Campaign was to demonstrate our vast power so that no one would ever again challenge us. No one had defined any other goal so satisfying to the public. Our attack on Rio had unleashed a side of our nation seldom if ever seen: our thirst for revenge seemed beyond satisfaction. As we debated where to attack next, it is no overstatement to say the world shivered in fear.

The question was soon decided in favor of the lands east of the old Black Sea. Intelligence had suggested a certain coincidence between members of the enemy's fighting groups and this region. Subsequent research has shown these coincidences to be overstated, but even a remote coincidence seemed enough at the time. One might have thought the decision to launch the campaign had been made rather casually, indifferently even, as if nothing mattered but to act, as if against whom we acted, or where we acted, really made no difference.

The rest of the world was relieved to learn the Black Sea region had been chosen for our first real campaign. The truth was that certain countries had been maneuvered into assisting the enemy. Fear on their part, as well as acquiescence on the part of the rest, had made a conspiracy seem the best way to avoid trouble from either side. As usual, neutrality proved to be a mirage. Ever since the first attacks, those countries were afraid their double-dealing would be discovered. As weakness is a poor foundation for solidarity, inevitably one of them came to us with the story, hoping for forgiveness. We were hardly in a forgiving mood.

For these and other reasons, the rest of the world pretended to keep the war at a distance. Nations still calculated how they might avoid being involved in the war at all, but that was a vain hope. Sooner or later all nations would be hurt in some way. In the early days, however, it was still possible to hope, because we began the war virtually alone. Our armed power was so vast that it outstripped the capabilities of even the second-ranked world powers by several orders of magnitude, and this was so even before the military establishment awoke itself to fighting a truly global war. This meant that even if allies wanted to take the field with us—and none did—they would have only detracted from the powerful forces we set in motion.

Over the years we had grown accustomed to operating alone anyway. We were quite forthcoming about this, while our allies prided themselves on being allowed to participate in some of our operations. Anyone who could keep up with our pace and sophistication was much admired by the other nations. And it was just possible that an ally would benefit in some way by being a useful friend. Because we asked for so little in the normal way of things, when the Grand Campaign was finally launched, 115 of the world's 205 nations lost no time in aligning themselves with us. In practical terms, that meant little. None of the nations were obliged, or felt themselves obliged, to participate in the fighting. What we had in mind was beyond the reach of our allies in any case. Thus, alone and full of hate, our nation launched itself into the wastelands of Central Asia, now officially designated as a "strategic focal point."

The term may have been the invention of our first Grand Commander, or, as everyone referred to him after his appointment, "the GC." He did not seem like an extremist. Nothing about his appearance suggested that he was anything other than what he seemed: a man of middle height and middle age with a soldierly trim. In dress and habit, he had a taste for plainness, suggesting a kind of contrary vanity—itself remarkable at a time when our professional soldiers festooned themselves with all manner of insignia and ribbons. The false occasion, the kind of high state affair in which our politicians gloried, made him very uncomfortable. On reviewing platforms, he was often restless, looking about, obviously bored. And he very much disliked having to deliver the speeches he had been provided for these occasions.

After his appointment, our political authorities decided the GC should spend as much time in the public arena as possible. He tolerated this assignment, but only just. Much to the consternation of his superiors, the GC took to editing his speeches as he delivered them, often directly contradicting policies so painstakingly concocted by the organs of state. But this practice of his seems to have been merely an indulgence because being worshipped bored him. His supposed independence of mind was thus only a bit of acting. The GC was in perfect accord with the aims of his government, which were that the cultural and social structures of the Black Sea region should be completely dismantled, or better yet, destroyed utterly. Even if the region could hardly support itself, much less a war against us, the region was to be the target of our first outing. The GC set himself to achieve these ends, and with a vengeance.

As international law then required, the GC issued an official declaration of war aims. He announced that he aimed to eliminate the possibility that the enemy could conduct hostile operations of any kind, against anyone, ever again. He therefore intended to reduce the enemy's social organization until it reached a point of agricultural subsistence. He disclaimed any interest whatever in the number of enemy dead his campaign might be required to produce; such results were merely a side effect, not the point, of the war, he insisted. The enemy population "was really not worth going out of the way to kill"; he would be happy with any number of casualties as long as the number was high.

The number was very high. When the stench of the dead was finally too strong to ignore—all the sources agree the casualties around the Black Sea had gone past five million, counting all categories—protests arose from around the world, demanding an armistice. First Rio and now this. Ancient resentments and modern anxieties converged. All these calls for peace were ignored, met by our cold official silence. Nations began realigning themselves. The old global consensus was disintegrating under the strains of this war.

The GC knew that public sentiment would turn against the war sooner or later. He said the war had to educate world opinion, and that when the world understood the real meaning of this war, all the energy consumed by fear and hatred and guilt would be translated into purpose and resolve to fight to the bitter end. Thus, the GC said, he must stand with the strategy he had been given.

The GC accelerated his attacks—he called them "raids," which were usually initiated with what were then designated "atmospherics." Atmospherics could be directed against several cubic miles of enemy atmosphere and made to ignite. Some said at the time that these were the most fearsome weapons of all, but even the scant historical record we have makes clear that these were only one of an arsenal of fearsome weapons. It is true that atmospherics were used more often than the other hyperweapons, but they had real technical limitations too: these determined the size of targets they were sent against. They were most effective against small cities and various military sites. In modern war, small cities usually were regarded as irrelevant, but as this was a war of revenge, smaller cities were simply vaporized as a way of driving up casualty figures. Still, the GC said that as these figures were swollen with noncombatants, they should be disregarded.

In saying this, perhaps the GC intended to terrorize the enemy and intimidate our allies into doing more. The impossibility of sorting combatants from noncombatants made atmospherics exactly the right weapon for his purposes. Carefully designing his strategy along the lines of our policy, he used these weapons deliberately, precisely. What was not destroyed was taken under his control. Once the GC's principles were understood, merely the threat of destruction seemed to be sufficient encouragement for the population to submit.

The government finally ordered the GC to suspend operations. He seemed to agree, but then continued anyway. The war cabinet sent a special envoy to insist. The GC told the envoy he was "in the process of stopping." He said he could not turn complex military operations on and off like a faucet. The envoy departed. Enemy casualties rose at the same rate as before. Expecting further protests, the GC reminded his superiors that a quarter of a million people had been killed and several million dispossessed of their homes by the battle of Washington alone, and that a final count of casualties from the other great cities still had not been made. By those measures, he insisted, the enemy had not been paid a fraction of the revenge that was owed it. His message was to have been highly confidential, but it was made public. Then the war cabinet learned that the public agreed with the GC. The war went on as before.

When most of the world is unfit for sustained habitation, imagining a time when the opposite was true is difficult. In those days, the designation of the smallest part of the earth as uninhabitable created a global outcry, so solicitous were we of our natural surrounds. Where a few hundred thousand square miles had been declared "lost," it was usually only because of some accident. Indeed, the historical record shows only two significant instances of loss attributed to self-poisoning.

The Grand Campaign had a fundamental effect on our present ways of living because it was the first time environmental attacks were employed in war. We have records in which the GC is heard saying that the enemy's part of the world "had never counted and never would." He was the one who broke the taboo on environmental warfare. He observed later that since all the other taboos had been broken it made no sense to observe the last one remaining. He said that history would decide the issue, and by then he would be long dead. Present-day judgments would not deter him.

Needless to say, the campaign suffered when he was taken prisoner. For the moment, the war slowed down, as if somehow the world were catching a breath. The enemy had been planning his capture for some time. During one of his visits to the operational area, they had interfered with his navigation system and redirected his flight over their territory, where he was forced to land. After some days of uncertainty about the GC's fate, the enemy announced he was in their hands and would be tried for his crimes against peace.

The enemy claimed the authority of common international law. We accused the enemy of using international law for their own purposes. In turn they replied: if not for their purposes, then whose? We demanded the GC's trial be moved to a neutral place. The enemy extolled the virtues of their legal system. We demanded safe passage for any lawyers we might contribute to the GC's defense. The enemy extolled the virtues of their lawyers, saying the very best defense had been assigned to the defendant. In every one of these pretrial disputes, international authorities had decided the question in favor of the enemy. Then, in his opening statement before the War Crimes Tribunal, the general himself (and at the trial he was never referred to except by his military rank) argued that international law was defunct both as a concept and as a reality. He said that if the enemy merely wished to kill him, they should go ahead without the bother of a corrupt trial.

In a formal reply, intended as much for the world audience as for the one before him, the Chief Prosecutor argued that the general was being tried "by right of power." This curious phrase he explained to mean that as the general was held already under threat of summary execution as an enemy combatant, any treatment short of that was the privilege of the power holding him prisoner. In plain language, the enemy had the right to exercise its power over the general any way it chose. And the enemy chose to exercise its power through the medium of its own ancient legal customs. The general permitted himself a bitter laugh, saying that he was happy the Chief Prosecutor was convinced of his own argument.

Entertaining as these antics might have been, or however enlightening for scholars of law, they made little impression on the general. He was perfectly composed and, as the prosecutors noted, not at all contrite. He had shown no mercy and asked for none now. He happily agreed he was the true author of the campaign's strategy and went on to say he had paid special attention to designing the environmental offensive that had poisoned the Black Sea. "Black enough now," he laughed. The trial's videoscripts show the general in a long technical exchange with the Chief Prosecutor, concerning the "excellent returns" on all the environmental weapons research.

One should not be misled to characterize the general's testimony as in any way a justification or rationalization of his actions. One can clearly see in the videoscript how the general has managed to detach himself from his all-too-obvious fate. All around him in the courtroom, from the jurists' bench to the select audience, eyes are looking at him as though he is already dead. As his prosecutors sat transfixed, the general incriminated himself even more profoundly, recounting how in all the long years of his career he had passed his time in useless headquarters of useless military formations and war colleges, putting his imagination to the task of building a new form of warfare.

As if revealing a great secret, the general's voice dropped to a near whisper, so low that several times the Chief Prosecutor asked him to speak up. At some undefined juncture in the past, the general said, warfare had quietly and without drama transcended reason. A war of unimaginable violence was now possible, a war of violence so extreme there was no other reason for its being other than its own existence. An age-old soldier's dream had been realized, he said: war could theoretically sustain itself on its own violence.

The general had told no one. The thought of such a war mesmerized him and terrified him. He kept this idea locked away in his mind, as far from his professional duties as he could. But he could not force himself to forget what he had learned; this was the kind of war that always came back to him in his dreams, in idle moments, in times when he thought about some other matter, his imaginary war would appear, unbidden. Each time, he could see the war more and more distinctly. What began only as a slight tugging at the edge of his consciousness was now a wholly recognizable vision. Later, in private conversations with himself he called this vision "trans-rational war." After his appointment, however, his vision was officially approved as the basis of our grand strategy.

For centuries, the general said, war had been jailed by peace. From time to time, war had been paroled, but only on condition it behave in a civilized manner—this last phrase, the general pronounced with decided irony. The common assumption grew that war was a crude and ultimately defective way of expressing a people's interests. Surely, the assumption went, humans now had many better ways of resolving their discontents.

This kind of thinking was delusional, the general said; it confused hope with reality. War is an indelible feature of human life, he said. To suppress war was merely to compound its severity when it escapes the confinements of civilization. Here the Chief Prosecutor allowed himself to be caught up in the general's argument. War was savage only when we decided to make it so, he said. The purpose of war was to reach a viable peace, he argued. We must exercise some control over war or we cannot use it, he said.

The present war is proof of what I say, the general replied. All around the world people said they did not want this war, and many others decried its beginning but rationalized its continuance. Still others were secretly happy, but for their own reasons advocated an armistice. The first offensives had frightened everyone. These measures seemed inhuman, they complained; they were unbecoming of modern civilization. The general said these sentiments were nonsense. Humankind had proved itself equal to any kind of savagery. No matter how horrible the weapons, we had employed them with happy abandon. The general thought that more recent wars—he did not say which—had been quaintly limited but also surprisingly successful in that they had decided matters for a time. After a few such wars, war itself was regaining its reputation as a decisive instrument of statecraft. So when this war began, the ambitions of all the combatant nations drove the level of violence to unimagined heights.

As for him, the general said, he was a professional soldier and thoroughly reconciled to the fact of war. He likened this war to a storm; he knew it would happen, and he knew it would express itself more through sheer violence than deliberation. Yet with all that he knew about war, not until he actually took command did he realize the war had command of him. His words came slowly and distinctly, so as to impress his audience to understand. Here, at this exact point, the videoscript shows the general's face change its aspect, as though a cloak of sadness had fallen over it.

"It was as if I had mounted a wild horse and she carried me into a tumult, toward an obscured precipice," he said quietly.

The general never spoke again.

His public execution was gratuitously horrific, carried out in the most theatrical manner on the premise that, when the war was ever finished, "a lesson for the learning would be available to the people of the world," as the Chief Prosecutor later explained. He said his nation's traditions required such an answer to such crimes as the GC had committed. But beyond showing the rest of the world they really had not progressed much beyond the tribal fires, one cannot imagine their reasons were to be taken seriously. Whatever the enemy thought, their calculations were disastrously wrong.

The Grand Commander's successor was announced right away. The original GC had terrorized the enemy with his extremist style, and so—having no ideas of his own—his successor found it necessary to publicize his own devotion to the old GC's views on transrational warfare. He was everywhere in the days before the ill-fated Second Grand Campaign, never passing an opportunity to be seen and heard.

The second GC certainly looked right; indeed, by all accounts his success owed much to the way he looked. Physically, he was far more prepossessing than the original. He was described as "germanic" in appearance, a remark apparently meant to be taken as a compliment in those times. And he dressed to be noticed as well. No award was too insignificant for him to have won. A story, perhaps apocryphal, has a doyen of society approaching the GC when he was in full dress, pointing to his many medals, asking, "Which of these is for gardening?" The old GC was said to have a delicious sense of humor. The new GC had none at all.

In official circles, whispers were heard that this new commander was merely an epigone. The old GC's charm and intellect had the strange effect of rendering his extreme theories palatable. How could anyone so vicious be so likable? The new GC had no such charm. He happily proclaimed himself a simple mechanic of war, hoping he would be taken for the opposite—a great military artist, yet unsung, but famous soon enough. He proclaimed his task to be the optimal application of national power. As for what he referred to as "higher meanings," he said he would leave those to his superiors.

As is usually the case with such people, the GC was almost pathologically insecure. His public heartiness concealed the most deep-seated hatred for those who were more thoughtful and were not embarrassed by it. He was suspicious of everyone, but he reserved the outer reaches of his contempt for his own fellow citizens. As for the enemy, they were not human beings at all, but a kind of thinking pest.

The new GC had every intention of seeing his way through to victory by any means. His strategic plan has been preserved; strangely, the document was one of the first to be uncovered in Kansas. He meant to outdo his predecessor, whom he despised, in every respect. After a lifetime of waiting patiently in the shadow of those who were supposedly his masters, he would prosecute the war to a most ferocious end.

This he meant to do by fighting right past the enemy's armies, into the enemy's urban agglomerations. He knew, as everyone did, that most of these areas could not be defended at all; by attacking them remorselessly, he could interrupt the enemy armed forces' source of power. In effect, he wanted to strand the enemy's armies, leaving them with little to fight for—or with. Once that point was reached, he estimated he could eradicate the most dangerous military formations at times and places of his own choosing.

This strategy was hardly original, but it had not been employed for years. Although successful in certain cases, the use of this strategy left the victors with such a vile reputation that they almost always lost the peace. The idea fell from favor among professional soldiers. The new GC, knowing or caring little for what had been done before, believed the new strategy was his invention, and actually said so, much to the amusement of those who knew better. Thus, his scheme to collect as much acclaim as possible before he began campaigning was foiled. He was infuriated, but he did not quite know why.

We may assume, therefore, that in his final hours he was not happy. He had not been in command a month before an enemy operative killed him. Posing as a staff officer, the operative shot him to death with a guard's pistol.

By then, the number of war dead had passed seven million for this campaign alone. The Second Grand Campaign stalled. No one had confidence in the GC, or in his strategies. From several sources, I have learned that even on our side the general's death was greeted with some relief. Many of his comrades in the higher ranks were secretly embarrassed by his crudity. Now, these same sources said, we thought we could learn from our mistakes, find a GC who was not so enamored of extremist strategies. They were wrong. They hoped that common men, with the commonest of minds, could actually extinguish this war. The commanders who followed the second GC were so colorless they disappeared into the greater drama of the war. The war proved to everyone that it could subsist on a succession of mediocrities.

That was how the war took command of itself.

Our enemies, more inventive than powerful, played their part by fighting on. Our military and domestic defenses had been reformed in a near frenzy after the battle of the cities. The enemy's enthusiasm seemed to cool as well. Their campaign plan at this point was to keep up a certain level of civic anxiety to go hand in hand with operations in the battle zones. As for our new domestic arrangements, the enemy simply ignored those, contenting themselves with episodic attacks. Our people did not know this, naturally, so every domestic attack reawakened memories of the grand attacks that began the war. No one could ever really say if the new attacks were opening shots of a more serious enemy drive. As usual, ignorance gave rise to fear.

At the front itself, all parties struggled to keep the war in motion, doing what they could to avoid a stalemate. History has told us of wars in which the combatants assumed a wary consensus on why and how a war might be waged, how victory would be defined, on which weapons would and would not be used, where it would be fought and where not. As time passed, war decided less and decided it for a shorter time, so that the usefulness of war gradually declined. This, one presumes, was what the original GC meant when he told his captors that war had been "jailed" by peace, that war was so over-controlled it was of no use at all. A stalemate amounted to the defeat of war itself. If war lost its power to create victory, what then? This philosophy was of the most futile sort, but it was not some imaginary military-academic construct. To some high-ranking soldiers, the problem was quite real. If reason had no control over war, what did?

Meanwhile, a new "doctrine of equitability" made its appearance in the enemy's councils. The doctrine codified the enemy's desire to reduce us to the rank of an ordinary power. The doctrine held that, as a matter of principle, no one power in the world should be permitted to reach an imperial stage of development. Nations should guide themselves to aim for parity with all others and no more. The risks of imperial pretension were just too great. The irony of this doctrine was lost on the enemy. They were presuming to dictate to the rest of the world, just as they had accused us of doing.

Too, the enemy's doctrine seemed rather self-serving, since they would never ascend to our magnitude of power. Anyway, some said, the rank of world power was not so easily broken. Nor was this kind of power something a nation simply wished for. Vast and complex combinations of events and chance made such power. Our theoreticians said our power went beyond rational calculation. Nor was this power easily given up. A world power could not relinquish its strength by degrees so that the anxieties of its competitors could be allayed. Our power was the sum and substance of everything we were and everything we would be. History itself, they said, had brought us to this place and time.

The rest of the world seemed unimpressed by our arguments. They decided once and for all that it was fruitless; they said our love of power was almost religious.

So the war went on, but that is not to say that it remained the same. The scope of our campaigns grew, and with them the war's velocity.

Along with the changes in the general shape of the war, its minor forms changed too. At first even the enemy's part of the war had gone along crisply and elegantly. The professional and military classes at the academies propounded views on what all this meant for the future of war. Some military professors insisted history had outgrown the ancient rituals of battle in which huge armies blundered into one another over a vast ground. But the war disappointed everyone by growing more violent, more destructive, and even less decisive. The war had been poorly thought out from the beginning, so now it would be poorly fought out as well. As a measure of our intellectual bankruptcy, the phrase most often heard in those days was that the war "would burn itself out eventually."

Now the war entered its longest and least productive period. The dependability of the violence forced the people to arrange their lives around the idea that they could die at any moment. Civilian casualties were just so close to true randomness, one could imagine—if one so wished—that statistical probabilities offered a certain protection. So far, the probabilities were slightly in favor of an ordinary citizen surviving the war. None of the combatant nations could sustain intense levels of violence for very long, however, and so the war took on certain rhythms, pulses.

Civilian philosophies arose to accommodate these changes in circumstance too. One school of thought held that humankind should completely forget about the future, while another encouraged everyone to think of nothing but the future. Still another advanced the concept of a wholly inner life, separated as far as possible from present realities. One of the spiritual movements—no political movements were allowed—called for the world to return to its pretechnocratic stage, to what was called a "New Eden." The so-called Edenic Movement was resolutely apolitical as well; one of the movement's basic tenets was that politics had brought us all to the edge of catastrophe, and that politics should be banished forever. Even the armed forces advanced their own kind of pseudo-philosophy, a pastiche of militarism and romanticism that appealed to the immature mind. In the early days of my career, I myself subscribed to "the Military Ethos," as it was called.

As the casualty lists exceeded five hundred million, no school of philosophy seemed of much help. We were losing our grip on the world. After several years, the casualty lists seemed the only news being produced by the war. No other news seemed at all important.

I was at the academy by then. My classmates and I were little interested in grand questions of any sort, much less those to do with the war. Above all, we were interested in ourselves. Nor were we trained to be curious. Curiosity in those days was thought bothersome, disruptive, and possibly even dangerous. Just how and by what methods we imbibed these views, I cannot say. Nevertheless, after our time in the academy our formation was complete. Our mission was to apply the military power of our nation, nothing more. Strategies, operational plans, even larger tactical plans meant little to us. We were the ones who made these abstractions come to violent life.

Our prejudices were many and casual. When we bothered about

the enemy at all, our thoughts never wandered beyond the stereotypes with which we had been indoctrinated. The enemy was everywhere and nowhere. And although the enemy had been very successful against us so far, it was only a matter of time before we would once more take the offensive that would, completely and finally, kill them and all their cowardly friends.

The reality of the time was that the enemy had not become encumbered as many armies do during the course of a war. He could not dispense altogether with bases and production facilities, but these were small and mobile and easily replaced. As the enemy's successes accumulated, more and more sites were available for his use. They were very numerous now, very widely dispersed from continent to continent, including our own. The state of affairs would have presented any number of stimulating problems to any real student of modern war, but neither we nor our professors were interested.

When a graduate or someone associated with the academy was killed, an announcement was posted, a recent development since we had too many casualties to continue holding memorial assemblies. We would have been on permanent funeral duty, or so it seemed to us. We all thought these assemblies a great nuisance, but the school's commandant and his underlings took them seriously. They gloried in any occasion where we could dress out in our finest uniforms. In retrospect, ceremonies seem to have been more important than anything else that happened in the academy when I was there. Now, I simply wonder how we came to think we knew so much.

The closer we came to our day of graduation, the more sharply the war was defined in our imaginations. Subsisting on little information other than the official bulletins, we began analyzing the casualty lists. If several thousand of our casualties came from a particular locale, say, the Erevan District, or the Moab Plains, we marked it down as a sharp action and speculated about what had brought it on. Over several months we began to see the outlines of the different campaigns under way around the world and at home. We thought we were so clever. We strutted about the school as though we possessed a vast storehouse of operational secrets. Now I know that all the information given on casualties, even the numbers, had been altered for reasons of security. Our understanding of the war was based on lies.

During our final year, more familiar names came out on the casualty lists. Some names had been prominent in our games. Others had been singled out—by some mysterious process—as great and natural leaders. Yes, he will be Chief some day, one of us would say knowingly, for being able to predict such success implied that you were privy to the mysteries of greatness yourself. I know of no instance in which such predictions ever came true. The most promising student, so popularly proclaimed, was immediately killed when he arrived at his new base of operations. An atmospheric detonated as he was getting off the transport. Whether great or common, they all died, all the same.

Only one really remarkable incident remains in my memory from those days. A professor at the academy was dismissed for criticizing something. He had exceeded his brief as a member of the faculty, which was chiefly to manage the flow of information. As the professor was decidedly unpopular, it was no surprise that his students were the ones who denounced him. Exactly what the professor had said was never reported. Much later I heard a rumor that he had been killed, leading an enemy fighting group, but that was not so unusual by that part of the war. What most impressed me was how small an impression the affair made at the time. The chain of command had acted. All the decisions of the chain of command were by their nature correct. Neither the professor nor his misdeed was ever spoken of again. It was if a tear in the historical fabric had been crisply and efficiently repaired. Conformity had been safely restored.

That was why it was not until I joined my first formation that I began to learn the true state of the war. The most shocking news I heard was not really news at all but two pieces of intelligence passed along by a former classmate. My friend made some offhand reference to operations in the Rockies that I did not understand.

Seeing my confusion, he said, "Oh, I thought you knew: the enemy has managed to establish quite a few operational bases in the West." I was still puzzled. "Well, you do know that a large number of our people have gone over to the other side?"

With some heat, I said I thought it all very well to protect our fellow citizens from the news, but keeping this from one's own kind was going too far. This news changed my whole view of the war, I said.

"If you didn't know about these developments, I should think it would," he said cheerily, and then went about his duties.

My first operational base was situated in a mountainous region not far from the site of the first Grand Campaign. Of course, by the time I arrived, the region was a vast wasteland, depopulated for a thousand miles in every direction—the handiwork of our first GC. Our commander, speaking to all of us newly arrived officers, said Groznyy Station was as defensible as any of our bases, and safer than most. The mountainous terrain would interrupt the worst effects of any really large weapon the enemy might try against us. If we could avoid those, he said, we had a good chance of fending off any precision attack. He did not think there would be much ground action.

As the most junior of officers, of course I spent no time at all in the commander's private company, but my impression was that he was quite happy with the situation as it stood. I never once heard him speak of launching offensive operations, nor did our various formations ready themselves to do so. In the brief period we were at Groznyy Station, we did little more than polish our equipment. The commander said he was not satisfied with the state of our fortifications, so we devoted most of our energies above ground to extending and calibrating our defenses. I spent most of my time in the subterranean training halls with my own troops. Along the ramparts above, little was left to look at besides snowless mountains and arid plains.

We were not fated to operate out of Groznyy Station. After only a few months, the so-called Grand Redeployment was ordered. We did not know at the time that all our forward formations had received the same order. Everyone was coming home. From my lowly position, the whole movement took on the air of an emergency. And so it proved to be.

Our command's policy had been to quarantine us from any home news whatsoever, a common practice in those days meant to protect us from distractions. We were constantly reminded to focus on our preparations for combat—although at Groznyy this injunction seemed vaguely contradictory. No other activities were permitted. But soldiers will always trade rumors, and some would invent rumors for no other reason than to start the most outrageous gossip.

The most popular rumor by far at Groznyy told of a Lost Civilization, a part of the world that was miraculously untouched by war. This civilization had been "set aside" by common agreement of the warring powers as a place from which to fashion a new beginning once the war was over. Many of us professed to believe this even as we knew very well no such place existed, or was likely to exist. We would spend the few free minutes we had, imagining what this civilization must be like, what languages its people spoke, what habits moved their society, what their buildings were made of, and how they managed to make the weather perfect and how their seas were clean and beautiful. The Lost Civilization was a useful fantasy, as all fantasies are; it was the only fantasy available to us then. Of course, fantasies could not take the place of real news. We had no

idea of what awaited us on our return to the continent. We assumed
it was more or less the same as when we left.

The first warning we had that all was not the same was when our
transport made an urgent combat approach to landing at our new
base. The maneuver—which was rather sickening—surprised us,
but we landed without mishap. Many other transports had been intercepted and shot down. Still others were captured intact when they
landed at bases that had been overrun.

Compared to our old base, the new base was crude, one might
even say primitive. Groznyy Station had been a finished, fully functional operational base with its full complement of troops and
equipment. As such, that base was nearly impregnable, immune
from all but the most catastrophic attacks. In the earliest days of
Groznyy Station, the enemy had attempted to seize it by main force,
but the casualties were so high they never tried again. Our new base,
by contrast, was under constant threat.

The base, Fort Hood Station, no longer exists. The base had been
established some time in the twentieth century. Few signs of those
days remained by the time of our arrival. On the surface, one could
see wreckage left from old attacks. Not one structure, not a tree, was
left standing. A hot wind blew constantly across the ugly terrain.
Our bunkers were only a few hundred feet deep and thus quite vulnerable. This meant that we must defend our whole operational
area, keeping the enemy at arm's length if we could. The base itself
was no protection. During enemy raids, the exit galleries of our
bunkers were crowded with troops. No one wanted to be buried by a
direct hit. When the enemy used chemical explosives, the troops had
to be forced into the bunkers so that the doors to the main vaults
could be closed. So frequent were the raids, we were always on
alert. Several times a day we would be forced out of our positions
above ground and down into the bunkers. When the firing subsided,
we rushed above ground as fast as we could to meet any ground at-

tack. The ground attack never came, however. The enemy simply wanted to keep us suspended at a high degree of tension.

Thus, the Grand Redeployment, now celebrated as the opening move to rescue some small part of our continent, was not so grand after all. From that time until the last gasp of the war, I felt as though we were constantly on the defensive, constantly retreating.

Any reasonable observer would have agreed with me. Repeated attacks had rendered several great coastal "belts" virtually uninhabitable. The North Atlantic Belt followed the coast from near old Boston almost to Cape Fear, with an inland depth in some places up to a hundred miles. The Great Lakes Belt ran along the western coast of Lake Superior, through old Chicago all the way to old Detroit. Almost all of the Michigan Peninsula was dead. The topography of the region allowed for a much more efficient dispersal of weapons effect, so that this zone reached an inland depth of 150 miles here and there. Prevailing winds carried effects farther along the southern coast of Lake Ontario and farther southeastward.

The Gulf Coast from old Pensacola to old Corpus Christi was the southernmost belt. Owing to the prewar stationing of military stores in this region, as well as its high concentration of petrochemical industrial areas, the Gulf Belt was especially poisonous. The belt had witnessed vicious fighting in the middle decades of the war. The fighting had been augmented by an unusually high ratio of the most intense weapons. So now a poisonous cloudbank lies over the whole region, shifting north and south with the seasonal wind patterns. The effect is cruel. The winter's northwesterlies give the impression that all is clear, encouraging people to migrate toward the coastline, where they can feed themselves. No sooner are they settled than the summer patterns drive the cloud onshore again, forcing evacuation. This belt, like all the rest, is supposed to be quarantined, but policing it is impossible. The poor people who evade the authorities have little understanding of the nuances of thermoradiological poisoning.

Assuming they somehow survive the cloudbank as well as the marauders and scavengers, they will die in a few months anyway.

Along the Pacific Coast, the North Pacific Belt reaches from old Vancouver to old Portland. South of the Columbia River barrier, the coast region is still viable all the way to just north of old San Francisco. There, the South Pacific Belt begins and continues toward Mexico, terminating roughly south of San Diego. The southern part of the South Pacific Belt is very toxic also. As the home station of a considerable number of ground and naval forces, this region was one of the first "purely military" targets, and it was repeatedly attacked until the entire coastline was a poisoned desert.

One more such place, the so-called North Slope zone, had been the target of repeated attacks. Unaccountably, the enemy spent enormous energy in this region. The oil reserves were almost extinguished already, and few nations used that form of power anyway. The place was a frozen wilderness; few people lived there. But in the years before the war, the North Slope had acquired a certain nostalgic fame; it came to represent the old days, long before the war when the world was not forced to ration power. Aside from a certain psychological influence, one has difficulty understanding what these attacks accomplished. They seemed such a waste, all around.

As the geography of the nation was being rewritten by the war, what was left of our population was blown from place to place. As I have mentioned, refugee camps first grew up on the perimeter of the most dangerously poisoned cities. From that time we have the origins of New Chicago, New Houston, New Boston, and so on. For the most part, however, these camps were places where people could regain their senses, make new plans, and recover their health if possible. Those whose injuries prevented further movement died in these camps. Slowly, the dead replaced the living in "the perimeters," as the camps were sometimes called. Every one of the old cities is surrounded by graveyards now. Those who lie there are referred to as "the advance dead." If you are so unfortunate as to return to a dead city, these graves will be your first sight. Inside the cities themselves, the dead are present but graves are not required.

Naturally, the living drifted away from the perimeters in search of happier climes. Others gravitated toward little settlements that grew up beyond the gates of our operating bases, very unwisely, as it happens. These utterly defenseless people suffered thousands of casualties even when they were not attacked directly, simply as a secondary effect of weapons. Population clusters were not considered high-value targets by either side, in fact.

And as for the bases themselves, even they could hardly be considered places of refuge. We had few of them left. Most of those were heavily defended fortresses whose original purpose had been to act as a platform for offensive operations. Now the high command saw them only as the final places to be fought over. The enemy directed all his remaining strength against the bases. We used all our strength protecting them.

We had lost several important bases already. Quebec Station and Atlanta Station had fallen quite early. Without topographical protection, no base could survive for long. Santa Fe Station and Denver Station had not been so exposed, but the enemy found a way to use the mountains to advantage when they attacked, flying close to the slopes and down defiles to pour out onto our positions from unexpected directions. For our part, we found ways to improve our defenses. Since the dead zones were impassable, we used them as anchors for our defensive positions. Both my base and Seattle Base backed up to poison belts, protecting our rear areas. No attacks from those directions were possible.

We still had two submaritime bases out of the original fourteen, the Cape Fear and the Key West Stations, which were sited underwater on the Hatteras Plain about 500 miles east of the cape, and in the Puerto Rico Trench, some 750 miles southeast of the original station. Strategists of the day liked to speak of the opportunities presented by the "Savannah Gap" between these two stations. They speculated that this area could serve as a kind of lodgment from which to expand our operations into the interior. They were impressed that the enemy had not established a presence in this region. If the enemy was not at a place, and we were not at a place, our strategists worried that the place was not "under control." The enemy never seemed to think this way; he was not interested in controlling anything. He only wished for our complete and utter destruction.

As the war went on, the enemy seemed to learn while we seemed only to draw on the knowledge we already had. Well after the event, it is possible to see where these two trends crossed to spell our ultimate future. The enemy adopted our own strategy and executed it far better than we did. Their first attacks were relatively simple, but they grew in sophistication. The first attacks employed largely undifferentiated violence. Each passing offensive revealed a new stage in their strategic and operational development. Their attacks became more refined, precise pulses of violence, aimed for specific effect. And they rarely missed their aim. As we were to learn, these techniques were the foundation for the battle of the libraries.

The battle of the libraries was the only really large engagement in which I took part. As was so often the case, the battle was misnamed; the action was more in the nature of a campaign to sever the remaining connections between our armed forces and our nation. The idea was to drive us into defensive laager so that we might be prevented from defending our country. That having been done, the enemy intended to destroy or disrupt all the remaining networks of social cohesion. One important part of this larger campaign was meant to eliminate all the repositories of knowledge and information left in North America.

These "libraries" were actually huge banks of data that had been distributed throughout the continent at specially prepared sites. As military targets go, the repositories were unimpressive. No one saw the need to defend large caverns, filled with rows on row of data storage. We called the sites "libraries" for want of a better name, although we understood the real meaning of the word to refer to large collections of old books. Such of these as we had were destroyed at the beginning of the war. Everyone professed to regret this loss but saw it as one of the lesser tragedies besetting us. Most people were unimpressed by the prospect of doing without knowledge. You see where knowledge has taken us thus far? said one leading social commentator. Our highest authorities, however, vowed to come out in force against the barbarians, but our weakness made jokes of warnings like these now.

In my sector the war was quiet even after the enemy began the new offensive. More because of a restless nature than any other reason, I volunteered for patrol duties. Really big battles were rare now and the forces marked for those spent their days in tedious tactical rehearsals. Those of us in the patrol units referred to the others as "the bridesmaids."

My patrol area ran northward from Fort Hood Base for a thousand miles or so, a vast, mostly treeless tract of low hills, utterly deserted. Our maps designated it as the Plains. The few militarily significant places in the Plains had been destroyed long ago, but no one claimed the Plains and certainly no one would fight for them. The Plains became a million-square-mile exercise ground for both sides. On patrol we always hoped to meet the enemy counterpatrols. Then we could throw ourselves into short and sharp fights and play at our never-ending game of war.

And then our intelligence officers reported strange rumors coming out of the Plains. Just along its easternmost rim, along a great river where the forests began, a settlement had been seen. The inhabitants were supposedly near a small ruin, which they had started to excavate. What they were digging for no one could possibly imagine. In the officer's mess, we decided this was another of those rumors fabricated for our amusement, a variant on the Lost Civilization rumor.

One day, however, the rumor acquired substance. An artifact, purportedly from the excavation, came into our possession. The story was that traders had passed it from hand to hand until it arrived outside our gates. The artifact was from the covering of an ancient book made of paper. Paper had been out of use so long, no one at the base had ever seen any. This piece was very badly weathered and showed signs of having been buried in damp earth. Only with difficulty could one make out printing on the piece: *Vom Kriege*. Exactly what this meant was by no means clear. Some speculated the writing was in one of the ancient national languages, but that was rejected as far-fetched.

Our intelligence officers admonished us not to make too much of this tattered fragment. The piece could have come from anywhere, perhaps even be part of an enemy deception of some sort. However, when pressed, they admitted they had retraced at least part of the fragment's journey, back toward the settlement in question.

The war suddenly seemed less important to me. The news from the Plains was strangely affecting. Never curious or given to day-dreaming, I found myself excited by the idea of this settlement. How did they live there? What did they do? What were they digging at? What did the writing on the fragment mean? Did the fragment have anything to do with their work? Frustrated with my ignorance, I pressed the intelligence officers to agree on a quick, unobtrusive investigation.

As it happened I knew this part of the Plains as well as anyone. Few of my comrades configured their patrols here because the area was close to one of the heavier enemy concentrations, at the so-called Little Egypt Base, not far northeast of old St. Louis. But I had come to regard the great river as a guide of approach deeper into the region, and I had grown fond of the Plains; their vastness had a soothing effect on someone like me, who had been confined in one way or another for his whole life. Until now, I had not noticed that I looked forward to my patrols and designed them to last longer and longer.

I collected ten volunteers to go along. In short order, we assembled our battle kits and deployed to a small valley just west of the settlement's reported location, taking care to make a quiet approach. While the rest of the party worked on temporary defenses, I climbed to the top of a small ridgeline.

The ridge watched over the great river, whose valley is more than a mile wide at this point. The river was just as wide in some places too, punctuated with small sandy islands. Here and there it seemed one might walk across the river without much trouble. Wildlife was everywhere. From some quarter down below came a tinkling of bells. And smoke. I could see a hundred or more hutments arrayed around an open commons. People were walking about during the day without the slightest apparent concern. The whole settlement seemed defenseless.

Nearby was what I took to be the ruin itself, a great mound into which was dug an entrance. Close by the entrance an open-air shed with work tables held even more people. The scene was so inviting it seemed only natural that I walk down the hill and join them. Much to my sorrow, I did.

As I was in battle kit, I am sure I presented an alarming sight. But I was alarmed too. Almost everything I saw was unfamiliar to me. Until that day I had never seen a dog; now all different sizes and shapes surrounded me in a riot of sound and motion. Walking past an enclosure of horses, I realized I had never seen one of these either, although I remembered seeing images of one. All were much larger than I had suspected. As I went past the houses I felt people looking at me from the darkness inside. Slowly, children ventured out to stare and walk along. Then they jumped, step by step, trying to match my longer stride.

The lane gave out on to the common area. A group of people had gathered there, as if awaiting my arrival. None of them was armed. As a friendly gesture I removed my helmet so they could see my face. The tallest man stepped from the group toward me.

"Welcome to Kansas," he said. "We've been watching you since you landed in Salt Creek."

When he saw my confusion, he laughed. "No, we don't think you landed in a creek. That's just what we call the valley—Salt Creek Valley."

"What is Kansas?" I asked.

"Well," he said, "that's a bit more difficult. That is the ancient name for this place, but we have adopted it to mean everything here. And we just refer to the dig that way too."

Then he asked me where we were from. When I told him, he said, "Oh yes, Texas."

When I asked the meaning of Texas, he smiled, "that is the ancient name for your place. We think these names were used for specific regions. People in the old days felt they belonged to their place. Quaint, don't you think?"

I agreed that it was.

"What brings you to Kansas?" he asked.

I explained about the rumors we had heard, and I told him about the artifact.

"I know the book that piece comes from," he said right away. "What you saw was trash. I have no idea how it traveled that far south. One of the traders probably thought he could get something for it. I hope he did too. We have the complete book. We have about 200,000 other books too."

Two hundred thousand real books! How could so many have survived so long? Who had collected them and to what purpose? Why had these people come together to unearth them? What would be done with the books when their work was done?

As if reading my thoughts, the tall man said, "Well, you see, we are building a library—or rebuilding it, to be precise."

I could only shake my head. Then I realized that at some point in the conversation I had sat down at a table. A drink of some sort was in my hand. A child, shrieking happily, ran by with my helmet on.

"Yes, it does seem a little eccentric, I admit," the tall man said cheerfully. "To make matters stranger, the library's collection is rather narrow. Most of the books seem to do with war, which of course we all know far too much about. But every now and then we come upon a book that had real value. Then we stop working and read it. Or someone reads it to us as we do our chores." He laughed again, "That's why the excavation is taking so long. We are learning as we go."

"Why just books about war?" I wondered.

"Our best guess is that there was an officer's school here. You are an officer. Do you know what a staff college is?" he asked.

I confessed I did not. Anyway, what would an officer's school be doing in such a faraway place?

"Never mind," the tall man said. "It isn't important. The right lessons weren't learned anyway."

"How long . . . ?"

"Oh, the first of us arrived here fifteen years ago, I'd say. We think another twenty or thirty years should see the end of the excavation."

I asked for a closer look. The tall man looked in the direction of his comrades, who then departed on other business. He took me to the main dig. A shaft had been carved into the side of the mound, which the tall man said was only debris from the original site that had been grown over by vegetation.

He and his comrades thought the site consisted of several buildings of some size, only one of which actually contained books. A few books had been retrieved from outlying sites, but these were thought to have been carried there by some sort of explosion. Near the entrance to the main shaft, a separate gallery had been carved out of the mound. The "rescued books"—that was the phrase the tall man used—were kept here.

I never imagined so many books, stacks and stacks. Here and there a stack had tipped over, revealing their softly colored insides. I wandered through the stacks, letting my hands brush over the covers, some dull, some rough, some polished like a stone. Some books were huge, others so thin. Many had images, maps, charts, lists of numbers and words. I felt as though each book had a voice, and that they were all speaking to me. I wondered if I was in the presence of wisdom.

I have no feeling for how long I stayed in the gallery. When I finally looked up, the tall man had gone. I was still in the gallery when the raid commenced, surely the only reason I survived.

The enemy attacked with his usual ruthless skill, destroying the settlement and all its inhabitants in one pass. Across the ridgeline, in the Salt Creek, the defenses my own party had prepared were insufficient to protect them. They were all killed as well.

I was to blame. I had failed to switch my own combat locator system to stand-by. The enemy had intercepted my signature, decoded it, and tracked it to my position. After that, only programming the targets remained. The wonder is that the strike took so long to execute. As I said, we were all enfeebled by the war.

Nothing remained of the settlement when I came out into the light. The ground had been swept clean by the intense heat. In a few months, the vegetation would return, and Kansas would be invisible once more.

As my locator was still working perfectly, a relief patrol soon arrived and returned me to Fort Hood Base. There, I was placed under arrest.

At my court martial, I was held responsible for the deaths of all those in the settlement as well as those under my command. My commission was rescinded and I was discharged without honor from the armed forces. The usual punishment for my offense was death, but my award for valor in the assault on the Malakoff Redoubt swayed my judges toward leniency.

I could not have been freer, so I headed back to Kansas. Following the traders' routes, one after the other, I finally reached the old settlement. The ground was covered in snow. Rather than waste time and effort constructing a shelter, I moved into the excavation that had saved my life, into the book gallery.

From time to time during the first winter, friends from Fort Hood Base found an excuse to come by the site, drop off supplies, and talk about what I was doing. Because of their friendship, I was allowed to go about my work for the first several months with little worry about my survival. After some years, other people arrived and then decided to stay, just as the first ones had. Some would stay for a time and pass on, taking news of our work along with them. In this way, the settlement slowly grew up again.

I thought about my project for some time before I actually began to work. Above all, I promised myself, I should not hurry. I would lavish time on my project as though I were rich in time. Nor would I concern myself with how my project would eventually be received. The doing of the thing was now to be the point of my life.

I would make a book from among the books about me. I would set about reading and studying as well as I could. And when I found books whose writing spoke to me of how war had been born and grown and come to be the way it is now, I would copy some of it down and fasten all the pieces together. I would make a book on war so I could understand war.

Did it really happen? I thought it happened. I remembered it to the edge of forgetting. In my mind, it all lived. I am satisfied now.

So much of my life is a dream that I do not need to sleep. I travel through my dreams inside my little history book. Now I ask for pages long torn out. I hunt for characters known and sadly set aside, glide over tragedies, spark new alarms, and trace the lost smiles of contented labor.

I will not leave this book. My doctors say my gift had its price. Kansas was poisoned long ago. Anyone who lived among the books was doomed. Had I known, would I have returned? Oh yes. I preferred to die among my books. Which I would have done but for the visit of an old friend, who brought me here. My book is now in his hands, to do with as he will.

My poison—I think of it as mine—no longer permits me to function. I blink my eyes yes or no when nurses ask me questions. Now I can only think, but not much longer. So I think about my stories. Are they true? They have been true to me. And as true to war as I could make them.